Climate Change Solutions

Climate Change Solutions represents an application of critical theory to examine proposed solutions to climate change. Drawing from Marx's negative conception of ideology, the authors illustrate how ideology continues to conceal the capital-climate contradiction or the fundamental incompatibility between growth-dependent capitalism and effectively and justly mitigating climate change. Dominant solutions to climate change that offer minor changes to the current system fail to address this contradiction. However, alternatives like degrowth involve a shift in priorities and power relations and can offer new systemic arrangements that confront and move beyond the capital-climate contradiction. While there are clear barriers to a systemic transition that prioritizes social and ecological well-being, such a transition is possible and desirable.

Diana Stuart is Associate Professor in the Sustainable Communities Program and School of Earth and Sustainability at Northern Arizona University.

Ryan Gunderson is an Assistant Professor in the Department of Sociology and Gerontology at Miami University.

Brian Petersen is Assistant Professor in the Department of Geography, Planning and Recreation and Program in Sustainable Communities at Northern Arizona University.

Climate Change Solutions

BEYOND THE CAPITAL-CLIMATE CONTRADICTION

Diana Stuart
Ryan Gunderson
Brian Petersen

University of Michigan Press
Ann Arbor

Published in the United States of America by the
University of Michigan Press
Printed and bound by CPI Group (UK) Ltd, Croydon, CR0 4YY

First published July 2020

A CIP catalog record for this book is available from the British Library.

Library of Congress Cataloging-in-Publication Data

Names: Stuart, Diana (Diana Lynne), 1979– author. | Gunderson, Ryan (Ryan Michael),
    author. | Petersen, Brian (Brian Craig), author.
Title: Climate change solutions: beyond the capital-climate contradiction / Diana Stuart,
    Ryan Gunderson, Brian Petersen.
Description: Ann Arbor: University of Michigan Press, [2020] | Includes bibliographical
    references and index.
Identifiers: LCCN 2020001736 (print) | LCCN 2020001737 (ebook) | ISBN 9780472131983
    (hardcover) | ISBN 9780472038473 (paper) |ISBN 9780472126804 (ebook)
Subjects: LCSH: Climate change mitigation. | Greenhouse gas mitigation. | Environmental
    policy—Philosophy. | Critical theory.
Classification: LCC TD171.75 .S88 2020 (print) | LCC TD171.75 (ebook) | DDC 363.738/746—
    dc23
LC record available at https://lccn.loc.gov/2020001736
LC ebook record available at https://lccn.loc.gov/2020001737

To our daughters, for whom we hope another way is possible.

Acknowledgments

DIANA WOULD LIKE TO thank the coauthors for a tremendously fulfilling collaboration over the past few years. She would like to thank her father for encouraging her love of nature and respect for nonhuman life, and her mother for instilling and supporting her love of writing. She also thanks her students who keep asking the big question (how do we get there?) and the scholars, writers, and activists working to show us the way.

Ryan owes thanks to many colleagues, friends, and students for discussions related to climate politics, environmental social science, social theory, and related topics who cannot be listed here for fear of forgetting anyone. Two friends and former mentors deserve special thanks: David Ashley for introducing him to critical theory and graciously offering countless hours of time for conversation during a defining and cherished period of life, as well as Thomas Dietz for his commitment to, and passion for, seeking democratic and fair solutions to environmental issues, and for helpful comments on an earlier version of chapter 8. He also owes special thanks to his family for their love and support. Finally, he thanks Diana and Brian for being ideal collaborators and good friends.

Brian thanks Diana and Ryan for collaborating on a dynamic research agenda that has culminated in this book. He also thanks all the students, colleagues, and citizens who have heard his public talks and have asked excellent questions, provided critical feedback, and demonstrated the urgency and necessity of sharing this book's arguments and messages. He wants to thank all those working to address climate change and social injustices, exposing inequities, and demanding social transformation. He hopes this book and the coauthors' ongoing work can contribute to this exciting and imperative cause.

We thank and acknowledge the publishers of the below articles that we authored prior to writing this book. We used ideas and text from these articles in specific book chapters as follows:

Chapter 1 features ideas and revised text from the following articles:

> Gunderson, Ryan. 2014. "The First-Generation Frankfurt School on the Animal Question: Foundations for a Normative Sociological Animal Studies." *Sociological Perspectives* 57 (3): 285–300.
> Gunderson, Ryan. 2017. "Ideology Critique for the Environmental Social Sciences: What Reproduces the Treadmill of Production?" *Nature and Culture* 12 (3): 263–89.
> Gunderson, Ryan, Diana Stuart, and Brian Petersen. 2019. "Materialized Ideology and Environmental Problems: The Cases of Solar Geoengineering and Agricultural Biotechnology." *European Journal of Social Theory*.

Some sections from chapters 1, 2, and 5 are revised and expanded from:

> Gunderson, Ryan, Diana Stuart, and Brian Petersen. 2018. "Ideological Obstacles to Effective Climate Policy: The Greening of Markets, Technology, and Growth." *Capital & Class* 42 (1): 133–60.

Ideas and adapted text from chapter 3 were originally published as:

> Stuart, Diana, Ryan Gunderson, and Brian Petersen. 2019. "Climate Change and the Polanyian Counter-Movement: Carbon Markets or Degrowth?" *New Political Economy* 24 (1): 89–102.

Some sections from chapter 4 are revised and expanded from:

> Gunderson, Ryan, Diana Stuart, and Brian Petersen. 2019. "The Political Economy of Geoengineering as Plan B: Technological Rationality, Moral Hazard, and New Technology." *New Political Economy* 24 (5): 696–715.

A different version of chapter 6 was originally published in:

Gunderson, Ryan. 2019. "Work Time Reduction and Economic Democracy as Climate Change Mitigation Strategies: Or, Why the Climate Needs a Renewed Labor Movement." *Journal of Environmental Studies and Sciences* 9 (1): 35–44.

A different version of chapter 7 was originally published in:

Gunderson, Ryan, Diana Stuart, Brian Petersen, and Sun-Jin Yun. 2018. "Social Conditions to Better Realize the Environmental Gains of Alternative Energy: Degrowth and Collective Ownership." *Futures* 99: 36–44.

A different version of chapter 8 was originally published in:

Gunderson, Ryan. 2018. "Global Environmental Governance Should Be Participatory: Five Problems of Scale." *International Sociology* 33 (6): 715–37.

Chapter 9 features revised paragraphs from the following article:

Gunderson, Ryan. 2019. "Dialectics Facing Prehistoric Catastrophe: Merely Possible Climate Change Solutions." *Critical Sociology*.

Contents

Digital materials related to this title can be found on the Fulcrum platform via the following citable URL: https://doi.org/10.3998/mpub.10052020

CHAPTER I

Introduction

Climate change is fueling wildfires nationwide, new report warns

NEW YORK TIMES: NOVEMBER 27, 2018

Midwest flooding highlights national security risk posed by climate change

CHICAGO TRIBUNE: MARCH 22, 2019

Floods, tornadoes, snow in May: extreme weather driven by climate change across US

USA TODAY: MAY 29, 2019

MANY WHO READ the news about climate change may silently fear the end of the world is approaching. Events are commonly described as unprecedented and record-breaking, threatening our ecological and social systems. "Climate disasters" in 2018 caused $14 billion in damages in the United States alone and included hurricanes, cyclones, floods, and fires (National Oceanic and Atmospheric Administration [NOAA] 2019). While the impacts of climate change are already unfolding, scientists are also warning that if we do not act boldly *now* we could be headed toward a "Hothouse Earth" scenario of catastrophic warming (Steffen et al. 2018). In a 2018 special report, the Intergovernmental Panel on Climate Change (IPCC) called for "rapid, far-reaching and unprecedented changes in all aspects of society" over the next ten to twenty years in order to keep Earth's temperature within 1.5 degrees Celsius (C) above preindustrial levels (IPCC 2018). As climate change impacts increase and continued greenhouse gas (GHG) emissions lock us into a warmer and warmer future, we face a narrowing window of opportunity to act.

Government efforts to reduce GHG emissions have thus far focused on carbon markets and increasing the use of green technologies. More recently, scientists and politicians are pushing forward research in geoengineering, proposed as a Plan B to save society from the impacts of climate change if reducing emissions fails. However, for many of us, these proposed solutions to climate change are far from comforting. Will they be enough? If they are not enough, what else is necessary? Is another way possible?

In this book, we examine proposed solutions to address climate change and their potential to quickly, effectively, and justly reduce GHG emissions. We analyze proposals already being implemented as well as those that are less commonly discussed because they entail more fundamental changes in society. In any case, climate change will fundamentally change society. However, rather than waiting for that to happen, certain changes made now could significantly reduce future climate impacts. These changes would involve shifts in our priorities, in the balance of power in our society, and in our ideology. We use critical theory to examine the weaknesses of approaches to address climate change that maintain the goals, social relations, property structures, and culture of the current system and, more perniciously, delay the system changes that could radically reduce GHG emissions. We also evaluate alternative ways forward that could transform the current system in ways that would allow us to more effectively and justly address climate change. Our goal is not only to critique false solutions but to illustrate that alternatives that offer more effective mitigation pathways exist and are indeed possible.

THE CLIMATE CHANGE PROBLEM

There is overwhelming evidence that the global climate has warmed significantly since preindustrial times. The IPCC brings together leading scientists from around the globe to assess climate change, releasing its first assessment in 1990 and its fifth assessment in 2014. The latter report states: "warming of the climate system is unequivocal, and since the 1950s, many of the observed changes are unprecedented over decades to millennia" (IPCC 2014). For thirty-seven consecutive years, starting in 1976, annual average global temperatures have exceeded the twentieth century average (NOAA 2013). The ten hottest years on record have all occurred since 1998, with 2016 as the Earth's hottest year followed by 2017 (NOAA 2017).

The IPCC (2014) links this warming to human actions: "it is extremely likely that more than half of the observed increase in global average surface temperature from 1951 to 2010 was caused by the anthropogenic increase in greenhouse gas concentrations." Average annual mean carbon dioxide levels in the atmosphere have increased from 315 parts per million in 1959 to over 400 parts per million in 2013 (NOAA 2013) and reached 415 parts per million in 2019, the highest level in over three million years (Galey 2019). According to the IPCC (2014), approximately half of all anthropogenic carbon dioxide emissions between 1750 and 2010 occurred in the last forty years. GHG concentrations, including methane (257 percent of the preindustrial level), nitrous oxide (122 percent of the preindustrial level), and carbon dioxide (145 percent of the preindustrial level) continue to rise each year (World Meteorological Society 2017). Most GHG emissions are linked to the burning of fossil fuels: between 1854 and 2010, a mere ninety companies were responsible for two-thirds of all carbon emissions, and since 1988, twenty-five companies have been responsible for over half of all global industrial emissions (Heede 2014, CDP 2017).

Despite attempts to deny the existence of anthropogenic climate change (McCright and Dunlap 2010), the impacts are increasingly difficult to ignore. The observable effects of climate change include increased frequency and intensity of hurricanes and storm events, melting glaciers, sea level rise, droughts, heat waves, floods, wildfires, forest die-off, animal extinction, and the disruption of agriculture and food supplies (National Aeronautics and Space Administration [NASA] 2017, Union of Concerned Scientists [UCS] 2017). In addition, climate change has already increased civil conflicts (Hsiang et al. 2011) and could lead to the displacement of 150 million people by 2050 (Vidal 2009).

Scientists and world leaders have called for actions to reduce GHG emissions with the goal of "keeping a global temperature rise this century well below 2 degrees Celsius above preindustrial levels and to pursue efforts to limit the temperature increase even further to 1.5 degrees Celsius" (hereafter the "2 degrees C target") (United Nations Framework Convention on Climate Change [UNFCCC] 2015). The IPCC's 2018 special report makes clear that a 1.5 degrees C warmer world would be much less risky than a 2 degrees C warmer world, including lower mean temperatures in most regions; fewer hot extremes in most inhabited regions; a lower probability of drought in some regions; lower sea level rise; less biodiversity loss; and less health, food, water, security, and other risks to humans (IPCC 2018).

The social and ecological forecasts of a 2 degrees C world are grim, including the loss of almost all coral reefs (> 99 percent) and a less secure food supply. However, GHG concentrations continue to rise, and with each year, it becomes increasingly unlikely that even a 2 degrees C target will be met. As the impacts of climate change intensify, it will become critical to either dramatically reduce GHG emissions and adapt to the negative impacts of climate change.

Two proposed solutions dominate current policies and planning efforts to address climate change: green technology and carbon markets. In addition, geoengineering is increasingly being discussed as a necessary climate change response. While promoted as the solutions to climate change, each of these strategies has significant shortcomings, fails to address the root causes of climate change, and protects the current system that prioritizes the interests of economic elites. These solutions are framed as "win-win" scenarios and ways we can "green" or "techno-fix" business as usual. Yet these solutions conceal relationships that link our current political-economic system to GHG emissions. In this book, we review evidence showing that these strategies have been and will likely remain ineffective and, in the case of geoengineering, are highly risky. We draw from critical theory to illustrate how these climate change "solutions" reproduce the drivers of an inherently ecologically unsustainable society. Most importantly, we explore alternative solutions that have the potential to challenge the priorities of the current system and successfully mitigate climate change.

WHAT IS CRITICAL THEORY?

Critical theory typically refers to the work of scholars associated with the "Frankfurt School." In the early 1920s, a young and wealthy radical named Felix Weil established the Institute of Social Research in Frankfurt, Germany. The purpose of the Institute was to promote and further Marxist theory and research since Weil wished to bestow the Institute to a future, hoped-for German socialist state. However, Weil's plans were never realized, and the Institute took on a life of its own soon after its inception. The most influential and well-known first-generation members of the Institute were Max Horkheimer, Theodor Adorno, Herbert Marcuse, Erich Fromm (who left the institution in the late 1930s), and Walter Benjamin (an informal, outside member). Although there was enough theoretical diversity within this group that defining it as a coherent "school" of thought is problematic (Wheatland 2009), the group of thinkers associated with the Institute is popularly referred to as the Frankfurt School (see Jay 1973, Wiggerhaus 1994).

Max Horkheimer (1993c) gave his inaugural address as the director of the Institute in 1931. He called for interdisciplinary research to bridge social science and philosophy to generate ideas that could guide the development of a more rational and just society. This inaugural speech laid the foundations for what was later termed "the Critical Theory" (e.g., Marcuse 1968, Horkheimer 1972). Following in the footsteps of their greatest influence, Karl Marx, the critical theorists argued that social theory should be not only explanatory and descriptive but also practical, radical, critical, and normative. In addition to Marx's influence, the Frankfurt School incorporated insights from a vast range of thinkers, including Sigmund Freud, Max Weber, Georg W. F. Hegel, and Friedrich Nietzsche, among others. Their concerns about the economic and political systems of their time resulted in a sizeable canon of radical, sometimes abstruse, and often pessimistic analyses and critiques of a "totally administered society" (see Anderson 1976).

Early critical theorists argued that the domination of nature is intimately linked to the domination of other humans and internal human nature. Modern societies attempt to master nature with increasing efforts to harness natural forces for human aims, a form of interaction that is perceived as the only rational way to interact with the environment: "[w]hat men want to learn from nature is how to use it in order wholly to dominate it and other men. That is the only aim" (Horkheimer and Adorno 1969: 4). The proliferation of instrumental reason, production systems that maximize profitability, and unreflective technical progress not only makes the domination of nature more efficient but also leads to the domination of human beings. Humanity's attempts to master and control nature—a goal originally intended to free humanity from nature's supremacy—have paradoxically enslaved humans along with the rest of nature.

> The human being, in the process of his emancipation, shares the fate of the rest of his world. Domination of nature involves domination of man. Each subject not only has to take part in the subjugation of external nature, human and nonhuman, but in order to do so must subjugate nature in himself. (Horkheimer 1947: 93; see also Adorno 1967: 67)

For the Frankfurt School, the domination of nature is intimately tied up in the domination of the self and other human beings. The Frankfurt School investigated relations between humans, nature, capitalism, and technology and uncovered contradictions and systemic drivers of domination. The socio-ecological contributions of the early critical theorists have received a fair amount of discussion, with mixed reception (Leiss 1974; Balbus 1982; Bookchin 1982; Salleh 1988; Mills 1991; Eckersley 1992; Dobson 1993; Harvey 1996; Vogel 1996; Foster 2002; Biro 2005; Barry 2007; Wilding 2008; York and Mancus 2009; Nelson 2011; Gunderson 2015, 2016; Stoner and Melathopoulos 2015). We extend this discussion by drawing on many of the main arguments and concepts of the first-generation Frankfurt School, as well as their primary method of ideology critique, in order to examine current responses to climate change and more radical alternatives.

This book is a "critical theoretical" project in the sense that it employs a form of "oppositional thinking" to achieve "reflection on a system of constraints which are humanly produced" in order to overcome undesirable power relations and irrational social conditions (Connerton 1976: 16, 18). The form of oppositional thinking employed by critical theory is often termed "ideology critique," which, in social-ecological context, entails "immanent critique" (appraising and analyzing society from the perspective of its own values and categories), historicizing seemingly natural and immutable social conditions, and diagnosing social-ecological contradictions and crises in order to locate more rational alternative social futures existing within society (Gunderson 2017). Through ideology critique, critical theory seeks to explain and expose irrational aspects of society, "irrational" in the sense that contradictions and injustices carry on despite being avoidable, and to account for their perpetuation through examining how "societies hide their own potential from themselves, in order for the current system of economic and social domination to be perpetuated" (Granter 2009: 2–3). That is, critical theory seeks to explain the reproduction of irrational conditions. The purpose of theory is to both explain and describe social reality and, more importantly, to aid in the process of progressively altering it by discovering openings for change within contradictions and crises. Iris Young (2001: 10) describes the methodological implications of this framework well:

> [a] critical theory does not derive [normative] principles and ideals from philosophical premises about morality, human nature, or the good life. Instead, the method of critical theory . . . reflects on existing social relations and pro-

cesses to identify what we experience as valuable in them, but as present only intermittently, partially, or potentially.

Critical theory is well-placed to address two of the central problems related to interdisciplinary questions surrounding climate change: (1) why have societies, especially at national and international levels, failed to effectively respond to climate change, and (2) how might societies be able to effectively respond to climate change (Norgaard 2018)? We examine the policy mechanisms that aid in the reproduction of an inherently ecologically destructive social order as well as investigate social alternatives already present in the existing social order, but present "only intermittently, partially, or potentially" (Young 2001: 10).

In this book, we adopt a broad interpretation of critical theory, going beyond the specific members of the first-generation Frankfurt School to include thinkers with overlapping theoretical frameworks, methods, and goals. In addition to drawing from the most prominent figure of the Frankfurt School's second generation—Jürgen Habermas—we incorporate theoretical insights and empirical research from a diversity of scholars with the common goal of overcoming the domination of humans and nature to create a world in which the needs and powers of human (and other) beings are met and emancipated from oppression (Horkheimer 1972). We apply ideas from a range of sociologists, economists, and philosophers, including Karl Polanyi, Jorge Larrain, André Gorz, Göran Therborn, and more recent scholars such as Richard York, to illustrate why green technology, carbon markets, and geoengineering reproduce the social drivers of climate change instead of effectively addressing climate change, as well as how alternative approaches that challenge the current socioeconomic order can be more effective and just. While we draw from a diversity of critical theories throughout the book, the concept of ideology represents a key theme in our analysis.

IDEOLOGY, THE CAPITAL-CLIMATE CONTRADICTION, AND TECHNOLOGY

Ideology

Ideology is a thorny and elusive concept so it is important to clarify what we mean by the term. The word was coined by the French rationalist and anti-metaphysician Destutt de Tracy to refer to an emerging discipline: the scientific study of the genesis and content of ideas (for histories, see Mannheim 1936, Lichtheim 1965, Barth 1978, Larrain 1979). Today the term is most commonly used to describe systems of ideas and beliefs that make up a political position and/or guide the interpretation of everyday events (Therborn 1980). Environmental social scientists have examined the role of ideology in human-nature relations (e.g., Sunderlin 2003, Best 2009, Cutler 2016, McCright et al. 2016), either adopting a neutral notion of ideology as a general worldview (e.g., Mannheim 1936) or a conception similar to "sets of ideas by which men posit, explain and justify ends and means of organised social action, and specifically political action, irrespective of whether such action aims to preserve, amend, uproot or rebuild a given social order" (Seliger 1976: 11). The latter notion is often termed "political ideology"—all of those political "isms." For example, Dunlap and McCright (2015) argue that neoliberalism is a hegemonic ideology that underlies climate denialism. While we recognize the importance of neutral conceptions of ideology and draw from them, especially Therborn's (1980) theories of ideological transformation, our primary aim in this book is to illuminate ideas that obscure systemic contradictions related to climate change.

We apply a conception of ideology drawn from the Marxist tradition, where the term refers to ideas and practices that conceal systemic contradictions (Larrain 1979, 1982, 1983). Marx's conception of ideology was unique during his time and still is today due to the notion that ideology is to be understood in relation to real contradictions created through social practice. In their critique of the Young Hegelians, Marx and Engels (1977) famously argued that social problems do not result from the wrong ideas, but that a distorted consciousness results from a contradictory reality. Larrain (1979: 46) explains ideology as "a solution in the mind to contradictions which cannot be solved in practice; it is the necessary projection in consciousness of man's practical inabilities." Ideology, however, is not restricted to internal or shared states of consciousness. Contradiction-concealing ideas can be internal as well as material, in the form of reproductive practices, institutions (Althusser 1971), and text (Thompson 1984). In discursive form, ideologies conceal contradictions through descriptive, explanatory, and/or normative claims and implicit or explicit assumptions that (1) grant legitimacy to the social order (*legitimation*), and/or (2) conceive of the social order as natural and immutable (*reification*) (for similar formulations, see Lukes 1974, Thompson 1984).

There are a handful of studies containing arguments that approximate what we mean by ideology in the context of human-nature relations (e.g., Hornborg 2001, 2003, 2009; Bell and York 2010; Foster 2010; Nyberg and Wright 2013; Stoner and Melathopoulos 2015; Wright and Nyberg 2014, 2015). Wright and Nyberg (2014, 2015; Nyberg and Wright 2013) have identified many of the specific organizational-level mechanisms used by corporations to conceal contradictions related to climate change. For example, corporations incorporate critiques of capital's role in climate change through the creation of myths, such as corporate environmentalism—framing the corporation as a central climate change mitigation actor (Wright and Nyberg 2014). They maintain that criticisms are recuperated in a way that *reproduces* capitalism's unsustainable relation with the environment by *legitimating* the existence of corporate capitalism. This conception is akin to Bell and York's (2010) analysis of ideology as a legitimation process for coal interests in West Virginia, where the coal industry propped up a pseudo-grassroots organization ("Friends of Coal") to manufacture an ideological cultural and economic identity for the region.

Unlike social science approaches that focus on human ideation while overlooking the structural causes of the environmental crisis and exaggerate the "epistemic powers of actors" (Ollinaho 2016: 54; see Arponen 2013, 2015), ideology in the Marxist tradition is investigated as an organization of ideas and practices that reproduces contradictory material happenings through their concealment, not as an independent cause of material happenings. The Marxist conception of ideology has been applied primarily to explain why workers willingly accept an alienated existence contrary to their interests instead of revolting (Langman 2015). The negative theory of ideology can also be applied to help explain the parallel existence of what Stoner and Melathopoulos (2015: 22) call the "environment-society problematic": despite increased attention and public concerns about the environment, environmental degradation continues to increase. This paradoxical situation has led scholars to ask: why are we sustaining "what is known to be unsustainable" (Blühdorn 2007: 272) and "[w]hy is there no storming of the Bastille because of the environmental destruction threatening mankind" (Beck 2010: 254)? The paradox can be cast in even more explicitly Marxist terms: Which ideologies reproduce our current economic system's unsustainable relationship with the environment? To be clear, we do not argue that ideology is an *independent cause* of climate change. Ideological analysis is imperative to explaining the *social reproduction* of the *capital-climate contra-*

diction: the contradiction between the structural drive of capitalism to increase material and energy throughput to expand production, on the one hand, and the negative impacts this structural drive has on a condition of production, the climate system.

Capitalism and the Climate

Our current economic system is a capitalist system. Capitalism has been defined in different ways. Some have defined it as a market-based system rooted in private ownership, as opposed to public (cooperative and/or government) ownership and allocation of goods (although most systems are a hybrid of private and state ownership and of market-based and other mechanisms of allocation). One distinctive characteristic of capitalism when compared to all past modes of production is how the production process is organized: a large group of people who do not own the means to produce their own livelihood, the "means of production" (e.g., tools, equipment, natural resources), are paid wages by those who do own the means of production to produce goods, services, and new means of production. In addition to being a particular kind of class relation, capitalism is also unique as a system of generalized and specialized *commodity* production, i.e., a system to produce goods and services to sell on the market for a profit.[1] Capitalism is a system in which "production is for exchange; that is, it is determined by its profitability on a market" (Wallerstein 1979: 159). The goal of a capitalist system is to create profits and to keep creating more profits. Part of the surplus[2] created in the economic process must be reinvested to reproduce and *expand* this process (e.g., technologies that increase productivity, supervisors, advertising). Firms compete with one another and make strategic decisions to maximize profits. While many people associate capitalism with private property, market exchange, profit, and wage-labor, these are ultimately not its defining characteristics. As Wallerstein (2004: 23-24) explains,

> [c]apitalism is not the mere existence of persons or firms producing for sale on the market with the intention of obtaining a profit. Such persons or firms have existed for thousands of years all across the world. Nor is the existence of persons working for wages sufficient as a definition. Wage-labor has also been known for thousands of years. We are in a capitalist system only when the system gives priority to the endless accumulation of capital. Using such a definition, only the modern world-system has been a capitalist system.

Due to the prioritization of endless accumulation as well as the external structural necessity to self-expand, capitalist economies are *growth dependent*. Economies grow when profit maximization is compulsory, but other factors also contribute. Capitalism is perpetuated due to competition between firms and a pattern of lending, debt, and increased production to pay off debt. Investments in mass production infrastructure also lock businesses into producing excessive quantities of goods and advertising to get consumers to purchase these goods (Blackwater 2015). Our current society also continues to prioritize and fetishize economic growth (Stiglitz 2009). As we detail in chapter 5, capitalism's growth-dependency is an important feature in the environmental context. Growth entails increasing production, consumption, extraction, and pollution. Therefore, economic growth, predicated on the expansion of capitalism, is foundational to our environmental crises (Schnaiberg 1980, Gould et al. 2008)—including climate change. As we explain in Chapter 5, capitalism is growth-dependent, and growth is a major driver of GHG emissions. The ecological case against capitalism centers on highlighting the energy and material throughput needed for continually increasing profits as well as the pollution created in the process.

Although capitalism seems "natural" to us because we happen to live in a capitalist society (Lukács 1971; Harvey 1982: 9), it is a humanly created and historically contingent socioeconomic system worthy of critical examination. Capitalism, although relatively new in human history, has also become so normalized and alternatives so stigmatized that, as put by Jameson (2003: 73), it is "easier to imagine the end of the world than to imagine the end of capitalism." The historical experiments in socialism during the twentieth century primarily remained capitalist in the sense that state officials and bureaucrats replaced the role of private capitalists in appropriating surpluses created by workers ("state capitalism") (see Wolff 2012a: 81ff) and also remained "capitalist" in terms of economic growth and environmental degradation. However, as we will discuss later in the book, diverse forms of collective ownership combined with participatory democratic governance offer different opportunities to foster a system that prioritizes social and ecological well-being over profit and continual economic growth.

In this book, we focus on a key contradiction concealed by the dominantly proposed solutions to climate change: the capital-climate contradiction. This refers to the contradiction between capital's need to expand production, on the one hand, and the destructive effects expansionistic production has on the conditions of production, specifically the climate system, on the other. The capital-climate contradiction, which Wright and Nyberg (2014, 2015) accurately term a "creative self-destruction," is a specific example of O'Connor's (1998: 162) "second contradiction of capitalism," whereby "individual capitals defend or restore profits by strategies that degrade or fail to maintain over time the material conditions of their own production." The environment is conceived of as a condition of production as all commodity production depends on the biophysical environment, not only for inputs but also for its very existence and reproduction, including a livable climate system. Weis (2010: 318–19) has described O'Connor's second contradiction well in the context of climate change: "the failure to account for the atmospheric burden associated with fossil energy, and its impact on the Earth's climate system, represents one of the most fundamental biophysical contradictions of industrial capitalism." The capital-climate contradiction is built into the basic structures of modern capitalist societies. Indeed, the burning of fossil fuels for profit maximization is tied up in the development of capitalism (Malm 2016). The case that capitalism is the underlying driver of climate change is well-established. While this argument will not be detailed here, it is reviewed by Antonio and Clark (2015).

In this book, we move beyond an analysis of *causes* of climate change to an analysis of *social reproduction* and potential *solutions*. Our assessment of the underlying causes of climate change will be familiar to many and is in line with neo-Marxist, climate justice, and ecosocialist analyses (i.e., capitalism is a set of structural imperatives that increase throughput, which necessarily increases emissions). With a theory of ideology, we seek to conceptually *supplement*, not replace, this structural explanation. Without a theory of ideology, we cannot fully explain the reproduction of climate change drivers nor can we formulate an alternative way forward (e.g., see the assessment of climate justice discourse in Kenis and Mathijs 2014). Although we do not construct a utopia in this book, we locate some already existing concrete climate change responses that may help society move beyond the capital-climate contradiction (what we call "transitional mitigation strategies," outlined below).

Our argument is not that capitalism is incapable of minor improvements, but that it is systematically incapable of responding at the rate and scale necessary to stay within the 2 degrees C target. As we illustrate in the following chapters, green technology, carbon markets, and geoengineering solutions to climate change each fail to address the capital-climate contradiction. Instead, they *conceal* and reproduce the capital-climate contradiction. Following this critique, we examine more radical "transitional" solutions to climate change that have the potential to transcend the capital-climate contradiction, including degrowth, community renewable energy systems, and participatory global environmental governance. An underlying thesis of the book is that climate change mitigation requires social-structural changes. By "social-structural" changes, we mean changes in institutional arrangements underlying the distribution of power, including ownership, political governance, and class relations. This means changes in the ownership of, and control over, institutions and technologies that negatively impact the climate and/or have the potential for a more rational application in different social conditions.

We refer to climate mitigation strategies that have the potential to move beyond the capital-climate contradiction as "transitional mitigation strategies," which are characterized by most or all of the following features:

- Are "non-reformist reforms" (Gorz 1967) that may act as part of a "transitional program" (Löwy 2015: 37) out of capitalism, as opposed to minor reforms that reproduce the capital-climate contradiction. Kallis (2018: 136) describes non-reformist reforms as "reforms that, if they were to be implemented, would require the very contours of the system to change radically to accommodate them. And reforms that, simple and common-sensical as they are, expose the irrationality of the system that makes them seem impossible."
- Increase social well-being in a just manner as well as effectively decrease GHG emissions by reducing total material and energy throughput. In other words, transitional mitigation strategies are scenarios that increase human well-being, mitigate climate change, and protect the biosphere.
- Socialize and/or democratize the processes, institutions, and techniques that have significant climate impacts.
- Are desirable alternatives that already exist in pockets of the existing order "but as present only intermittently, partially, or potentially" (Young 2001: 10).

To situate the political strategies and policies we recommend in the second half of this book, we should note that our focus on socializing and democratizing the processes, institutions, and techniques that have significant climate impacts are in line with "ecosocialism" (Löwy 2009), and the goal of reducing total material and energy throughput in socially desirable ways is consistent with "degrowth" (see chapter 5). Our aim is not to examine every transitional mitigation strategy that has been proposed to address climate change. For example, the book does not deeply explore potentially transformative alternatives to industrial agriculture, an issue we have written about extensively elsewhere (Stuart et al. 2014, Stuart 2018, Stuart et al. 2018), or personal vehicle-dependent transportation systems. Instead, our goal is to put forth a *framework* that can explain the ineffectiveness of current mainstream approaches and examples of already existing strategies that have the *potential* to effectively and justly mitigate climate change. Because climate change responses often call for technological innovation and adoption, our analysis examines climate change-relevant technologies (hereafter, "climate technologies"), from renewable energy systems to geoengineering strategies. Critical theory offers a distinctive approach to technology assessment.

The Question Concerning Technology

Our assessment of climate technologies is informed by critical theory. A unifying theme in the critical tradition is attention to how technology develops out of unequal productive (class) relations and serves capitalist imperatives, namely the drive for capital to self-accumulate (for a brief review, see Malm 2018: 177ff). Put in more conventional language, "[t]echnology is the embodiment of values in artifacts" (Young, 2014: 293), specifically the historically particular "value" of capital accumulation built on historically specific productive relations. This is not inconsistent with Marx's own theory of technology, especially the late Marx (see Malm 2018), whose framework is far more dynamic and sociological than it is technological-determinist (e.g., MacKenzie 1984).

   Our technology assessment is especially indebted to Marcuse's critical theory of technology as expanded by Andrew Feenberg (e.g., 1999). Like his colleagues (e.g., Horkheimer 1993: 314–15, Horkheimer and Adorno 1969: 84), Marcuse (1989: 123) argued it was naïve to view the development of modern science and its applications in isolation from the development of capitalism. Further, he maintained that science and technology are, in modern societies, firmly fastened to the interests of capital and rationality is "bent to the requirements of capitalism" (Marcuse 1972: 60). Marcuse (1978: 138–39) conceptualized technology broadly, as the totality of late capitalist social organization, instruments/machinery, as well as the modern mode of technical thinking. He maintained that the thought and practice of advanced industrial societies had "replaced" the natural world with a technical one, where reality is interpreted in physical-mathematical formulas to help guide "the use and the methodological transformation of nature and . . . produce a universe controlled by the power of man" (Marcuse 1989: 120). This transformation of reality into a "calculable order" is underpinned by a "technological rationality" that distilled a "pure" instrumentality incapable of formulating substantive end goals (1989, 1964: 158). Science and technology are not independent, autonomous forces but are organized in capitalist societies—their pre-given reality—to serve the interests of capital. Embedded in a society of organized domination, technology is often utilized to further the domination of nature and humans: "[t]echnology is always a historical-social project: in it is projected what a society and its ruling interests intend to do with men and things" (Marcuse 1968: 223–24).

Common questions about technology from a critical perspective include the following (see Gunderson et al. 2019):

1. What historically contingent social conditions gave birth to the given technology, even if the designers and users of the technology are unaware of this social-structural backdrop? This question is a key step into developing a critical theory of technology: to historicize and sociologize the given technology. As Feenberg (1999: 87) put it, if "[t]he legitimating effectiveness of technology depends on unconsciousness of the cultural-political horizon under which it was designed" then a "critical theory of technology can uncover that horizon, demystify the illusion of technical necessity, and expose the relativity of the prevailing technical choices." One of critical tradition's central contributions to theorizing technology-society relations is attention to the way the narrow interests of capital enable and constrain technology design and use.

2. Is the technology being deliberately developed to mask a social-ecological contradiction and/or will/does its adoption and use conceal the existence of the given contradiction? What social alternatives are *not* being pursued while the technological solution is being pursued (see the following question)?

3. Does the given technology "leave existing modes of domination mostly intact" (Greenfield 2017: 8) and can one reasonably anticipate or project that the technology will reproduce or even strengthen the existing social order? Common ways that a technology can reproduce or strengthen the social order is by diverting resources or attention from possible social-

structural changes that could transcend the given contradiction and through benefiting those already in power.

4. Finally, can or will the given technology "ever truly be turned to liberatory ends" (Greenfield 2017: 8)? In other words, if embedded in a different form of social organization (e.g., if the technology were collectively owned and/ or democratically controlled), could the technology be implemented in ways that improve human-nature relations and increase well-being? This book repeatedly condemns misplaced hopes in curing social and environmental ills with techno-fixes and emphasizes throughout that technology is value-laden. However, these are not reasons to preclude cases in which technological possibilities constrained by capital can be "unfettered" and improved upon to serve more rational ends in different social conditions.

These questions are brought to bear on climate technologies throughout the book, especially in chapters 2, 4, and 7. Below we provide an overview of the book that summarizes our primary substantive points.

BOOK OVERVIEW

Chapter 2 focuses on green technology, which includes technologies to improve the efficiency of resource use as well as technologies that support the use of alternative energy sources. Green technology is widely promoted as a key solution to climate change, as described in IPCC reports and in the Paris Climate Agreement. While nations, cities, and communities continue to adopt green technologies, the general optimism about these solutions overlooks paradoxical outcomes and contradictions that limit their effectiveness. Often referred to as the Jevons paradox or the "rebound effect," efficiency gains through green technology are in many cases partially or completely offset by increases in consumption (e.g., see York et al. 2011, York and McGee 2016). In addition, increasing evidence indicates that renewable energy substitutes for fossil fuels do not result in a one-to-one substitution and may increase total energy use (e.g., see Zehner 2012; York 2012, 2016). These paradoxical outcomes indicate that the use of green technology without reductions in resource consumption will not successfully reduce GHG emissions. Evidence suggests that in order to realize the full potential benefits of green technologies, the drivers of high resource consumption must be addressed. Because economic growth driven by capital accumulation remains a priority, green technology solutions implemented alone will fail to transcend the capital-climate contradiction.

Chapter 3 examines carbon markets, including cap-and-trade and carbon offsets schemes, that have been widely proposed and increasingly implemented as a way to reduce GHG emissions. The European Union's Emissions Trading System (ETS) is the oldest and largest carbon market born out of the Kyoto Protocol. The ETS has failed to substantially reduce carbon emissions (e.g., see Nicolas et al. 2014). Efforts to increase the effectiveness of carbon markets attempt to "tweak" programs through adjustments in permit allocation and prices. However, these efforts overlook larger questions about the appropriateness of market-based schemes to address climate change. We draw from Karl Polanyi (2001) to examine if carbon markets represent a true countermovement to address climate change. Anthropogenic climate change has been caused by increased commodification and market expansion. Therefore, real solutions to climate change must challenge market supremacy—not further increase commodification through markets that benefit the economic elite. Carbon markets serve to further the reproduction of capitalism and economic growth and serve to conceal, rather than transcend, the capital-climate contradiction.

In chapter 4, we examine geoengineering strategies that are gaining increased political support. Geoengineering refers to the use of technologies that can alter the climatic system in an attempt to reduce the negative impacts of climate change. The most widely discussed strategy is stratospheric aerosol injection, which would entail releasing particles into the stratosphere to increase the reflection of solar energy and reduce global temperatures. This could allow for continued GHG emissions while mitigating the impacts of climate change. We also examine various approaches to "carbon geoengineering," a climate change strategy based on the removal of carbon from the atmosphere or sources of fossil fuel combustion. Drawing from Marcuse, we examine geoengineering technologies and how they are being promoted as the most economical solution, a techno-scientific achievement, and a means to preserve the current economic system. Those who greatly benefit from the current system and have denied climate change in the past are increasingly coming forward to support geoengineering (Klein 2014, Lukacs 2017). While geoengineering could reduce the symptoms of climate change, like green technology and carbon markets, geoengineering strategies fail to transcend the capital-climate contradiction. Instead, these three proposed solutions continue to conceal the existence of this contradiction, ultimately undermining the chances of effectively addressing climate change.

Chapter 5 marks a shift in the book where we focus on transitional mitigation strategies that challenge the supremacy of economic growth and move beyond the capital-climate contradiction. Drawing from a diversity of scholars and scientists, we present evidence that significantly reducing GHG emissions is incompatible with continued economic growth. Growth as measured by the Gross Domestic Product (GDP) has long served as an indicator of prosperity; however, prioritizing economic growth above social and ecological well-being has resulted in an abundance of negative outcomes, including climate change. If our social system continues to prioritize increasing production and consumption, there is little hope to reduce GHG emissions. Scientists, scholars, and economists increasingly argue that the decarbonization necessary to stay within the 2 degrees C target cannot occur while simultaneously increasing GDP (e.g., Stern 2006, Jackson 2009, Anderson and Bows 2011, Alexander 2014, Hickel 2016). Effective solutions to climate change, therefore, must challenge the growth paradigm.

The second half of chapter 5 focuses on "degrowth." Degrowth involves a planned contraction in economic growth among wealthy countries to a steady state (non-growing) economy. It also entails a total reduction in the extraction and use of energy and materials, including fossil fuels, and therefore supports decarbonization. The basic claims of the degrowth movement include: economic growth cannot go on forever due to ecological limits and, thus, wealthy societies should intentionally contract their economies in a socially sustainable way (e.g., see Latouche 2010, Schneider et al. 2010, Kallis et al. 2012, Weiss and Cattaneo 2017). Degrowth is about living with enough rather than reproducing a social system that demands the production and consumption of an increasing amount of commodities. Degrowth scholars have proposed a range of policies and lifestyle changes that can support a planned contraction of the economy to a steady state.

Chapter 6 discusses the importance of work time reduction (WTR), economic democracy, and a renewed labor movement in reducing GHG emissions. WTR has been proposed as a key component of degrowth: it can significantly reduce production, energy, and resource use, especially if coupled with low-impact leisure activities (Schor 2015). Labor movements have played a central historical role in WTR, and unions continue to push for reduced working hours in several European countries. We also examine economic democracy as a climate mitigation strategy. Democratic models, such as worker-owned cooperatives, not only increase participation in decision-making but are also more likely to support environmental goals and GHG reduction (Boillat et al. 2012, Bayon 2015). Lastly, we examine the potential for a revived and renewed labor movement to overcome the false antithesis between labor and the environment, becoming a new and powerful force fighting for the systemic changes necessary to address climate change.

In chapter 7, we explore transitional mitigation strategies where the full potential of alternative energy technologies and systems can be realized. Drawing from Marcuse, we examine how green technologies may be able to address the energy boomerang effect and reduce GHG emissions when embedded in different social conditions. We focus on "community renewable energy," or collectively owned renewable energy systems, that are often associated with degrowth. Because growth-dependency is in part predicated on the private ownership and control of productive technologies, addressing the issue of ownership and control is especially important to begin intentionally and sustainably contracting total energy use. Examples of community renewable energy systems continue to proliferate as more communities, especially in Europe, choose to reduce GHG emissions locally. In addition, there are increasing examples of remunicipalization, where citizens have mobilized to take the control of energy systems out of the hands of private companies, making energy a public good. Chapter 7 concludes by examining the role that governments can play in transforming the energy sector for GHG reduction, including nationalizing fossil fuel companies.

Chapter 8 explores new international governance mechanisms needed to facilitate democratic decision-making about climate change. One option is to promote global participatory governance. Habermas's ideas on participatory and deliberative decision-making provide guidance for a form of environmental governance that allows values and norms to evolve, minimizes the influence of powerful interests, can subsume cost-benefit analysis, and focuses on talking and pattern recognition instead of calculation (Dietz 1994). We examine four questions of scale that will be critical for the creation of a global-level participatory governance system for climate change. Such a system has the potential to level the playing field, reduce the power of special interests, and result in responses to climate change that are equitable and just.

In the conclusion of the book, we focus on the role of ideology to further strategies with the potential to transcend the supremacy of economic growth and capital accumulation. Therborn's (1980) conception of ideological transformation suggests that a fundamental battle in ideological transformation is to extend the belief that another system is possible. For social change to occur, people need to know that there are alternatives and that they can become the new reality. In addition, a large and unified social movement is necessary to catalyze the recreation of our economic and social systems in ways that reduce material and energy use and increase human and ecological well-being. While a post-capitalist degrowth society and a new system that can quickly and effectively address climate change is certainly possible, we identify the roadblocks that constrain the creation of a new social order. Despite these obstacles, to have a fighting chance at minimizing the impacts of climate change, the conversation needs to change from focusing on simple tweaks to the current system to creating a new system where social and ecological well-being is prioritized above economic growth. While radical alternatives continue to be dismissed as impractical or impossible, they may be the only routes to effectively and justly address climate change.

CHAPTER 2

Green Technology

NATIONAL CLIMATE POLICIES and international climate agreements continue to focus on changes in technology to mitigate climate change. This can be seen through reports from the IPCC (2014) as well as in Article 10 of the Paris Climate Agreement (2016). The use of "green" technology to address climate change typically refers to two commonly proposed technological solutions for reducing GHG emissions: (1) improving resource use efficiency, and (2) alternative energy development. Examples of the first strategy include energy-efficient appliances and fuel-efficient vehicles. A 2016 report from the American Council for an Energy-Efficient Economy (ACEEE) claims that energy-efficiency gains have put off the development of 313 additional large power plants since 1990, reduced carbon emissions by 490 million tons in 2015 alone, and could prevent 1 billion tons of carbon pollution while avoiding the need for 800 new power plants between 2016 and 2030 (ACEEE 2016). The second green technology strategy involves switching energy sources away from fossil fuels and instead using bioenergy, solar, geothermal, hydropower, ocean, and wind energy. The IPCC's 2012 report on renewable energy makes a strong case for its potential to mitigate climate change, illustrating how future scenarios that include widespread renewable energy use can reduce GHG emissions (IPCC 2012). Investments in green technologies totaled more than $348 billion globally in 2015 (Bloomberg 2017). China in particular continues to receive international attention for increasing investments in renewable energy. Private sector investments have also increased: Goldman Sachs (2017) forecasts that wind and solar development will reach $3 trillion over the next 20 years and by 2023 private investments will negate the need for government subsidies. While politicians and investors continue to promote green technology as a way to successfully tackle climate change, this widespread technological optimism serves to conceal contradictions related to technology and the underlying drivers of climate change.

Techno-optimism, the belief that "technological breakthroughs will serve as the means to address each and every environmental problem that arises," offers hope that society can use technology to overcome natural limits and address any challenges that emerge (York and Clark 2010: 481; e.g., Foster et al. 2010, Dentzman et al. 2016, Gunderson et al. 2018b). However, environmental techno-optimism tends to ignore the social dimensions of technological innovation, adoption, and use (Gunderson et al. 2018b). Technological innovation is social because the values and interests of a given society, especially of those in power, shape the kinds of technologies that will be developed (e.g., Marcuse 1964, MacKenzie and Wajcman 1985, Bijker et al. 1987). Technological adoption is social because factors such as power, social structure, choice, and values influence whether a given technology or system will be taken up by a society (e.g., Cottrell 1972). Along with its social impacts, technology use is social in at least two, and sometimes contradictory, ways: (1) technology orients values and sets a range of outcomes that social actors and groups can pursue (i.e., technology is not neutral and disinterested toward all ends) (e.g., Hornborg 2009, Whyte et al. 2017), and yet, at the same time, (2) societies, especially those in power, can make choices about the different outcomes within the range of options made possible by a given technology (e.g., Veblen 1939, Cottrell 1972, Feenberg 1999). Sometimes the alternative social futures made possible by technology are constrained by existing social structures.

As outlined in the introduction of this book, critical theorists have closely examined relationships between society, nature, and technology. At times, the alternative social futures made possible by technology are constrained by existing social structures. For example, radicals have long argued that advances in productive technology could be used to help free, rather than further dominate, human beings—yet existing structures impose particular outcomes (Bookchin 1971, Granter 2009). Capitalist systems constrain possibilities and result in contradictions: "the forces of production [including productive technologies] enter into the basic contradiction only as they are developed or limited by the capitalist production relations" (Young 1976: 201). Presupposing the Hegelian dictum that the present is pregnant with the future, or, rather, many possible futures, the argument is that already existing technology could be used for more rational ends in different social conditions yet these ends are constrained by existing social structures. Akin to the claim that there is a contradiction between the technical potential of adopting and using techniques that could reduce human toil, on the one hand, and the social relations that stand in the way, on the other, there is currently a contradiction between the technical potential of adopting and using techniques that have the potential to reduce environmental pressure, on the one hand, and the institutionalized social relations—i.e., capitalist class relations—that hamper this technical potential on the other (Foster 2002: 101, Gunderson et al. 2018b). We term this the "technical potential-productive relations" contradiction below. Due to the social nature of technology use, if technologies are to contribute to significantly reducing environmental pressure, they must also be accompanied by social and policy changes. We will illustrate how this contradiction relates to climate change through examining how green technology solutions without significant social changes have paradoxical outcomes that will fail to adequately address increasing greenhouse gas (GHG) emissions.

Both of the common "techno-fixes" for climate change, (1) increasing efficiency, and (2) alternative/renewable energy sources, have been shown to have unintended and paradoxical outcomes. First, there is a commonly found association between improved resource efficiency and increased resource use, often termed the "Jevons paradox" (e.g., Bunker 1996; Alcott 2005; Greening et al. 2000; Foster et al. 2010; Holm and Englund 2009; Polimini et al. 2008; Sorrel 2007; York 2010; York et al. 2009; York et al. 2011; York and McGee 2016). Second, there is growing evidence that alternative or renewable energy substitutes for fossil fuel-generated energy may not result in a one-to-one substitution and may even increase total energy use (one aspect of the "energy boomerang effect") (Zehner 2012, York, 2012, 2016). In this chapter, we explore these two paradoxical aspects of green technology in more detail. We then illustrate how proposed technological solutions conceal underlying contradictions and divert attention away from the significant changes needed in order for society to truly realize the benefits of green technologies. Although green technologies have been widely promoted to reduce environmental harm, technology is not an autonomous mechanism that will inevitably solve environmental issues when employed. In addition, green technology serves to benefit powerful corporations and individuals who profit the most from the current system, further extending the capitalist logic underpinning carbon emissions rather than addressing the root causes of climate change.

JEVONS PARADOX

The Jevons paradox is named after the economist William Stanley Jevons for his work illustrating that improved efficiency of steam engines increased total coal consumption in the nineteenth century (Clark and Foster 2001). It now more broadly refers to the commonly found association between increased resource use despite improved efficiency. It is called a paradox as a reasonable assumption is that improvements in efficiency will decrease total resource use because fewer resources are used per economic unit.

The association between improved efficiency and increased resource use is found in many contexts at various scales. Jevons noted this association in his famous essay, *The Coal Question*, from 1865. In it, he stated "the reduction of the consumption of coal, per ton of iron, to less than one third of its former amount, has been followed. . . . by a tenfold increase in total consumption, not to speak of the indirect effect of cheap iron in accelerating other coal consuming branches of industry" (Jevons 1906: 154). Many others have built upon this initial insight. For example, another famous case involved efficiencies in steel production. Madlener and Alcott (2009), quoting Rosenberg (1994), illustrate how the Bessemer process, an innovation that blew air through molten iron ore to remove impurities (National Iron & Steel Heritage Museum 2012),

> was one of the most fuel saving innovations in the history of metallurgy [but] made it possible to employ steel in a wide variety of uses that were not feasible before Bessemer, bringing with it large increases in demand. As a result, although the process sharply reduced fuel requirements per unit of output, its ultimate effect was to increase . . . the demand for fuel.

Richard York, a sociologist at the University of Oregon, has written widely on the Jevons paradox. In one paper, he uses automobile gas mileage to highlight the paradoxical outcomes related to efficiency. People concerned about climate change have long argued for legislation to mandate more fuel-efficient cars as a means to reduce oil consumption and associated GHG emissions. However, the assumption that higher fuel efficiency reduces oil consumption is problematic. York (2006) shows that increases in miles per gallon in the U.S. car fleet did not lead to less fuel consumed. This outcome occurred for several reasons, including a shift from small cars to trucks, but also because the number of cars per 1,000 people increased, as did the number of miles driven each year.

For cars and electricity production in particular, increases in efficiency have consequences far beyond resource use. Using cars as an example, Zehner (2012) has argued that increased fuel efficiency serves to extend and perpetuate a car-based society. A car-based society is associated with energy consumptive lifestyles and practices. Car-centric communities maintain and extend development policies and practices that perpetuate dependence on cars for transport. Similarly, creating more electricity makes more energy available and often at a cheaper price that then enables excess energy use. In both cases, more energy efficiency leads to more energy consumed, negating resource conservation and associated carbon emissions.

The Jevons paradox is related to the idea of the "rebound effect," which refers to when the benefits of efficiency gains are partially consumed by increases in total resource use due to improvements in efficiency (Santarius 2012).[1] A full realization of the environmental gains of improved efficiency means that there is no rebound effect (a 0 percent rebound effect). Rebound effects above 100 percent are termed "backfire effects" or "backfires." This means that total resource use is higher after improved efficiency. It is not the case that all of efficiency gains will be consumed by increases in use. Santarius (2012: 15) argues there is a "fifty-fifty rule of thumb," meaning that increased resource use due to improved efficiency will offset at least half of the possible savings of improved efficiency. The underlying quandary of the Jevons paradox and the rebound effect is that total resource use increases despite efficiency gains.

Journalist David Owen (2010, 2011) explains these paradoxical phenomena in depth, providing numerous examples that the general public can relate to. One example is a family replacing an old refrigerator with a new energy-efficient refrigerator only to move the old fridge into the basement or the garage where it will be used for several more decades consuming the energy the new refrigerator saves. While cars are much more efficient today than several decades ago, motorists' energy consumption has continued to increase as energy gains are reinvested in consumption (Owen 2010). Owen argues that instead of high-efficiency, money-saving vehicles with air conditioning and all the possible comforts to make commuting enjoyable, we need vehicles that are so costly and uncomfortable to use that no one wants to drive (Owen 2011). Due to Jevons paradox, reducing consumption would be much more effective than increasing efficiency.

Scholars have put forth several possible direct and indirect causes and pathways that may explain the Jevons paradox. York and McGee (2016) summarize the most common hypotheses (cf. Sorrel 2007, Santarius 2012):

- *Direct association explanations:* The most common explanation of a rebound effect is that improved efficiency reduces the price per unit of production and/or consumption, thereby stimulating production and/or consumption and, thus, resource use.
- *Indirect association explanations:* The most commonly theorized indirect explanation is when the money saved by producers and/or consumers due to efficiency gains is spent on other forms of resource use. Another proposed indirect association points to new high-resource use pathways following structural transformations in production and consumption due to efficiency improvements.
- *Structural explanation:* Capitalist firms aim to maximize profits through two routes: (1) reduce costs of production, and (2) produce/sell more, requiring resource use. Improvements in efficiency reduce costs, thereby increasing profits, which are reinvested to expand production, requiring higher rates of resource use.

It is important to place the Jevons paradox in a social-structural context (e.g., York et al. 2011, Foster et al. 2010, Freeman et al. 2016, York and McGee 2016). As capitalist societies move from manufacturing to service and finance, it becomes easier to "get a larger share of GDP from less energy-intensive sectors" (York and McGee 2016), despite the common finding that economic growth is a leading cause of environmental pressure (e.g., York et al. 2003, Jackson 2009, Hueting 2010, York et al. 2010, Jorgenson and Clark 2012). York and McGee (2016: 85) argue that improved efficiency may form and/or strengthen "developmental pathways that over time lead to rising resource consumption." For example, resource efficiency is a cost-reduction strategy that, by increasing profits, increases production. That is, rebound effects may operate through an indirect structural mechanism, which partially explains the common association between economic growth and environmental stress despite higher levels of efficiency, especially at the national level (e.g., York et al. 2011, Jorgenson and Clark 2012). Indeed, nations with higher levels of efficiency generally have higher rates of carbon dioxide emissions, electricity consumption, and energy use (York and McGee 2016). Needless to say, the Trump administration's call for the use of "more efficient fossil fuels" at the 2017 United Nation's climate conference will not succeed in significantly reducing GHG emissions (Friedman 2017).

THE ENERGY BOOMERANG EFFECT

Along with improving resource use efficiency, alternative energy development is another commonly proposed technological solution to environmental problems, especially for climate mitigation. The goal is to displace
fossil fuel energy sources with non-fossil fuel sources, thereby reducing GHG
emissions. However, the assumption that a unit of alternative energy will
displace a unit of fossil fuel-based energy is problematic (York 2012, Zehner
2012). York (2012) and York and Bell (2019) show that across many countries,
significant increases in energy produced from alternative energy sources has
not led to an equivalent displacement of fossil fuel use. In the past five
decades, there was only a "very modest" displacement of fossil fuel-generated
energy sources with alternative energy sources in most countries. On average, a unit of alternative energy displaced less than one-quarter of a unit of
fossil fuel-generated energy and a non-fossil fuel-generated unit of electricity
displaced less than one-tenth of a unit of fossil fuel-generated electricity
(York 2012). Relatedly, renewable energy-generated electricity may have less
of a suppressive effect on GHG emissions in affluent countries compared to
poorer countries because it suppresses nuclear-generated electricity, rather
than suppressing fossil fuel-generated electricity (York and McGee 2017).
The paradox is clearest in the following disconcerting finding: reductions in
carbon intensity have been associated with increases in total energy use and
electricity production for five decades (York 2016). Further, it is worth noting
that alternative energy development has a number of other environmental
impacts, such as potent GHG emissions released when producing solar panels, habitat degradation associated with dams constructed for hydroelectric
power, and biomass air pollution issues (Zehner 2012, Bell 2015).

Zehner (2012: 172–73) terms the paradoxical correlation between alternative energy production and increased energy use as one aspect of the "energy
boomerang effect," where alternative energy has unintended consequences,
including expanding development and energy consumption. The energy
boomerang effect presupposes a particular set of structural conditions best
understood in light of Schnaiberg's (1980) "treadmill of production" theory.
The latter posits that capitalist economies must constantly expand production, creating a production cycle (a "treadmill") that increases energy and
resource extraction ("withdrawals") and pollution ("additions") into the
environment. In relation to energy production and use, the treadmill of pro-

duction is built on a number of structural conditions, including (1) the private ownership of energy systems; (2) the imperative to utilize energy to increase economic growth (and, thus, energy throughput); and (3) the use of energy production itself as a capital accumulation strategy.

The energy boomerang effect relates to the underlying socioeconomic relationships that drive economic growth and consumption. It seems unlikely that the energy boomerang effect is due to the alternative energy converters themselves or to human nature. For example, there would not be increased demand for energy due to downward pressure on prices if the economy was not dependent on increasing energy throughput to increase economic growth. Assuming continued economic growth, and without policies to ensure reductions in overall energy use, "[a]lternative-energy production expands energy supplies, placing downward pressure on prices, which spurs demand, entrenches energy-intensive modes of living, and finally brings us right back to where we started: high demand and so-called insufficient supply" (Zehner 2012: 172). Further, in a growth-dependent economy, alternative energy sources are a capital accumulation strategy, as opposed to a resource conservation strategy. Corporations invest in technologies to decrease costs and increase profits, not to reduce resource use (York 2016). In short, the energy boomerang effect presupposes a particular kind of society that privately owns energy systems; has a built-in structural imperative to utilize energy to increase economic growth and, thus, energy throughput; and uses energy as a capital accumulation strategy. An increase in total energy use is not an inevitable feature of alternative energy development. That is, the energy boomerang effect is *not* an *independent* effect of alternative energy development (see chapter 7).

GREEN TECHNOLOGY: CONCEALING UNDERLYING CONTRADICTIONS

As reviewed, efficiency improvements and alternative energy development are not sufficient conditions for drastically reducing GHG emissions. As described in the introduction, to examine responses to climate change, we draw from Larrain's (1979, 1982, 1983) explication of Marx's "negative" theory of ideology. Here, we apply the concept of ideology to specifically examine how the promotion and implementation of green technology operates in ways that mask underlying contradictions. From this vantage point, we can more closely analyze how a focus on green technology becomes a denial strategy that maintains current relations of power and prevents the more substantial changes needed to address climate change.

The common promotion of green technology as an independent solution to climate change is only one instance of a prevalent techno-optimism in environmental politics, which exists in at least three distinct variants. First, those supporting ecological modernization focus on technology and the shift in the responsibility for environmental outcomes from a command-and-control state to a more central role for the market and other non-state actors (Mol 1995). Second, reformists, namely environmentalists and environmental nongovernmental organizations, seek solutions that fit within existing institutions (Demaria et al. 2013) rather than calling for alternatives to the reigning capitalist system. Regarding climate change, this means finding market approaches that facilitate and promote alternative technologies as a means to address climate change, a position captured by market logic that fails to see the futility in a platform predicated on growth-based alternative energy production. Lastly, policy elites and corporatists favor a neoliberal approach to governance that privileges entrepreneurial motives to meet societal needs by diminishing or eliminating governmental regulation and oversight to the greatest extent possible. Unlike ecological modernization proponents who see a role for government in a shift to new technology, this perspective seeks to drastically reduce or even eliminate government intervention in the market and instead rely on technological solutions to address climate change that come from the private sector.

Despite its prevalence in contemporary environmentalism, there are at least three fundamental shortcomings of techno-optimism in relation to human-nature relations: (1) it overlooks the wide body of research showing that environmental problems are influenced by social factors and are often partially caused by social-structural conditions, (2) unintended additional environmental problems often follow techno-fixes, and (3) techno-optimism ignores the paradoxical outcomes of techno-fixes (York and Clark 2010). Here, we stress a fourth, subtler drawback of techno-optimism in the context of climate change: it draws attention away from the underlying contradictions and causes of climate change, especially the "technical potential–productive relations contradiction."

As mentioned in the introduction to this chapter, there is currently a contradiction between the technical potential of adopting technology that aids in the reduction of GHG emissions, on the one hand, and the institutionalized social relations that hamper this technical potential, on the other (the "technical potential-productive relations contradiction"). The technical potential-productive relations contradiction was framed well by Foster (2002: 101) and can be broken down into three claims:

> [(1)] It is not technology that constitutes the problem [of ecological unsustainability] but the socioeconomic system itself. [(2)] The social-productive means for implementing a more sustainable relation to the environment within the context of a developed socioeconomic formation are available. [(3)] It is the social relations of production that stand in the way.

The basis for the first claim—that there is nothing essential about technological development that creates unsustainable relations with the environment—rests on the assumption that technologies are shaped and directed by social structures and group interests. The second claim is that society already possesses the productive technological means to bring forth a more ecologically sustainable society and, specifically in the context of climate change, reduce GHG emissions. While green technologies are not the sole solution to climate change, they have the potential to contribute to a reduction in GHG emissions when applied in different social conditions (e.g., see chapter 7). However, this potential depends on the social structures and interests that condition them. As stated by Rosa and others (2015: 52) in a recent review of the anthropogenic drivers of climate change:

> [o]ne of the most important overall lessons of sociological research on the anthropogenic forces driving global climate change is that it is necessary to look beyond technical fixes and consider the social, political, and economic structures that condition human behavior and resource exploitation. Developing more efficient and less polluting technologies without also altering institutions and social structures may not be sufficient to substantially reduce GHG emissions, since political-economic systems have many dynamic feedbacks that may prevent technological fixes from having their intended effects.

We agree with Foster's third claim that current institutionalized social relations are a barrier to using technology as a means to help reduce GHG emissions. By "institutionalized social relations," we mean the private ownership of productive forces for the incessant accumulation of capital, which reproduces the treadmill of production. As revealed by the Jevons paradox and the energy boomerang effect, green technologies within a capitalist system prioritizing economic growth will fail to reduce GHG emissions. Thus, the technical potential-productive relations contradiction is intimately connected to the capital-climate contradiction. Climate policies that attempt to use green technology within the constraints of the existing social order conceal the technical potential-productive relations contradiction. The effect of concealing this contradiction is twofold: (1) ineffective policy, and (2) the reproduction of an inherently unsustainable social order.

Green technology as it is currently promoted and implemented serves to benefit powerful parties who wish to maintain the current system of economic relations. Foster (2010) argues that the "technological fetishism" underlying mainstream solutions to the environmental crisis is one of several "strategies for denial." Focusing on technology as an independent solution to climate change will not only remain ineffective but represents a form of denial "that serves the vested interests of those who have the most to lose from a change in economic arrangements" (Foster 2010). Hornborg (2001, 2003, 2009) makes a similar argument regarding the contradiction-concealing character of faith in technology-based solutions to environmental destruction. For example, since around the mid-1970s, and especially since the 1990s, there has been a "discursive shift . . . geared to disengaging concerns about environment and development from the criticism of industrial capitalism" (Hornborg 2003: 207). The belief that green technology applied in the current social-economic system will successfully address climate change serves to reproduce the current system of unequal exchange (Hornborg 2003). Green technology conceals this reality as well as fundamental contradictions related to how the continuance of current social relations constrains the potential for technologies to play a role in GHG reduction. In a world-system and ecological context, Hornborg (1992, 2001, 2009) uses the term "fetishism" to describe the common illusion of the autonomy of productive technologies, which conceals various socio-ecological processes such as unequal exchange and the Global North's forgotten dependence on land.

Techno-optimists have put forth seemingly viable options to the challenges posed by climate change. These approaches, however, currently represent options aligned with the current socioeconomic order and not alternatives to it. The reliance on technology as the solution to the climate change problem comes in different variants, but all reflect an ideological position: they conceal the technical potential-productive relations contradiction. Perhaps the deepest illusion of techno-optimism is the belief that technology is neutral and disinterested, free to be used and shaped by rational individuals who are independent of social-structural context. This assumption is problematic for a number of reasons (see Feenberg 1999, Whyte et al. 2017). As Marcuse pointed out, the ends that technology serves are prepared by the "pregiven empirical reality" (2011: 152), or, "in line with the prevalent interests in the respective society" (2001: 44). In other words, technology embodies the values and power of the society for which it functions (for expanded discussion, see chapter 4). Techno-optimists view old technologies as the causes of climate change that can be reformed, rather than interpreting "dirty" and "green" technologies in a social-structural context. The latter perspective allows one to see that the potential of reducing GHG emissions depends on changing the social structures and interests that condition them (see chapter 7).

Although technological advances theoretically hold the potential to address the challenges posed by climate change, these approaches have limited viability in contemporary societies. By producing energy without fossil fuels, alternative energy appears as the most obvious means by which to reduce carbon emissions globally. For example, although they do not need fossil fuels to generate electricity after technological infrastructure is in place, alternative energy systems like wind and solar do not *necessarily* lead to diminished fossil fuel-derived emissions, at least at the levels needed to effectively address climate change. As reviewed above, York (2012) shows that although alternative energy production has increased, it has not proportionally displaced fossil fuel emissions from energy production. This does not bode well given energy demand projections. The U.S. Energy Information Administration projects a 48 percent increase in global energy consumption by 2040 and that, despite significant investment in renewable energy, fossil fuels will supply greater than 75 percent of total energy (Showstack 2016). As energy demand increases, especially for electricity, renewable energy production would have to grow at a rate faster than any energy technology in history to meet climate stabilization goals (Hook et al. 2012). In contrast to current trends, a switch to renewable energy (with current technologies) would require that we use less total energy, due to lower energy return on energy invested (Hall et al. 2014; see chapter 7).

In summary, the current focus on technological fixes to climate change represents an ideological, not a pragmatic, response because techno-optimists displace the technical potential-productive relations contradiction by viewing technology as neutral and disinterested, or malleable and applicable independent of social context. In other words, techno-optimism in climate policy and its failure to reduce GHG emissions partially results from a failure to recognize that continued use of technology in the interests of capital will drive forward more of the same social and ecological outcomes.

THE IMPLICATIONS OF GREEN TECHNOLOGY SOLUTIONS

By concealing the technical potential-productive relations contradiction, climate policy that depends on the greening of technology reproduces existing systems to the exclusion of social alternatives. Focusing on technological solutions in a capitalist system omits consideration of both more effective alternatives (discussed in later chapters) and, perhaps more importantly, ignores the institutionalized social relations that led to the problems in the first place. Even if proponents are unaware, climate policy that depends on green technology represents a continuation of a larger project to serve capitalist interests. It does so by relying on technology rather than technology *and* social change to reduce GHG emissions, thereby allowing the fossil fuel-based economy to continue unfettered. Technological solutions devised to alter social processes that lead to reduced emissions hold great potential (Keary 2016) but simply focusing on technology as the solution to climate change represents an ideological rather than a practical solution. Few proponents of renewable energy and energy efficiency prioritize total energy reduction or technologies that might guide social behaviors in a new direction. Instead, many focus on techno-fixes designed to increase economic growth and continue to conceal the technical potential-productive relations contradiction. This represents an ideological approach orchestrated to fit "solutions" into an existing economic paradigm rather than looking for effective, long-term alternatives.

As argued above, proposed solutions to climate change through the greening of technology fail to address the systemic drivers of GHG emissions and therefore represent false solutions that mask the more fundamental changes necessary for climate mitigation. These false solutions defend the status quo by proposing minor tweaks to the current system rather than rethinking social priorities and reconfiguring socioeconomic relationships.

In this way, green technology continues to conceal the technical potential-productive relations contradiction. To effectively reduce GHG emissions, green technologies would need to be adopted with substantial changes in society that reduce overall consumption and resources use (see later chapters on how this can happen).

In addition to concealing the technical potential-productive relations contradiction, a one-sided focus on green technology also conceals the broader capital-climate contradiction outlined in the introduction. Green technology, embedded in current social conditions, serves as a way for capital to expand production while claiming that it can do so while reducing the destructive effects of expansion on the environment. In other words, green technology provides a convenient mechanism through which those financially benefiting from the status quo can continue to do so while claiming that technology can effectively reduce GHG emissions and stave off climate change disasters. The continual concealment of these contradictions will reduce the likelihood of effectively tackling climate change because progress will be limited by the Jevons paradox and the energy boomerang effect. In other words, continued attention on green technology as the primary, independent, or only solution to climate change conceals the root causes of the climate crises.

Techno-optimism is a prevalent form of ideological content in mainstream climate policies that reproduces the conditions that cause climate change. In this chapter, we presented evidence that attempts to "green" technology and institutions that brought about the climate crisis will remain ineffective, conceal systemic contradictions, and continue to reproduce the same social order that has caused climate change. Energy efficiency results in increased energy use and renewable energy continues to be used in addition to fossil fuels, increasing total energy use. While considered solutions to climate change, the social context of capitalism makes them false solutions. This continued techno-optimism restricts our horizon of thinking about alternatives to capitalism. Only through increased exposure, awareness, and acceptance of alternatives to prioritizing capital expansion will society transform to use technology in new ways that can dramatically reduce resource use and GHG emissions. How society can transform to realize the potential of green technology and more effectively address climate change will be explored in later chapters.

CHAPTER 3

Carbon Markets

A GROWING NUMBER of climate change policies call for emissions trading or carbon markets, usually a combination of cap-and-trade and carbon offsets schemes. For example, Article 6 of the Paris Climate Agreement establishes a new carbon offset mechanism and leaves open the possibility for an international carbon market (discussed below). Carbon emissions trading schemes are being implemented in a growing number of countries and regions, including the European Union (EU), New Zealand, South Korea, Kazakhstan, California, and China. The EU Emissions Trading System (ETS) is the oldest and largest carbon market born out of the Kyoto Protocol (Lohmann 2005; Newell et al. 2013; Vlachou 2014; Vlachou and Pantelias 2017a, 2017b).

Carbon markets attempt to reduce GHG emissions through an imposed maximum emission limit (the "cap") and assigning tradable legal rights to emit (the "trade"). Carbon offset schemes refer to investments in climate mitigation projects outside of the jurisdiction(s) covered, often in the Global South, which allow the investors to gain carbon credits to emit GHGs inside the regulated area. In carbon markets, prices fluctuate according to supply, based on the cap, and are meant "to represent the value of the environmental impact of carbon dioxide emissions or the potential shifts in wealth as those emissions are constrained and property rights conveyed" (Newell et al. 2013: 125). As discussed below, the EU ETS has not substantially reduced carbon emissions (Nicolas et al. 2014; Vlachou and Pantelias 2017a, 2017b). While this may be partially due to the over allocation of permits and resulting low prices, a continued focus on how to "tweak" trading programs to improve effectiveness overshadows larger questions about the appropriateness of market-based solutions to address climate change and their relation to social-structural conditions. Before more closely examining if carbon markets are an adequate means to respond to climate change, it is important to understand the theoretical origin of carbon markets.

Assumptions from environmental economics underlie carbon market schemes. Assigning prices to natural entities to solve environmental degradation presupposes that environmental degradation and problems result from "unpriced" (non-commodified) resources being used/polluted without compensating the harmed human parties (van den Bergh 2001). These "negative externalities" (uncompensated/unpriced harms) are not accounted for either in the market price of the product or in the product's production costs (Fairbrother 2016). According to environmental economics, the solution is to internalize these negative externalities. One must think of the environment as a pool of commodified and not-yet-commodified resources, or "natural capital," in order to assign price values to natural entities or classes of entities (e.g., Hawken et al. 1999; for a critical overview, see Foster et al. 2009). In the case of carbon markets, the prices created through bargaining are supposed to represent how much society "values" the resource (Lohmann 2005, Newell et al. 2013).

Environmental economic valuation schemes and their various applications have been criticized by environmental ethicists, neo-Marxists, ecological economists, and others (e.g., van den Bergh 2001, Adaman and Özkaynak 2002, Foster 2002, Smith 2007, Foster et al. 2009, Kosoy and Corbera 2010, Robertson 2004, Stoner and Melathopoulos 2015, Wright and Nyberg 2015). Three common critiques are especially important: (1) it is problematic to reduce the totality of nature's value to price values, (2) increasing the scope of capital's penetration of nature will only serve to perpetuate the structural causes of environmental problems, and (3) technical market-based solutions implicitly demote alternative approaches. In this chapter, we contribute to these critiques through applying the work of the Hungarian economist Karl Polanyi (2001) to examine carbon commodification and markets. We argue that a market-based solution is inappropriate to address a problem caused by market expansion. We draw from Polanyi (2001) to argue that carbon markets do not represent a genuine countermovement to climate change and therefore will not be able to successfully address climate change. We illustrate how a real solution to climate change would involve subordinating economic systems to social and environmental goals. Furthering market expansion to address a market problem will ultimately result in increased environmental harm and social inequality.

POLANYI AND CLIMATE CHANGE

The expansion of markets in the current neoliberal era represents one of several waves of market expansion in recent history (Burawoy 2015). Karl Polanyi's seminal book, *The Great Transformation*, reflects upon two previous waves of market expansion: the first beginning at the end of the eighteenth century and the second beginning after World War I. In each case, counter-movements emerged to protect society from the negative impacts of commodification. Polanyi believed that the protectionist movement after World War II signified a new understanding of markets and a permanent end to their overextension; however, we find ourselves in the midst of yet another wave of market expansion that began in the late 1970s. While Polanyi warned about the destruction that a reliance on market mechanisms could cause to society and nature, he likely never anticipated the magnitude of the current threat posed by global climate change.

Three key theoretical concepts from Polanyi (2001) apply to our analysis of climate change and carbon markets: fictitious commodities, the double movement, and (dis)embeddedness. A large body of literature has examined, interpreted, and applied these three concepts (for clear explications and review of interpretations, see Dale 2010, 2016; Holmes 2012). In this chapter, we review these concepts only briefly and focus our attention on how they apply to our analysis of responses to climate change.

According to Polanyi (2001: 75), commodities are "objects produced for sale on the market." He argues that because they are not produced for sale, "labor, land, and money are obviously not commodities" and therefore, when they are traded on markets, represent fictitious commodities (Polanyi 2001: 75). When fictitious commodities are treated like real commodities, negative consequences will ensue. Here we focus on climate change, an issue most closely related to what Polanyi discusses in terms of land: "land is only another name for nature, which is not produced by man" (Polanyi 2001: 75). Anthropogenic climate change has resulted from the commodification of nature. Increasing quantities and types of fossil fuels have been extracted, priced, sold in markets, and subsequently burned. Fossil fuels were not created for the purpose of being bought or sold in a market but existed for thousands of years below ground, part of the land or nature. By incorporating fictitious commodities into market systems, Polanyi agues, we run the risk of destroying the social and natural dimensions of our world. Polanyi argues that without protections, "nature would be reduced to its elements, neigh-borhoods and landscapes defiled, rivers polluted, military safety jeopardized, the power to produce food and raw materials destroyed" (Polanyi 2001: 76). Many social scientists have already recognized carbon credits as a Polanyian fictitious commodity (Kaup 2015). It is not our intention to argue this point further. We focus on carbon markets as a furthering of this fictitious com-modification and representing a false countermovement.

While Polanyi states that treating fictitious commodities as genuine commodities can result in the destruction of society, he also describes why this has not occurred: "social history in the nineteenth century was thus the result of a double-movement: the extension of the market organization in respect to genuine commodities was accompanied by its restriction in respect to the fictitious ones" (Polanyi 2001: 79). Polanyi emphasizes the importance of the double movement: "human society would have been annihilated but for protective counter-moves which blunted the action of this self-destructive mechanism" (Polanyi 2001: 79). Countermovements emerged to protect nature and society from the consequences of the com-modification of land, labor, and money. Burawoy (2015) maps out three waves of market expansion and their countermovements including the third or neoliberal wave, which threatens ecological catastrophe. Carbon markets have emerged as a proposed countermovement to stave off ecological catas-trophe; however, we argue it represents a false countermovement that fails to address the underlying drivers of global climate change.

Lastly, Polanyi's notion of embeddedness is helpful for assessing the over-all purpose of a countermovement. The term embeddedness can be generally interpreted as the degree that economies/markets are directed or constrained by other social (non-economic) goals and institutions. While the concept of the embedded or disembedded economy has been greatly debated, we agree with other scholars that it is the idea rather than the reality of the disembed-ded economy that drives market fundamentalism (see discussion in Holmes 2012). In other words, market fundamentalism attempts to embed social and ecological processes into the logic of the free market: "the control of the eco-nomic system by the market is of overwhelming consequence to the whole organization of society: it means no less than the running of society as an adjunct to the market. Instead of economy being embedded in social rela-tions, social relations are embedded in the economic system" (Polanyi 2001: 60). Although markets never become fully disembedded from society, the idea of the "free market" drives policies that are increasingly destructive (Dale

2016). Market fundamentalism attempts to expand commodification and to subject society and nature to market rules. Countermovements thus should attempt to re-embed economic systems within the social-ecological sphere, prioritizing social and environmental protection.

Scholars have applied Polanyi to climate change arguing that (1) carbon-based fossil fuel is a fictitious commodity, and (2) a double movement has emerged surrounding the consequences of its commodification (e.g., Carton 2014, Kaup 2015, Osborne 2015). Carton (2014) adopts a flexible or "soft" interpretation of Polanyi that recognizes market-based strategies that increase commodification as a countermovement. Carton (2014:1007) argues that carbon markets represent a modern form of the double movement:

> it seems reasonable to conclude that in a society where social institutions have become embedded in economic relations—i.e., where norms, values, and interests have become tied in with a generalised market mechanism—those social and political forces constituting the countermovement might in part be consistent with the further expansion of market relations.

Thus, a market-based problem gets a market-based solution. Carton (2014: 1008) also adds, "countermovements need not be 'good for everyone' to be valid examples of the dynamics that Polanyi described." The author argues that the success of counter-movements now depends on their "compatibility with capitalist social relations" and that carbon markets "can be conceptualized as an example of Polanyian social protection" (Carton 2014: 1008–9).

In contrast, Fraser's (2014) interpretation of Polanyi offers a challenge to Carton's claim that carbon markets are a Polanyian countermovement and develops a critique of, rather than an apology for, carbon markets. Fraser (2014: 548) argues that "the structural reading of fictitious commodification foregrounds the inherently self-contradictory character of free-market capitalism." Fraser (2014: 548) argues that Polanyi identifies "three contradictions of capitalism: the ecological, the social, and the financial, each of which underpins a dimension of crises" (see also O'Connor 1998). She states that attempts to commodify labor, land, and money are contradictory and ultimately undermining, "akin to a tiger that bites its own tail" (Fraser 2014: 548). Therefore, further commodification only deepens these contradictions and causes further damage to society and ecosystems. In addition, Fraser's (2014) extension of Polanyi includes recognition of domination and sensitivity to hierarchy and exclusion. She illustrates how some protectionist movements can be used to further, rather than mitigate, domination and inequality in society. Applying Fraser's ideas to carbon markets reveals how increased commodification through carbon markets will fail to address climate change, further domination by elites, and ultimately increase risks to society. A genuine counter-movement to the commodification of carbon-based fossil fuel and emissions would restrict the market, address the underlying contradictions, and not further domination. In this chapter, we will illustrate that only an approach that re-embeds the economy into the social-natural sphere (subordinating economic growth to social and environmental goals) will have any success in addressing climate change.

CARBON MARKETS AS A COUNTERMOVEMENT TO CLIMATE CHANGE

The centrality of carbon markets as a climate policy mechanism is clear in Article 6 of the Paris Climate Agreement of the 21st Conference of the Parties of the UNFCCC (2015). Article 6 recognizes that national governments may utilize "internationally transferred mitigation outcomes," without explicitly using the terms "emissions trading" or "carbon market." The somewhat difficult wording of Article 6 "provide[s] the ability to create an international market if any Parties [of the Agreement] so desire" as well as "the means to create a process that may/will lead to the convergence of domestic carbon prices over time" (Marcu 2016: 6). Further, Article 6 establishes a carbon offsets scheme, widely referred to as the "Sustainable Development Mechanism."

Most research on the effectiveness of emissions trading has focused on the EU Emissions Trading System (ETS) launched in 2005 (for reviews, see Newell et al. 2013, Muûls et al. 2016). The most positive reports estimate a 2.4–4.7 percent reduction in total emissions from 2005–2007 and there have likely been slight decreases in emission intensity during Phase II (2008–2012) (for sympathetic overview of positive findings, see Muûls et al. 2016: 5). However, Carbon Trade Watch (2011) argues that the ETS failed to reduce total emissions, including during Phase I, and emissions reductions in the EU since the implementation of the ETS are primarily due to non-ETS variables, such as renewable energy production and the economic recession (Nicolas et al. 2014). Further, there is little evidence for resultant long-term investment in new technologies (Leiter et al. 2011). Many blame the overallocation of permits and resulting low prices. For example, one could trade a permit to pollute a ton of carbon for cents in 2007 due to an oversupply of allowances following industry lobbying, and the market collapsed in 2012 (Newell et al. 2013). There was a great deal of technical discussion on how to improve the EU ETS for the third phase, which started in 2013 (for review, see Newell et al. 2013), though the resulting model effectively reproduced the basic features of the first two phases (Carbon Trade Watch 2011). Although a 2017 EU agreement will likely result in slightly higher carbon prices, critics argue changes are minor, big industry will be paid to continue to pollute, and the deal makes the Paris Agreement meaningless (Reuters 2017). EU policy director Jong stated that the "deal ignores the urgency to reduce emissions quickly and hands out billions in pollution subsidies . . . the EU carbon market will continue to fail at its task to spur green investments and phase out coal" (Reuters 2017). In addition, carbon offsets have been called minor "green" updates to dirty factories that supposedly "offset" future emissions, a process Klein (2014: 223) describes as "running in place." For example, the Kyoto Protocol's Clean Development Mechanism (CDM) allows industries in overdeveloped countries to invest in emission reduction projects in Global South countries in order to buy carbon credits to increase emission caps. When coupled with cap-and-trade schemes, investing in carbon offsets allows polluters to emit more.

Along with the lack of success of the EU ETS to reduce emissions, there are a number of controversies surrounding carbon markets, most related to the CDM (for review, see Klein 2014: 219). The most notorious case relates to Chinese and Indian coolant plants. By installing cheap technological means to destroy HFC-23, a highly potent GHG byproduct, the factories were able to gain and sell emission credits worth millions of dollars. This incentivized the plants, which were already producing an extremely environmentally harmful commodity, to produce more HFC-23 in order to destroy it to gain emissions credits to sell to polluters (CDM Watch and Environmental Investigation Agency 2010; Klein 2014: 219–20). As Melathopoulos and Stoner (2015) argue in their critique of ecosystem service valuation, assuming that past limitations and inadequacies of carbon markets are due to technical issues neglects a larger question: the relationship of these programs to current social-structural conditions.

Carbon markets are best interpreted as an endeavor to expand the commodification of fossil fuels in order to address the capital-climate contradiction, yet they have had little impact beyond increasing capital accumulation and serving to (perhaps purposefully) stall more direct and effective mitigation strategies. The endeavor is paradoxical and harmful for a number of interrelated reasons, including: (1) the perpetuation of the structural causes of climate change; (2) attempts to control carbon emissions through markets may result in obstacles, surprises, and risks; and (3) the implicit and explicit undermining of alternative social futures and policies that have the potential to reduce carbon emissions. Carbon markets also (4) represent a response to climate change that benefits economic elites and furthers their domination of society. These four points are discussed in detail below.

Carbon markets perpetuate the structural causes of climate change by recommending the expansion of carbon commodification. Along with carbon-based fossil fuel being a part of what Polanyi called the fictitious commodity "land" or "nature," carbon credits represent a fictitious commodity as well, "because their very existence as something that can be bought and sold depends on making them both visible and tradable" (Kaup 2015: 291). As described by Kaup (2015), carbon markets are constructed by (1) deciding how much carbon can be released, (2) making invisible gases into measurable credits, and (3) creating a market where they can be traded (bought and sold). Carbon markets represent an attempt to address climate change that furthers capitalist expansion, attempting to convert nature into capital (Knox-Hayes 2010). However, because carbon is a fictitious commodity and carbon markets do nothing to address the underlying contradictions between the climate and capitalism, carbon markets are bound to cause increasing problems and deepen existing contradictions. Foster et al. (2009) analogize carbon market schemes to the Greek myth of King Midas, to whom Dionysus granted his wish for everything he touched to be turned to gold, later to find that he could not eat or drink. In this analogy, the god of the practitioners is their pre-existing conditions, a socioeconomic system that persists through profit maximization via commodification and the expansion of production, and the unintended consequence is as follows: "putting price tags on species and ecosystems will only serve in the end to subsume nature to the endless growth of production and profits" (Foster et al. 2009: 1090). In the same way that "the modern businessman sees in the landscape an opportunity for the display of cigarette posters" (Horkheimer 1947: 104), carbon-based industries see the climate system as an accumulation strategy (Smith 2007). In short, climate markets rely on the historically contingent and problematic attempt to reduce the value of fossil fuels and carbon emissions to a "sum of private values" (van den Bergh 2001: 7) without recognizing the degrading outcome of expanding the use of a condition of production.

Because they fail to address the capital-climate contradiction, carbon markets increase risks to society and the environment. Attempts to commodify carbon are flawed and possibly dangerous. Drawing from Marx's conception of formal and real subsumption, Boyd et al. (2001) convincingly argue that the more capitalism attempts to incorporate and control aspects of nature, the more obstacles and surprises will emerge. Attempted commodification of nature and transforming nature into sites of production can result in unexpected and catastrophic outcomes: "efforts to further control and subordinate biological systems to the dictates of industrial production will almost inevitably generate new risks and vulnerabilities for the production process, not to mention unforeseen externalities" (Boyd et al. 2001: 561; see also York and Clark 2010). While the risks associated with fossil fuel combustion are already clear, addressing these impacts through attempts to commodify, quantify, and control are also risky. Already, attempts to quantify and control carbon face obstacles and surprises. For example, Osborne (2015) examines carbon storage in forests and finds that unforeseen biophysical processes, such as pest infestations, can significantly reduce carbon storage and invalidate expected offsets. In addition, models of global carbon sources, sinks, and movement are plagued with unknowns. In general, carbon and climatic systems are still not fully understood with uncertainties remaining in terms of nonlinear relationships, feedbacks and thresholds that can undermine the ability to set a "safe" limit in a cap and trade program (Lohmann 2010). Inserting carbon into a market mechanism assumes humans can control carbon and ignores risks and unknowns, leaving open a range of potential obstacles and surprises. Falsely assumed control over the carbon cycle will increase social and environmental risks.

Carbon markets also increase risks to society by preventing or delaying alternatives with the potential for transformative reductions in GHG emissions. Carbon markets demote or undermine alternative policies and alternative social futures that would be more effective. Lohmann (2005) provides evidence for this happening in the context of the Kyoto Protocol. After the United States introduced the idea of emissions trading, this redirected intellectual and financial resources from innovations and social changes that had the potential of reducing emissions. Environmental criticisms of Kyoto's emphasis on establishing a carbon market were scorned as taking a "do-nothing" stance, input and ideas from nonprofessional and noncorporate groups were minimized, and alternative pathways were marginalized. The corporate watchdog nonprofit Corporate Europe Observatory (2015) argues that the existence of the EU ETS has undermined the ability of new emissions regulations to take hold and its negligible targets act as a "ceiling" rather than a "floor" for national climate policies. In short, another ideological outcome of emissions trading is the reproduction of the capital-climate contradiction through the implicit disavowal of alternative social futures. By accepting capitalism as a given, market-based solutions demote alternative social futures that may be able to more successfully address climate change.

The creation of carbon markets as a response to climate change represents a defensive maneuver from economic elites to preserve the status quo and further the accumulation of capital (Klein 2014). It is a political (i.e., not neutral) strategy influenced by substantial financial interests (Bryant 2016). The further commodification of carbon creates profits, and the vast majority of these profits are going to the same people already profiting from the current neoliberal system. Lohmann (2010) details how carbon markets are dominated by the same institutions active in derivatives trading, including Goldman Sachs and other big banks. Carbon markets are dominated by speculators and supported by the largest actors in finance as well as industry, who prefer a more flexible and capitalist mechanism to address GHG emissions (Kaup 2015). Large banks and corporations are already reaping profits from trading carbon. If carbon markets represent a countermovement to climate change, it is a movement that will further domination, hierarchy, and inequality. This reality spurs Carton (2014: 1008) to specifically explain, "countermovements need not be 'good for everyone.'" In contrast, Fraser's (2014) interpretation and extension of Polanyi incorporates domination, power, and hierarchy and calls for countermovements that restore justice as well as social protection.

Lastly, we draw upon Polanyi's concept of embeddedness to examine carbon markets as a countermovement to climate change. Carbon markets further embed society and nature into market relations; whereas, a genuine countermovement would work to embed markets into the socio-natural sphere. As Polanyi never indicated that nature and society are separate, Kaup (2015) calls for a neo-Polanyian approach to socio-natural embeddedness where markets are subjugated to goals of social and ecological well-being. In contrast, through attempting to subject nature to a market mechanism, carbon markets further commodification, domination, and risks to society. A genuine countermovement would involve prioritizing social and environmental goals over market expansion and would protect society and ecosystems from harm in a way that is just and equitable (Fraser 2014). As stated by van Griethuysen (2010: 3), to avoid social-ecological collapse, we must "shift from the property-based hierarchy where social and ecological considerations are subordinated to the capitalist economic rationality towards an eco-social rationale, where economic activities are subordinated to social and ecological imperatives."

CHALLENGING THE SUPREMACY OF THE MARKET

In a world where markets are presented as the solution to all problems,
an ideological challenge to the supremacy of the market is a crucial
preliminary to any effective countermovement.

BURAWOY 2015: 24

The work of Karl Polanyi has taken on increasing relevance in recent years. As Fraser (2014: 544) argues, today's crises are part of a "great transformation redux"—the current neoliberal era has unleashed the same crises described by Polanyi. Crises linked to market expansion have not only been recognized by academics but also by activists, politicians, and public figures. Applying a structuralist interpretation of Polanyi (Fraser 2014), we have illustrated why carbon markets do not represent a genuine Polanyian countermovement. They further expand the market mechanism, increase domination and inequality, and will be unable to successfully address climate change in a way that protects the majority of global citizens from harm. Carbon markets will not succeed in significantly reducing GHG emissions because they fail to address the underlying causes of climate change and instead further subject society and ecosystems to market logic that prioritizes economic growth.

Similar to our analysis of green technology in the last chapter, market-based solutions to climate change conceal the capital-climate contradiction. In contrast, carbon markets help to reproduce the capital-climate contradiction and are therefore unlikely to adequately address climate change. The ideological assumptions presupposed in emissions trading schemes may be the basis of their failure to reduce total emissions. The assumptions underlying emissions trading schemes conceal the nature of the contradiction by, for example, recommending the expansion of the commodification of the environment rather than its reduction or dissolution. The latter type of thinking, calling for the reduction or dissolution of nature commodification, is only possible if one recognizes the historical contingency of current conditions (i.e., not reifying what is). Monetary valuation schemes do not understand the inherent contradiction in reducing nature to "natural capital." Recognizing this contradiction would lead to a radically different approach to climate change policy: decommodifying the environment, as opposed to its further commodification.

Climate policies that rely on market reforms distract attention away from social alternatives that may actually address the capital-climate contradiction (discussed later in this book). Alternative social futures that lie outside national allowances of now-commodified carbon dioxide pollution and other reified categories are marginalized. Market-based solutions provide the illusion that we can address climate change while still expanding markets and economic growth. They offer an easy way for those benefiting from the current system to slightly tweak it to "solve" climate change. However, due to underlying contradictions, market mechanisms will be unable to adequately address climate change. Maintaining the current system that prioritizes economic growth will continue to result in similar outcomes. Hoffmann's (2011: 13) analysis of the EU ETS and similar schemes summarizes this well: "[w]hile well intentioned at first sight, such measures run the risk that they perpetuate the systemic flaws of the system."

CHAPTER 4

Geoengineering

POLICY MAKERS AND CLIMATE SCIENTISTS are increasingly discussing the development and deployment of geoengineering, defined by the IPCC as "a broad set of methods and technologies that aim to deliberately alter the climate system in order to alleviate impacts of climate change" (Boucher et al. 2013, IPCC 2014). The IPCC held an "Expert Meeting on Geoengineering" in 2011 and the IPCC Fifth Assessment Report discusses the possible role of geoengineering in climate change mitigation (IPCC 2012, IPCC 2014). The addition of geoengineering to the 2014 IPCC report marked a clear shift as geoengineering moved from the fringe to the mainstream of the climate change policy debate (Hamilton 2015). As policies to curb GHG emissions show discouraging results, advocates of geoengineering claim that the 2 degrees C target will be difficult or impossible without engineering the climate (Keith and MacMartin 2015, Conolly 2017). Geoengineering is also receiving increasing support since the election of Donald Trump as the U.S. President. Trump's first Secretary of State and former ExxonMobil CEO, Rex Tillerson, referred to climate change as "an engineering problem" and added enthusiasm for geoengineering "appears to be growing" among other high-level officials in the administration (quoted in Lukacs 2017). In November 2017, a U.S. congressional sub-committee held a hearing on geoengineering that demonstrated increasing Republican support to use geoengineering technology to reduce the impacts of climate change (Temple 2017). In addition, controversial outdoor solar geoengineering experiments are now moving forward (Rosen 2019).

Geoengineering can be divided into "solar geoengineering," sometimes called "solar radiation management" (SRM) and "carbon geoengineering," with some of the latter strategies referred to as "carbon dioxide removal." Solar geoengineering strategies aim to reduce global temperature increases through deflecting solar radiation, for example, through mirrors in space or aerosols in the atmosphere. Carbon geoengineering aims to reduce atmospheric GHG levels through removing carbon from the atmosphere or from sources of fossil fuel combustion and then storing the carbon either in oceanic or terrestrial reservoirs (IPCC 2014). In this chapter, we focus on two of the most prominently discussed geoengineering strategies: stratospheric aerosol injection (SAI) (a form of solar geoengineering) and different forms of carbon geoengineering. Geoengineering schemes are being increasingly promoted as essential climate change response strategies.

Given the possible risks and the extent of unknowns associated with geoengineering (details below), it seems unreasonable to many that it is being seriously considered. Calling attention to the uncertainty and risks associated with geoengineering, Liao and others (2013) argue that if engineering the climate is posited as a real solution to climate change, we should first have a discussion about engineering people, whose cumulative behaviors are causing climate change. They argue, with some satire, that engineering meat intolerance, intelligence, altruism, and body size can alter human behavior and environmental impacts on an individual basis—which is much less risky than altering the whole planet. The authors acknowledge how preposterous human engineering is and then question why, given its greater risks (especially SAI), geoengineering is being considered as an option. Why is geoengineering considered a reasonable response to climate change when there is an ongoing unwillingness to address GHG emissions (the root cause)? The answers are social and, thus, require a critical social analysis.

While most discussions of geoengineering continue to focus on the specific technologies and how we could implement geoengineering, we focus on the political-economic and social reasons why geoengineering is being seriously considered as a solution to climate change and what this means for alternatives. The "whys" are not as straightforward as expert-analytic appraisals suggest. In a systematic analysis of geoengineering appraisals, Bellamy et al. (2012) found that all appraisals framed the problem in narrow, mostly technical terms and most commonly as an issue of climate change emergency conditions, insufficient mitigation efforts, or climate change impacts. The "obvious exclusions" in the general framing of geoengineering are the wealth of social and ethical issues (Bellamy et al. 2012: 605). However, recent analyses have more closely examined the social, legal, political, and ethical dimensions of geoengineering (e.g., Corner and Pidgeon 2010; Gardiner 2011; Preston 2012, 2016; Sikka 2012a, 2012b; Hulme 2014; Burns and

Flegal 2015; Hamilton 2015; Payne et al. 2015; Stilgoe 2016; Clingerman and O'Brien 2016). We follow a growing body of literature that examines the political economy of geoengineering by drawing from critical theory and explicitly situating its development in the capitalist context (e.g., Foster 2018, Gunderson et al. 2018a, Ott 2018, Surprise 2018).

Applying critical theory means connecting the forms of rationality justifying geoengineering to social-structural conditions. We focus particularly on the work of Herbert Marcuse for a perspective that is neither technophobic nor naively Promethean. Sikka (2012: 113) briefly described what a Marcusean perspective may bring to the debate: "geoengineering technologies would be viewed as a further set of invasive and dehumanizing artifacts oriented to continued control and subordination." We significantly expand on this claim through a critical examination of the structural forces and forms of rationality that have driven the recent agenda for geoengineering. Before we examine SAI, a specific form of solar geoengineering, and various forms of carbon geoengineering, we set the stage for our analysis through further describing Marcuse's work on technology and how it informs this discussion.

TECHNOLOGICAL RATIONALITY

As discussed in the introduction, the Frankfurt School argued that science and technology in capitalist societies—as embedded social projects—are largely utilized to dominate the environment and human beings; however, they maintained that these institutions have the potential to be reformed in a more rational society. Marcuse was critical of technological rationality in its current form for a number of reasons (e.g., Leiss 1974: Appendix, Feenberg 2004), three of which are important for theorizing the social dimensions of geoengineering. First, Marcuse argued science and technology are fastened to the interests of capital (e.g., Marcuse 1972: 59–60). He was aware of the ecological havoc caused by capitalist societies (e.g., 1972, 1994, 1992) and argued this was directly aided by technological rationality's inability to see nature as anything but "stuff of control and organization" (Marcuse 1964: 153). Capitalism and technological rationality are wedded in contemporary societies. In both, the cosmos must be reduced to quantifiable and calculable order to be mastered and both are organized by the common principle of efficiency (Marcuse 1989: 123). Second, Marcuse argued that the progressive goals of science and technology have been lost and "neutral" scientific projects are utilized to further the domination of nature and human beings. Individual scientists become engrossed in calculation and the progress of knowledge without reflecting upon the outcomes that their experiments and findings serve (Marcuse 2011). In other words, the scientific project is narrowly concerned with "how" questions—impressed and captivated by the achievements of scientific progress—without reflecting on sometimes destructive outcomes. Third, the repressive result of technology as a totalizing "ensemble" devoid of substantive goals creates a "one-dimensional" population marked by "a system of thought and behavior which represses any values, aspirations, or ideas not in conformity with the dominant rationality" (Marcuse 1989: 119). Because technical achievements primarily serve giant industries who "deliver the goods," technological rationality continues to support the status quo. Marcuse argued this compliance impedes ideas and actions that could usher in a qualitatively different society. Technological rationality reproduces the existing system and works against radical alternatives. For Marcuse, technological rationality will remain irrational until technologies are used to free human beings from harm and protect the environment, rather than blindly dominate it.

Focusing on geoengineering, Marcuse's work on the relationship between technological rationality and capitalism leads to important questions. Is geoengineering an example of Marcuse's assessment of the irrational core of a purely instrumental rationality? Have discussions about the technical means for mastering nature prevailed over setting substantive end goals? Is geoengineering an attempt to use technology to further the domination of nature rather than to protect the social-ecological world? How does capitalism shape the reality of developing and implementing geoengineering? To examine these questions, we move beyond dominant discussions focused on *how* to develop and implement geoengineering and instead ask *why* certain parties are supporting geoengineering as an approach to address climate change.

With these questions in mind, we turn to examine SAI and carbon geoengineering strategies. Our analysis should not be read as a critique of the intentions and meanings of individual geoengineering scientists and proponents. Instead, we are concerned with the social-structural forces underlying the case for geoengineering and why prominent justifications appeal to elites with a vested interest in selling and burning fossil fuels to accumulate capital. We follow others who argue that there is good reason to hypothesize that geoengineering implementation is relatively plausible in capitalist societies (Gunderson et al. 2018a), especially the variant of neoliberal capitalism in the United States (Ott 2018), due to social structural conditions.

STRATOSPHERIC AEROSOL INJECTION

Stratospheric aerosol injection (SAI) is considered the most economical SRM strategy and is the most widely discussed geoengineering strategy overall. SAI was inspired by volcanic eruptions: sulfur aerosols in the atmosphere from eruptions reduce incoming solar radiation and global temperatures. The Mt. Pinatubo eruption in 1991 led to dimming that cooled the earth by 0.5 degree C for one year (Robock et al. 2010). Injecting sulfur particles (or compounds with similar properties) into the atmosphere would represent an attempt to emulate this process. Planes, balloons, or ground cannons could release particles into the stratosphere where they would combine with dust and water, forming aerosols that increase albedo (reflection). Aerosols would likely last for about one year; therefore, this strategy would require continued deposition (Keith 2013). In his 2013 book, *A Case for Climate Engineering*, Harvard scientist David Keith made a strong case for developing SAI, and his ideas are quickly moving from theory to reality. Partially funded by Bill Gates, Keith and his collaborators are working on the Stratospheric Controlled Perturbation Experiment involving the launch of balloons containing aerosol particles—likely to be conducted in New Mexico as early as 2019 (Rosen 2019).

Although geoengineering options have the potential to contribute to climate stabilization, they come with significant risks. SAI could certainly block incoming radiation, but what other consequences might arise? It remains unclear how it may affect weather patterns, especially precipitation and, therefore, ecological and agricultural systems (Robock 2008a). According to models, the pumping of aerosols into the stratosphere may result in drought in South America, Asia, and Africa (Ferraro et al. 2014).[1] As stated by a leading geoengineering scientist (Keith 2013: 58): "used recklessly, geoengineering could threaten billions with starvation." Although a recent study suggests that these potential risks can possibly be abated with more moderate SAI approaches and finding the "right" level of geoengineering (Irvine et al. 2019). Others have highlighted how aerosols do nothing to address ocean acidification and could exacerbate the ozone hole problem, increase acid rain and air pollution, have unknown impacts on plants and clouds, and reduce radiation for solar power—in addition to risks associated with human error, commercial control, military use, and many other possible risks (see Robock 2008b, Robock et al. 2009, Boucher et al. 2013, Ciais et al. 2013, Weisenstein et al. 2015).

Perhaps the gravest risk associated with SAI relates to continued carbon emissions. Implementation could reduce incoming solar radiation, allowing for continued GHG emissions. If the intervention works initially but falters or if the project cannot be maintained, temperatures could increase rapidly due to a buildup of background GHG emissions, a risk known as the termination effect (Robock et al. 2010, Zhang et al. 2015). One modeling study found that implementing SRM for 25 years and then stopping could abruptly increase temperatures by 4 degrees Celsius, with severe impacts to agriculture and biodiversity (McCusker et al. 2014). Scientists have warned that political instability could abruptly halt SRM and result in a rapid temperature spike (Kintisch 2010). As David Keith (2013: 67) acknowledges, SAI is "a powerful and frightening tool."

In general, much of what is "known" about SAI is from computer models (Boucher et al. 2013, Ciais et al. 2013). Scientists acknowledge that models do not represent reality (Keith 2013). Models rely on many (potentially problematic) assumptions. In addition, while they may capture big picture patterns, most models fail to capture the details. Climate modeling is especially bad at predicting precipitation patterns (Keith 2013). David Keith (2013: 56, 63) explains, he has "no confidence in the precise numbers" from models and "we can never be certain of the efficacy and risks of geoengineering from models alone." As so much of what is understood is currently based on models, many risks related to SAI will remain unknown unless or until the strategies are implemented. Still, momentum is growing for SAI and SRM research in general, with the U.S. National Academy of Sciences launching a study to guide future SRM research and the IPCC already planning to focus more attention on SRM in its next assessment report in 2021 (Rosen 2019).

CARBON GEOENGINEERING

The recent IPCC special report (2018) highlights the important role of negative emissions strategies, which "include afforestation and reforestation, land restoration and soil carbon sequestration, BECCS [bioenergy carbon capture and storage], direct air carbon capture and storage (DACCS), enhanced weathering and ocean alkalinization." These strategies, along with post-combustion carbon capture and storage (CCS), sometimes confusingly referred to as just "carbon capture," are together referred to as "carbon geoengineering" strategies.[2] Land management strategies, such as afforestation/reforestation and restoring ecosystems (National Academy 2018) are sometimes called "natural climate mitigation" strategies and should be supported for reasons beyond climate change, including critically needed biodiversity conservation. While these "natural" strategies have the potential to be highly effective (Monbiot 2019), they have received a tiny amount of attention and financial investment compared to "high-tech" negative emissions strategies. News coverage of the IPCC special report focused largely on carbon removal as a way to "tweak the carbon cycle to reduce emissions" (Irfan 2018). In addition, following the release of the report, tech companies working on carbon geoengineering received increasing levels of financial investment (Magill 2018).

In this section, we briefly review some of the carbon geoengineering strategies gaining attention and funding. In our review, we purposefully include several approaches that are questionable carbon geoengineering strategies and strategies clearly not resulting in negative emissions. We do so because these strategies are being promoted and funded as part of a carbon geoengineering solutions portfolio. Identifying these false solutions is critical.

Post-combustion CCS involves capturing CO_2 at the point of generation, compressing it into a fluid, and then sequestering it for long-term storage underground or under the ocean (Leung et al. 2014). In this way, post-combustion CCS can theoretically result in carbon neutrality for fossil fuel-based power plants. To date, only a handful of demonstration projects exist. One example, is NRG Energy's Petra Nova coal power plant in Texas, which captures 1.4 million tons of CO_2 per year that is injected underground into oil wells to help push out more oil (Stone 2018) (see below). Here, the primary purpose is to increase fossil fuel extraction and increase profitability. After decades of research, they have yet to show that post-combustion CCS projects are economically viable and both private and government investment has remained minimal (Reiner 2016).

Ironically, CO_2 enhanced oil recovery (CO2-EOR) continues to be promoted as an important storage strategy for captured carbon (Biello 2009, IEA 2015). CO2-EOR involves injecting CO_2 into depleted or near depleted oil and gas reserves to extract otherwise unrecoverable reserves. It has been used for decades in the oil and gas industry. However, the "net" carbon storage referred to by proponents is defined within the boundaries of the stand-alone EOR project and fails to consider the CO_2 emitted from the combustion of recovered oil. For example, looking at data from multiple CO2-EOR projects, Jaramillo et al. (2009) find that between 3.7 and 4.7 metric tons of CO_2 are emitted for every metric ton of CO_2 injected. The motivation for EOR is not carbon mitigation but profit. This "win-win" strategy is increasingly supported by the U.S. government: the Department of Energy announced new funding for EOR projects in October of 2018, only days after the IPCC released their special report (DOE 2018).

Bioenergy combined with CCS (BECCS) is the carbon geoengineering strategy most widely incorporated into current integrated assessment models used to guide climate policy and international agreements (Anderson and Peters 2016). Of all the scenarios showing a high likelihood of staying within a 2 degrees Celsius target, 87 percent include widespread BECCS (Fuss et al. 2014). BECCS involves carbon being sequestered in plants that are then burned for power generation while capturing and storing the carbon emissions from combustion. However, BECCS remains primarily theoretical with the only empirical evidence from separate bioenergy and CCS facilities and a single ethanol-based BECCS demonstration plant (General Social Survey [GSS] 2016, Anderson and Peters 2016, Turner et al. 2018). Analyses of BECCS illustrate that finding suitable land, storage basins, and biomass will limit negative emissions, and there are serious concerns related to competition with agricultural land uses (Baik et al. 2018, Fridahl and Lehtveer 2018, Turner et al. 2018, National Academy 2018). Given the constraints and unknowns, Anderson and Peters (2016: 182, 183) argue that the prominence of BECCS in emissions scenarios and policy formulations is "disturbing" and represents a "high-stakes gamble."

Lastly, direct air capture (DAC) and storage involves taking carbon directly from the atmosphere and sequestering it. DAC technology can transform CO_2 into either a solid sorbent or a liquid solvent (National Academy 2018). Carbon geoengineering companies with DAC facilities, including Carbon Engineering, Climeworks, Global Thermostat, Infinitree, and Skytree, have focused on converting CO_2 into a usable product for sale (Siegel 2018). This process is only carbon-negative if atmospheric CO_2 is turned into a stable product that provides long-term storage. However, due to the higher costs associated with a solid product (Keith et al. 2018), most DAC projects involve turning CO_2 into a short-lived liquid product, primarily "carbon neutral" transportation fuels that return captured CO_2 back into the atmosphere upon combustion.

In summary, carbon geoengineering strategies are far from a panacea to global warming. Due to prioritizing profit above climate change mitigation, the most promising strategies currently result in temporary storage and function as a carbon neutral, rather than a negative emissions, strategy. In an alternative political economic context, where mitigation was the priority, increased funding could support projects with long-term storage potential. However, many carbon geoengineering strategies are still in the early stages of development, face logistical challenges (in addition to financial constraints), and many unknowns and risks remain. Given these realities, the reliance on carbon geoengineering technologies in almost all models driving climate change agreements and policies is risky and alarming.

WHY GEOENGINEERING?

This section discusses some of the political-economic and social forces driving the geoengineering agenda and forms of rationality employed to support it. We are most concerned with arguments that are likely to appeal to those in positions to make political decisions related to climate change. These arguments/rationalities include techno-optimism, maintaining the political-economic status quo, and appeals to cost effectiveness and potentials for profit. While we discuss both SAI and carbon geoengineering here together, we are aware of their differences (see above) and distinguish between these strategies when necessary.

A social basis for geoengineering's appeal is viewing it as an impressive techno-scientific achievement, perhaps the ultimate symbol of man's domination of nature. This can especially be seen in discussions regarding the potential of SAI. Some proponents, even scientists, have stated or indicated that the technologies should be implemented or at least developed simply because we have the ability to do so. Astrophysicist Lowell Wood, a strong and vocal proponent of geoengineering, stated that: "[w]e've engineered every other environment we live in—why not the planet? (quoted in Hamilton 2013b). David Keith states that, "[w]e may use these powers for good or ill, but it is hard not to delight in these newfound tools" (Keith 2013: 173–74). For them, the development of SAI technology represents the advancement of scientific progress. Even with the great number of possible risks, some scientists argue that the only way to proceed is with larger scale testing and deployment (Keith 2013, Hamilton 2013a), with one stating that, "we don't know how to ride a bicycle when we start, but we end up doing it" (Kintisch 2010: 179).

Scientists have long sought out techno-fixes to alter the environment, looking for levers that can be switched to change nature (Kintisch 2010). To some, SAI represents the ultimate trump card. Scientists and entrepreneurs are also discussing moving beyond SAI as a way to address climate change, exploring how they can use the technology to tailor the climate to optimal conditions (Hamilton 2013a). While SAI continues to be described by some proponents as the ultimate techno-fix to master nature, this portrayal overlooks associated risks as well as the powerful parties that are promoting geoengineering as a way to prevent changes to the current socioeconomic order.

In contrast, others have used different metaphors to illustrate the fallacy in the above reasoning, saying that geoengineering is like using dialysis to treat alcoholism, using a corset to treat obesity, or adding padding inside a car to fight drunk driving (Kintisch 2010, Nerlich and Jaspal 2012, Keith 2013). These alternative depictions suggest that developing and implementing geoengineering is not the appropriate means to address climate change as it will fail to address the root causes of the problem (Kiehl 2006). As expressed by Hamilton (2013b): "[t]he idea of building a vast industrial infrastructure to offset the effects of another vast industrial infrastructure (instead of shifting to renewable energy) only highlights our unwillingness to confront the deeper causes of global warming—the power of the fossil fuel lobby and the reluctance of wealthy consumers to make even small sacrifices."

Others support geoengineering, and SAI in particular, for economic reasons. According to Crutzen (2006), stratospheric sulfate approaches would cost about $25–50 billion per year, over one hundred times less expensive than emissions reduction (Keith 2010). As stated by the two leading scientists and dominant voices in current geoengineering discussions, Caldeira and Keith (2010: 57), "geoengineering could be the only affordable and fast-acting option to avoid a global catastrophe." Compared to other approaches, SAI is especially being touted as a cheap and easy fix for climate change, and while the exact costs are still uncertain, they could be in the range of $700 million per year (Keith 2013). Smith and Wagner (2018) more recently estimated a $3.5 billion start-up cost followed by $2.25 billion per year operation costs. In the November 2017 congressional hearing on geoengineering, Texas Republican Representative Lamar Smith stated, "instead of forcing unworkable and costly government mandates on the American people, we should look to technology and innovation to lead the way to address climate change" (quoted in Temple 2017).

A related political-economic driver of geoengineering support is its potential to reproduce the status quo. Even if geoengineering scientists support mitigation, geoengineering strategies in social context can be viewed as climate change strategies that protect and reproduce the current fossil fuel-powered capitalist order. Post-combustion CCS, for example, is an appealing solution because it maintains the status quo and its logic makes alternatives that significantly alter society unnecessary. CCS is supported by fossil fuel industries, especially oil and gas. For example, Chevron played a role in developing the IPCC's Special Report on Carbon Dioxide Capture and Storage (2005), the EU CCS Directive, and Australian, Canadian, and U.S. policies related to CCS and also participated/invested in the Gorgon (Australia) and Quest (Canada) CCS projects (Chevron Greenhouse Gas Management). Major oil and gas companies have also worked closely with government agencies to try to advance CCS technology.

A potential benefit of CCS for the fossil fuel industry is that it "provides a vision" of a "carbon-constrained future" that still allows for fossil fuel use: "CCS changed the way the fossil fuel industry envisioned their future challenges" (Stephens 2009: 36) by, for example, reducing the threat of reducing carbon emissions (Gibbins et al. 2006). CCS was embraced by the Bush administration "as an alternative to government regulation, emissions pricing and mandatory emission reductions" (Langhelle and Meadowcroft 2009: 237). As the former Chairman and CEO of Chevron, John S. Watson, stated in a 2010 speech:

> instead of pursuing complex regulatory schemes that can be very costly and lead to unintended consequences—from land use to trade flows—the world may be better served to turn our attention to basic R&D. . . . One technology that is getting a lot of attention is carbon capture and storage.

Kruger (2017: 63) explains that CCS allows energy companies and governments with fossil fuel resources to continue to reap profits and accumulate wealth:

> [t]he presumed dominance of fossil fuels is actually one of the main reasons put forward in favor of CCS. Social structures are consolidated as unchangeable constants. Mitigation options are assessed against the background of the prevailing power relations and the current production and consumption patterns. With these preconditions CCS is valued as an important instrument to reduce the emissions caused by burning fossil fuels.

In these ways, some carbon geoengineering technology is used to protect and further fossil fuel extraction and further increase profits. Anderson (2016) calls negative emissions technologies in general "mitigation on methadone" because they allow us to continue along a path of high carbon emissions.

Beyond carbon geoengineering, fossil fuel companies, wealthy individuals, and climate change deniers increasingly support geoengineering in general, including SAI (Kintisch 2010, Hamilton 2013, Klein 2014). Hamilton's book *Earthmasters* (2013) contains some of the most convincing evidence of support from the fossil fuel industry: Canadian oil billionaire, N. Murray Edwards, who has a financial interest in developing Alberta's tar sands, invests in David Keith's company Carbon Engineering Ltd.; Royal Dutch Shell funded a study of liming the seas; a top BP scientist chaired a geoengineering meeting in 2009; and ExxonMobil employed a scientist who has contributed to government reports on geoengineering. More recently, Hamilton (2015) identifies Shell and ConocoPhillips as having invested in geoengineering. These fossil fuel companies have much to lose if world leaders decide to aggressively reduce GHG emissions. This explains their participation in campaigns to counter climate science and deny that climate change is occurring (McCright and Dunlap 2011). Geoengineering represents an approach to address climate change while continuing fossil fuel extraction and consumption. Geoengineering may buy these companies time to extract the remaining accessible fossil fuel resources (especially new sources in the arctic) and maximize profits from this extraction. At the very least, geoengineering discussions could further delay emissions reductions approaches.

Some geoengineering supporters staunchly support free market capitalism. Efforts to reduce GHG emissions run counter to free market ideology, as they demand government intervention, regulation, and potentially taxes. This has led Bjorn Lomborg to support geoengineering and condemn cap and trade policies (Kintisch 2010). Modifying human systems and behavior could address climate change, but the policy intervention necessary to support these changes threatens free market ideology, a core conservative belief (Klein 2011). David Keith (2013: 143) asks in his book: "[m]ust we fix capitalism in order to fix the climate?" While he does not see a direct connection between capitalism and environmental degradation, others have answered this question with a resounding yes. GHG emissions reduction would require significant political and economic changes. Geoengineering solutions to climate change, however, do not threaten conservative worldviews that free market capitalism is the best way to organize society. In contrast to requiring government intervention into markets, geoengineering offers the illusion that free markets and unfettered capitalism can continue indefinitely. However, this indeed is an illusion as many free-market supporters overlook the fact that the deployment of strategies like SAI would require considerable state planning and intervention.

Geoengineering has led to a seeming paradox in which climate change deniers have embraced a response to climate change (Kintisch 2010). For example, the Heartland Institute rejects climate change but supports geoengineering (Klein 2014). This has also been the case for the American Enterprise Institute and the Hoover Institution, who challenged climate science but now promote geoengineering (Ellison 2018). While Reynolds et al. (2016) state that only "a handful of actors on the political right have indeed voiced support for SRM," this number seems to be rapidly growing. Recently, a rising number of conservative politicians who denied climate change have come out in support of geoengineering, including Lamar Smith, Randy Weber, Newt Gingrich, and attorney David Schnare—a Trump appointee (Bajak 2018, Ellison 2018). As explained by Kintisch (2010), geoengineering offers a middle ground for climate change deniers to concede that the world is getting hotter but perpetuate the myth that this is not primarily caused by human activity, or more importantly, fossil fuels. To counter warming, they can propose a low-cost geoengineering strategy while, at the same time, criticizing opponents for opposing what they claim will be a quick and effective solution. Klein (2011, 2014) argues that conservatives realize that climate change represents a serious threat to free market capitalism and they have therefore fiercely opposed its existence to maintain the current system. With increasing pressure to admit the reality of climate change, geoengineering offers a way forward that does not threaten the supremacy of capitalism (Klein 2014). In addition, as argued by Hickel (2017), it has become increasingly clear that the emissions reductions necessary to stay within the 2 degrees C target would require a contraction in economic growth, making technological approaches much more favourable for those who benefit from the current system. By supporting geoengineering, conservatives may be able to protect capitalism while still appearing to address the increasingly visible impacts of climate change. As the impacts of climate change become more difficult to refute, it is no coincidence that U.S. Republicans are showing increased support for geoengineering (Connolly 2017).

These motives to avoid GHG emissions reduction and preserve the current system have been publicly identified by geoengineering scientists. In response to increasing support for geoengineering from U.S. Republicans, climate engineers have expressed concern that geoengineering may be exploited by those opposed to GHG emissions reduction (Connolly 2017). Due to the known and unknown risks of geoengineering strategies, leading geoengineering scientists (including David Keith) have responded to the sudden increase in political support for geoengineering with great concern, recognizing the danger involved in the rapid and reckless use of these technologies (Connolly 2017, Orcutt 2017, Temple 2017). David Keith stated, "[o]ne of the main concerns I and everyone involved in this have, is that Trump might tweet 'geoengineering solves everything—we don't have to bother about emissions'" (quoted in Connolly 2017).

Recent political support for geoengineering as a means to avoid regulating industry lends support to the "moral hazard" argument, which runs as follows: "major efforts in geoengineering may lead to a reduction of effort in mitigation and/or adaptation because of a premature conviction that geoengineering has provided 'insurance' against climate change" (Royal Society 2009: 39). Because society is "insured" by geoengineering research and the hazards associated with climate change may be reduced by geoengineering, societies are (1) less likely to implement emissions reduction strategies, (2) likely to invest fewer resources in adaptation strategies (Royal Society 2009: 44–45), and/or (3) likely to increase emissions above business as usual projections (for summary, see Hale 2012). Many geoengineering scientists and technology firms continue to argue that we need to develop a "Plan B" but at the same time work on emissions reductions—one approach does not and should not curtail the other (Keith 2013, Hamilton 2013a). The case for geoengineering as Plan B, or, that geoengineering research should be conducted now because geoengineering may be necessary in a climatic emergency following insufficient GHG emissions reductions, is "[t]he dominant narrative surrounding geoengineering" (Corner et al. 2013: 945; for an extensive critique of the Plan B frame, see Fragnière and Gardiner 2016). However, continued financial investment in geoengineering, along with support from conservative movements, suggests that as geoengineering efforts ramp up, efforts to address GHG emissions will subside. This is a view shared by environmental organizations who oppose geoengineering, while other environmental groups have publicly agreed that at this point a Plan B (e.g., that could be used to save vanishing arctic ecosystems) has become a necessity. In 2015, Rex Tillerson stated that a "plan B has always been grounded in our beliefs around the continued evolution of technology and engineered solutions" (quoted in Lukacs 2017).

As geoengineering continues to be promoted, the public will be increasingly exposed to arguments involving the above reasons why geoengineering should be developed and/or deployed. Some people will likely be persuaded by the economic efficiency argument. Others may be lured by the promise of the ultimate techno-fix that allows for the further mastery of nature through science. Portrayed as a means to control nature, geoengineering will seem like the ultimate techno-scientific achievement and the rational way forward. As put by Hamilton (2013a: 174): "technologies gather added political momentum because we live in societies predisposed to seek technological answers to social problems." While some embrace the idea of geoengineering as a viable Plan B that allows a fossil fuel-powered capitalism to lumber on, others maintain that economic interests should be subordinated to ecological and social needs and that the continued technical mastery over nature is not only impossible, but such hubris will only lead to further harm. Therefore, it is time to transcend the current order, rather than reproduce its basic structures.

In contrast to SAI, we believe there are possible effective options for carbon geoengineering, but these options remain constrained by our current social order. For example, current DAC projects create carbon-neutral products due to the profit-imperative. Thus, they represent another example of the contradiction between the potential of technologies to reduce environmental pressure and the social relations that hamper this technical potential (see chapter 2). In a social order transitioning out of capitalism, however, the government could fund widespread implementation of DAC projects, possibly through taxes on carbon. In addition, a rapid expansion in solar and wind energy, while simultaneously shrinking fossil fuels, could potentially power a network of DAC plants, depending on the latter's future energy demands (which are currently very high). However, in our current social order, the profit-motive continues to prevent such actions. And, not coincidentally, the "natural mitigation strategies" focused on reforestation and restoration, while possibly highly effective and good for humans and wildlife, are not profitable and are not receiving much attention or investment.

While we acknowledge a potential role for carbon geoengineering in a different social context, it is far from a "silver bullet." Due to energy demands, high-tech carbon geoengineering will likely not create the negative carbon flows required to return atmospheric CO_2 levels back to the "safe" level of

350 parts per million (Wennersten et al. 2015). In other words, DAC alone, even used at maximum effectiveness, would not represent an ultimate techno-fix to mend the rift in the global carbon cycle. In addition, there are concerns about the potential environmental and political impacts of carbon geoengineering (e.g., Coninck and Benson 2014, Cuellar-Franca and Azapagic 2015). These concerns are summarized well in Greenpeace's 2008 assessment of post-combustion CCS: (1) CCS will develop too slowly to avoid dangerous climate change, (2) CCS is an energy-waster, (3) underground carbon storage is risky, (4) CCS is too expensive and "undermines funding for sustainable solutions," and (5) CCS comes with serious liability risks (Greenpeace International 2008; cf. Stephens and Markusson 2018: 509ff). These risks need to be considered and undoubtedly reducing emissions is more energy efficient and safer than CCS and other forms of carbon geoengineering.

MOVING BEYOND THE IRRATIONALITY OF PURE TECHNOLOGICAL RATIONALITY

Failure to consider the end goals and consequences, while focusing instead on technological progress and immediate economic growth associated with geoengineering, results in another instance of what Marcuse (1964) called the most "vexing" aspect of advanced capitalism: "the rational character of its irrationality." A low-cost, high-tech, and industry-friendly solution appeals to reason, but the use of technology to solve problems is irrational when it does not address the root causes of problems and the technological means overshadow the ultimate outcomes, casting aside the required social changes. Marcuse would see proposed techno-fixes as means to solve environmental crises through the same institutions that caused them. Geoengineering is the crowning realization of this contradiction. Marcuse's notion of technological rationality also helps us explain why geoengineering schemes, and technological fixes at large, are taken seriously among policy makers and scientists. Marcuse argued that in a one-dimensional society, where technical achievements primarily serve giant industries who "deliver the goods"—and, in this case, deliver the solutions—there is a tendency to identify with the system and dominant rationality. This way of thinking inhibits forms of thinking and acting that could create a qualitatively different social formation. In the case of geoengineering, technical fixes not only fit the dominant rationality and social order, but simultaneously exclude alternative paths that lay outside both. The technology of geoengineering does not contain the potential of transcending the existing social order; it maintains it. Increasing support for geoengineering further illustrates Adorno's claim that, "we live in a world in which we can no longer imagine a better one" (in Adorno and Horkheimer 2011: 107–8).

Geoengineering is a product of a society very much aware that large-scale changes must occur to mitigate climate change but structurally incapable of making the necessary social-structural changes to do so. Just as technical efforts to prevent an atomic catastrophe during the Cold War "overshadowed" public examination of the root causes and solutions (Marcuse 1964: ix), the technics of geoengineering overshadow the drivers of environmental catastrophe. The case for geoengineering outlined above is rooted in a "pregiven reality": an ecologically destructive social formation incapable of overcoming itself. As Feenberg (2004: 5) put it, modern "technology cannot simply be 'used' to realize radical ends. What sense would it make to try to turn the assembly line into a scene of self-expression, or to broadcast propaganda for free thought?" Indeed, what sense would it make to inject millions of tons of sulfate aerosols into the stratosphere in a society capable of casting off growth-dependence, organizing production to meet needs, and interacting with the biophysical world in nondestructive ways? Technological rationality is still irrational when used to serve a destructive society. Geoengineering is an inept—not to mention highly risky—means to solve ecological problems through the same instrumentality that has created them. We predict that geoengineering strategies will increasingly be considered principal means to combat climate change, perhaps even as alternatives to emissions reductions. When promoted as an economically efficient, high-tech, and market-friendly strategy due to insufficient emissions reductions, the "whys" of geoengineering reflect a society that cannot set substantive goals through reason and transform technology and economic production in ways that provide better outcomes. Such a condition echoes the early Frankfurt School's chief thesis: technological or instrumental rationality remains irrational.

Returning to Marx's negative conception of ideology, geoengineering represents another techno-optimist solution to climate change that conceals the underlying contradictions related to economic growth. Geoengineering offers the illusion of an easy "techno-fix" to overcome the capital-climate contradiction: using technology to further economic growth while addressing the symptoms of climate change. However, it does nothing to address the root cause of climate change and, due to known and unknown risks, its implementation could be catastrophic. Geoengineering is a mistaken attempt to transform the problem—the domination of nature through technology in the service of capitalism—into the solution. It represents a reckless attempt to treat the symptoms of climate change in order to maintain the current economic system. Increasing support for geoengineering from the Republican Party and the Trump Administration reflects a desperation to preserve the status quo while acknowledging, if only implicitly, the irrefutable evidence for climate change. Although geoengineering offers a convenient response for those profiting from the current system, transcending the capital-climate contradiction requires addressing the root cause of climate change: the prioritization of economic growth over other social and ecological goals. Drawing from Marcuse, it is not that technology will inevitably cause harm, but that we need to foster the development of a new social order where science and technology can protect the environment rather than blindly dominate it.

CHAPTER 5

Challenging the Growth Paradigm

Every society clings to a myth by which it lives. Ours is the myth of economic growth.

JACKSON 2009: 5

STARTING IN THE 1950S, economic growth became a policy priority for the United States and other nations (Victor 2010a). This growth has been measured by the Gross Domestic Product (GDP), which adds up the market value of all goods and services produced. GDP in the United States has increased on average about 3 percent each year since World War II. During his campaign, President Trump promised a 4 percent annual increase in GDP (Cohen 2018), illustrating ongoing political goals to increase economic growth. When it comes to the economy, nearly all politicians, newscasters, and citizens would likely agree: growth is good. Modern economics "believe[s] not only in the possibility of continuous material growth, but also in its axiomatic necessity" (Georgescu-Roegen 1977: 266).

In this chapter, we question the growth paradigm and ask: Is continued economic growth desirable for people and the planet, and is GDP an appropriate metric to design our social and environmental policies around? We first examine the idea of "green growth" that proposes addressing environmental issues while also growing the economy. We then explore the argument that economic growth is fundamentally incompatible with reducing GHG emissions and discuss how "green growth" is another ideology concealing the capital-climate contradiction. An increasing number of scholars and activists are now challenging the growth paradigm, arguing that the only way to address climate change is to stop prioritizing economic growth. Instead, they call for policies that abandon GDP as an indicator of progress and instead focus on reducing material and energy use and increasing social well-being. As stated by ecological economist Herman Daly (2013: 24), it is largely believed that "without economic growth all progress is at an end." He counters this belief by asserting, "[o]n the contrary, without growth . . . true progress finally will have a chance."

GREEN GROWTH

Green growth—alternatively, the "green economy" (United Nations Environment Programme [UNEP] 2011) or the "green transition" (Association of Academies of Sciences in Asia [AASA] 2011)—is a recent and increasingly popular (Jacobs 2013) addition to climate policy frameworks. The basic premise is that there can be a "win-win" relationship between economic growth and environmental sustainability. Green growth is believed to be possible through three policy mechanisms: (1) green stimulus packages, (2) market-corrective or price-based policies, and (3) green industrial innovation (Jacobs 2013, Bowen and Frankhauser 2011, Organisation for Economic Cooperation and Development [OECD] 2011, Hallegatte et al. 2011). The argument is that all three policy mechanisms are good for the economy and the climate. In short, "[g]reen growth is about making growth processes resource-efficient, cleaner, and more resilient without necessarily slowing them" (Hallegatte et al. 2011: 3).

When compared to other climate policy frameworks, what differentiates green growth is its ability to draw from nonclassical economic perspectives (e.g., Keynesian) (Bowen and Frankhauser 2011) and framing environmental protection as an economic opportunity, rather than an economic burden. The distinctive claim of green growth is that there are a series of "synergies" between environmental protection and economic growth, or economic capital can benefit from the protection of "natural capital" (Bowen and Frankhauser 2011, Hallegatte et al. 2011, Jänicke 2012, Jacobs 2013, Mathews 2012). Highlighting the economic benefits of environmental protection has gained traction through reports and recommendations from a number of international institutions: the EU Commission (2010), the Association of Academies of Sciences in Asia (AASA 2011), the United Nations Environmental Programme (UNEP 2011), the Organization for Economic Co-operation and Development (OECD) (e.g., 2011), and the World Bank (e.g., 2012).

Green growth strategies depend on the decoupling, or separation, of environmental pressures from economic growth. Green growth advocates claim that decoupling can be attained through a transition away from material goods and toward a service and information-based economy as well as through the use of green technologies that are more efficient and based on alternative energy sources (Hoffman 2016). Jackson (2009) makes the distinction between relative and absolute decoupling. Relative decoupling refers to reduced environmental impact per unit of economic output, whereas absolute decoupling refers to the overall reduction of environmental impacts. While relative decoupling (per unit output) can be seen in many cases, increases in total production continue to increase overall environmental degradation—making absolute decoupling elusive. However, it is absolute decoupling that is necessary to address environmental degradation, including climate change (Jackson 2009).

Despite its unique and promising features as a policy framework, green growth has been met with criticisms (e.g., Jackson 2009, Yun 2010, Hoffmann 2011, Santarius 2012, Dale 2015, Dale et al. 2016, Hickel and Kallis 2019). In the context of climate change, Hoffmann (2011) provides a number of reasons why green growth is an "illusion" of "false hopes." Greening growth at the scale and pace needed to limit global warming to 2 degrees C by 2050 is infeasible for a number of reasons, including: (1) carbon intensity would need to be reduced by at least 21 times (assuming 2 percent GDP increases per year, a low estimate) and up to 128 times (assuming 2 percent GDP increases per year coupled with Global South countries "catching up" to Global North countries)—reductions that seem infeasible through green growth mechanisms; (2) decoupling seen in a given Global North country often results from outsourcing environmentally destructive industries to Global South countries (cf. Santarius 2012); (3) it is highly unlikely that renewable energy will completely displace fossil fuels (cf. York 2012); (4) consumption habits will need to be radically altered; and (5) increased efficiency may increase the consumption of fossil fuel resources (i.e., the Jevons paradox; cf. Santarius 2012). Further, since the implementation of South Korea's National Strategy for Green Growth—*the* case study of green growth policy (Mathews 2012)—carbon emissions and energy use have *increased* (Bluemling and Yun 2016: 125, Gunderson and Yun 2017).

The idea of decoupling represents green growth's Achilles heel. The success of green growth relies on absolute decoupling (Jackson 2009, Victor 2010b), something that has yet to be realized in a way that can address climate change. There is little evidence that it is possible to increase economic growth while reducing total energy and material throughput. As stated by

Hoffman (2016: 36), "dematerialized growth remains an illusion under the prevailing capitalist accumulation imperative." Daly (2013) explains that decoupling is limited by the interdependence of production between different economic sectors and by the fact that expanding service and information sectors will not substantially reduce the use of energy and material goods. Studies using empirical data have also illustrated how modest decoupling in developed nations has been a result of increased carbon-intensive production in developing nations (e.g., Jorgenson and Clark 2012, Knight and Shor 2014). In other words, environmental impacts are being exported. Knight and Shor (2014) report, "[w]hile we find some reduction in the linkage between economic growth and territorial emissions, once we account for high-income countries' offshoring of emissions, there is no evidence of decoupling." The most damning evidence against green growth may be the recent work of Hickel and Kallis (2019), who illustrate that not only is there no evidence of green growth occurring but that it is likely impossible to ever achieve.

The idea of green growth prioritizes GDP-measured growth and perpetuates issues related to the use of this indicator. Economic growth is generally understood as an increase in GDP, which has been identified as a highly problematic indicator of progress and well-being (van den Bergh 2011, Victor 2010b). Several key issues with GDP have been identified: it does not distinguish between costs and benefits; it only includes flows of money, not stocks of resources; it fails to include activities with no market value; and it does not provide information on how wealth is distributed (O'Neill 2011). Alternative indicators have been created that take these issues into account, such as the Index of Sustainable Economic Welfare (ISEW) and the Genuine Progress Indicator (GPI). Applying these indicators illustrates how GDP growth can continue to increase while the ISEW or GPI level off or even decrease (Daly 2013). In other words, increased production does not translate into increased social well-being. Easterlin et al. (2010), among others, have shown that economic growth that goes beyond satisfying basic needs does not lead to increased happiness (for review, see Sekulova 2015). Similarly, economic growth does not seem to increase human well-being per unit of environmental pressure after a certain level of affluence (Dietz et al. 2012, cf. Dietz et al. 2009), despite the fact that mainstream economics views "increasing affluence . . . as essentially equivalent to human well-being" (Dietz 2015: 125). Further, O'Neill (2011) explains how GDP is a "quantitative abstraction" that has been used to guide policies and how its application has actually undermined qualitative goals, such as social and ecological well-being. Despite the fact that GDP is widely recognized as a poor measurement to prioritize, it remains fetishized in our society (Stiglitz 2009). As explained by Daly (2013), GDP is an index of production and is also our best index of total resource throughput; therefore, increasing GDP translates into an increase in energy and material use.

These limitations of green growth stem from its failure to address the capital-climate contradiction. Green growth is the union of the ideological greening of markets and technology, coupled with a supposedly environmentally conscious and exceedingly technocratic Keynesianism. The common example of contradiction in Marxist scholarship is the repeatedly failed attempt by labor to sustain improved relations with capital (i.e., to find "win-win" policies). The claim is that these policies often fail to make long-lasting and significant changes, with capital usually triumphant, because the interests of labor and capital are irreconcilable. We find a similar situation with the green growth strategy, which recognizes that there is a tension between capital and the climate, but attempts to conceptually weaken the contradiction by reconciling elements that are irreconcilable in reality (i.e., continued economic growth and adequate reduction in GHG emissions). While the technical potential for a sustainable society exists, attempts to sustain current institutionalized social relations block this potential (see chapter 7). The very notion of green growth epitomizes "a solution in the mind to contradictions which cannot be solved in practice; it is the necessary projection in consciousness of man's practical inabilities," i.e., an ideology (Larrain 1979: 46). Green growth as a solution to climate change ignores, and therefore fails to address, the underlying incompatibilities. As explained by Victor (2010a: 371), "[a]s long as economic growth remains so important to global policymakers, humanity is hopelessly constrained: the environmental policies we need face the unreasonable political hurdle that they must also be shown to promote economic growth. This must change."

AN INCOMPATIBILITY PROBLEM

Increasing evidence indicates that continued economic growth is incompatible with significant reductions in GHG emissions. The association between economic growth and GHG emissions is well-established (e.g., Stern 2006, Jorgenson and Clark 2012, York et al. 2003). This makes sense since GDP growth correlates with material production, including carbon: a GDP growth of 1 percent equals a 0.6 percent growth in material use (Wiedmann et al. 2015) and a 0.5–0.7 percent increase in carbon emissions (Burke et al. 2015—both cited in Kallis 2017). In his famous 2006 review, Stern recognized an important trend: reduced economic growth associated with recessions resulted in a total decrease in GHG emissions. He concluded that decarbonization of more than 3–4 percent a year is impossible in a growth-dependent economic system. Victor (2010a) explains the difference in reducing GHG emissions in a growing versus steady-state economy: "[t]o reduce greenhouse-gas emissions (GHG) by 80% over 50 years, an economy that increases its real gross domestic product (GDP) by 3% a year must reduce its emissions intensity—tonnes of GHG per unit of GDP—by an astonishing 6% a year. For an economy that does not grow, the annual cut would be a still very challenging 3.2%."

Given the challenge of reducing GHG emissions even in a steady-state (non-growing) economy, scientists and activists are increasingly acknowledging the need to purposefully contract the economy to address climate change (Kallis et al. 2012). Two climate scientists studying carbon budgets, Anderson and Bows (2012), state that overall reductions in economic growth are necessary to effectively address climate change. In other words, the reductions in GHG emissions necessary to avoid catastrophic climate change are not only incompatible with continued economic growth but demand that we reduce growth below current levels. As described by Alexander (2014): to stay within the carbon budget, wealthy countries must cut carbon emissions by 8–10 percent a year over the next few decades, a task that will require not only supply-side changes in technology but also demand side reductions in consumption and an energy descent. Decarbonization is not compatible with the current size of the economy and requires shrinking of global resource use (for more details, see chapter 7).

In order to reduce GHG emissions and stave off catastrophic climate change, we have to reduce production and consumption below current levels. This makes sense in terms of "ecological overshoot." Our current use of natural resources and energy already surpasses biophysical limits (Jackson 2009, Daly 2013), therefore, wealthy societies that produce and consume more than is necessary must contract their economies. Without this contraction, the economy may eventually collapse due to ecological overshoot—climate change possibly being the ultimate limit. As explained by Schmelzer (2016: 357), after a comprehensive historical review of economic growth: "[t]he growth paradigm is ultimately unstable and self-contradictory since the expectation it raises of continually increasing levels of material production run up to the ecological limits of a finite planet." Based on the undeniable biophysical limitations of the Earth, Jackson (2009) argues it is not a matter of *if* the economy will contract but *when*. It can happen by choice through new priorities and policies that guide a transition, or it can happen due to catastrophic environmental crises, resulting in devastating impacts to society. Trainer (2012) similarly states that global society has over-appropriated resources and that a transition away from growth is inevitable. As put simply by Kallis (2017: 10), "decarbonization and dematerialization are incompatible with economic growth [and] strict policies for decarbonization and dematerialization will have a negative effect on growth. This requires thinking how to manage without growth."

In order to minimize the negative consequences of reduced growth, a transition will require implementing policies to ensure stability and well-being (Martínez-Alier 2009). Scholars, activists, and scientists who agree that economic contraction is required and also inevitable have called for "degrowth" as a necessary transition (Research & Degrowth 2010, Kallis et al. 2012). Degrowth represents a planned reduction in production and consumption and a transition into a new economic system that is compatible with decarbonization (Schneider et al. 2010, Kallis 2011, Assadourian 2012, Weiss and Cattaneo 2017). While many incorrectly assume the goal of degrowth is to reduce GDP, the primary goal of degrowth is to reduce material and energy throughput to a level within ecological limits. This process, however, would undoubtedly *result* in a reduction in the GDP, if the indicator was still to be used (Hickel 2019).

DEGROWTH

The term "degrowth" emerged in the 1970s as a political slogan in France and has quickly developed into an "activist-led science" (Martínez-Alier, et al. 2011) and an "academic paradigm" (Weiss and Cattaneo 2017), underpinned by the assumptions that economic growth cannot go on forever and societies must intentionally contract their economies in a socially sustainable way (Latouche 2010, Martínez-Alier et al. 2010, Research & Degrowth 2010, Schneider et al. 2010, Kallis 2011, Assadourian 2012, Kallis et al. 2012, Demaria et al. 2013, Weiss and Cattaneo 2017, Hickel 2019). Degrowth refers to "an equitable downscaling of production and consumption that increases human well-being and enhances ecological conditions at the local and global level, in the short and long term" (Schneider et al. 2010), or, put more simply, it is a "socially sustainable and equitable reduction of society's throughput" (Videira et al. 2014: 59). Since biophysical limits are being surpassed by the "over-developed" economies in wealthy nations, degrowth entails a contraction only in these over-developed economies while at the same time helping nations in the Global South to sustainably achieve an improved quality of life (Kallis 2017). To again clarify a common misunderstanding, the point of degrowth is not to reduce GDP. However, the changes required to reduce total material and energy throughput *would* result in a shrinking of the economy as measured by GDP (Hickel 2019) (see more below).

Degrowth represents a movement and research program that challenges the ideological positions embedded in growth-oriented politics and economics. It has emerged as a political response to address a multidimensional crisis that involves social, financial, and environmental threats (Kallis et al. 2012). The root cause of these threats is unsustainable economic growth driven by the structural imperative to accumulate capital. Activist groups rallied around degrowth starting in 2001 (Baykan 2007), and it has taken on greater importance and influence since, notably in Spain following the Great Financial Crisis (Prádanos 2018). Rather than an economic paradigm or ideology, Demaria et al. (2013: 193) argue that "degrowth has now become a confluence point where streams of critical ideas and political action converge." Whereas market-corrective measures, techno-optimism, and green growth represent capitalist approaches, degrowth represents a critique of capitalism and takes a decidedly noncapitalist approach to addressing societal problems (Kallis 2017). Latouche (2009) characterizes Western development as a mental construct, one taken up by the global community that has had disastrous consequences. Degrowth challenges the supremacy of the growth mindset, whether supposedly green or "brown," by calling for intentional economic downscaling to create a global society that no longer exceeds biophysical boundaries (Kallis 2011).

Barcelona, Spain, has emerged as the epicenter for current degrowth research, education, and activism, although degrowth-related activities are occurring across the EU and even in the United States. The Autonomous University of Barcelona is home to prominent degrowth scholars and now offers a graduate program in political ecology, degrowth, and environmental justice as well as a summer graduate program with a similar focus. The academic collective "Research & Degrowth" coordinates networking among degrowth scholars and activists. In 2008, the first global degrowth conference was held in Paris and has been followed by five other conferences held in the EU (Research & Degrowth 2018). Degrowth-related activism includes oppositional activism (e.g., political squatting, civil disobedience), building alternatives (e.g., local currencies, barter markets, cooperative living), and reforming existing institutions (e.g., introducing new policies related to work, debt, and energy) (Demaria et al. 2013). Most of these activities have occurred in and near Barcelona, as well as in France, Germany, and Italy.

Degrowth in Practice

Degrowth initiatives that reduce energy and material throughput have been implemented at various scales. Most focus on the household and community level and involve living in "voluntary simplicity" in a way that reduces consumption and energy use (Alexander 2011), a focus that we find limiting for reasons explained below. Despite concerns about scarcity, degrowth starts from the premise "that we do not need to 'develop' to get enough, because we already have, and in a sense always had, enough. What we need is to struggle for the institutions that will allow us to live with enough" (Kallis and March 2015: 8). Therefore, degrowth is about living with enough rather than supporting a consumer culture that demands an increasing amount of material goods. This harmonizes with what Juliet Shor (2010) calls *Plentitude*: living simply, sharing, and having enough rather than always more.

Lifestyle changes in-line with degrowth include working less, home provisioning, fixing things rather than replacing them, low-energy leisure activities (e.g., playing guitar instead of computer games), using low-energy transportation methods (e.g., biking instead of driving), and in general using more low-energy strategies to take care of personal needs and household chores. Alexander and Yacoumis (2016) estimate that through these types of changes total household energy consumption can be reduced by 49 percent. Community-level initiatives have involved developing new energy systems that use renewable sources of energy and less energy overall, barter markets to encourage reusing goods, increasing infrastructure for public transportation and cycling, community-supported agriculture, time banking, local currency, collective ownership, cooperative childcare, increased sharing, and cohousing (Kallis et al. 2012, Bloemmen et al. 2015, Kunze and Becker 2015, Jarvis 2017). An increasing number of families and communities across the globe are participating in "nowtopias," voluntarily experimenting with low-energy, low-consumptive, and noncapitalist ways of living (Kallis et al. 2012).

In his recent book, Kallis (2018) describes the importance of these "grassroots" degrowth practices. Whether explicitly described as a degrowth-oriented approach or not, there is an increasing number of examples across the globe of individual and community practices that embody degrowth goals, including solidarity economy practices and local food and currency systems. These initiatives are important because they represent alternatives to the dominant capitalist logic. These practices can have some impact on reducing resource consumption, but more importantly, they show us how we can create beneficial alternatives that could flourish in a new political-economic system. Further, they also highlight the value of care and relationships as well as the importance of deep democratic processes. Kallis (2018: 136) acknowledges that these projects "do not always abolish power dynamics," but they are important because "they represent and nourish alternative value systems that are in tension with the dominant value form of the capitalist economy." We agree that these alternatives existing in the "cracks" of the current system (Wright 2010) are not enough to adequately address climate change, yet they show us how alternative models are both possible and beneficial.

Policies for Degrowth

National and global level policies have been proposed by degrowth scholars and activists. Policies proposed include significant carbon taxes (without loopholes) that would go along with a declining annual cap on carbon emissions and allocating emissions on an equal per capita basis globally, abolishing fossil fuel subsidies, divesting from the fossil fuel industry, rapidly switching to community-based renewable energy, work sharing, reduced working hours, basic and maximum incomes, consumption taxes, reduced advertising, citizen debt audit, zero interest rates, and abolishing GDP as an indicator of economic progress (Kallis et al. 2012, Alexander 2014, Kallis and March 2015, Kallis 2017).

Upon reviewing the literature containing degrowth-related policy proposals, Kallis (2018) identifies four of the most commonly supported approaches, which he calls critical leveraging points: work, fiscal reform, monetary reform, and environmental limits. He highlights the importance of work sharing and work reduction to decrease production and consumption levels (see chapter 6). Tax reform, Kallis (2018), argues is critical for addressing inequality, limiting resource use, and reducing carbon emissions. Public banks can help put the control of money and investments in the hands of the people. Lastly, Kallis (2018) states it is critical to have a global climate agreement that sets an absolute limit for emissions that reduces over time (a diminishing cap), and that "cap and share" programs, where shares are divided up equitably, can be used to limit resource use in general.

As illustrated, there are an abundance of policy ideas to reduce energy and material throughput. The challenge remains getting those ideas implemented at national and global levels. Kallis (2018) describes degrowth as a "concrete utopia" because solid evidence supports that degrowth is indeed "doable." However, admittedly, there are substantial barriers to implementing degrowth-oriented policies in the near future. In the following three chapters, we take a closer look at several degrowth-related strategies taking place at various scales and then discuss prospects for a meaningful social transition that would allow for justly addressing climate change. Before moving onto these topics, we conclude this chapter by discussing criticisms of degrowth and how our interpretation and additions in this book address some of these limitations.

CRITICISMS OF DEGROWTH

There have been numerous criticisms of degrowth, many that have already been addressed in the degrowth literature. Some critics have argued that certain economic sectors, namely alternative energy, will need continued growth to meet climate change demands (Schwartzman 2014) as well as pushing the degrowth movement to recognize that it is currently only overdeveloped countries that must "deaccumulate" and to align itself with an explicitly socialist agenda (Foster 2011). Alternative energy will certainly play an important role in the future (see chapter 7). Degrowth focuses on constraining economic expansion and fitting energy production into a new set of social relations. Further, degrowth thinkers recognize that the material economic well-being of Global South populations would need to increase while simultaneously shrinking the global economy at least by a third (Assadourian 2012). Like others, we only recommend degrowth for overdeveloped economies. Relatedly, at an individual level, it is important to note that richer individuals are responsible for more carbon emissions than poorer individuals on average (e.g., Gore 2015), leading to calls to "tame the few" (e.g., Brand and Boardman 2008) through policies such as a maximum wage (Alexander 2015).

Another critique of degrowth is its focus on reducing GDP. Van den Bergh (2011) argues that instead of GDP reduction through "degrowth," we should adopt "a-growth" that ignores GDP altogether. Indeed, as discussed above, there are many issues with focusing on GDP as an indicator. However, degrowth strictly as "GDP reduction" is a misinterpretation (Kallis 2011): "[d]egrowth entails but is not reducible to GDP decline" (Kallis et al. 2012: 175). Most all recent work in the degrowth literature specifically emphasizes that reducing GDP is *not* the goal (O'Niell 2012). Most degrowth scholars agree that we need to move beyond GDP as a measurement of progress all together (Kallis et al. 2012, Kallis 2017). If GDP is continued to be measured, it is likely that prioritizing the reduction of energy and material throughput will *result* in a reduction in GDP. However, degrowth remains focused on reducing production and consumption levels (not GDP) in order to address environmental crises and improve quality of life. Again, GDP reduction would be a secondary consequence, not the primary goal.

Other criticisms relate to ambiguity, scale, and confronting capitalism. Van den Bergh (2011) critiques degrowth for having imprecise definitions of what degrowth means and entails. Much of this apparent ambiguity has been addressed elsewhere (see above; cf. Kallis 2011). In addition, Schwartz-man (2012: 119) states, "the degrowth program is highly problematic because of its failure to analyze the qualitative aspects of economic growth and its emphasis on the local economy without recognizing the urgency to address global anthropogenic change form a transnational perspective." This echoes Burawoy's (2015) call for a global approach to our current crises. Similarly, Romano (2012) argues that degrowth focuses on local initiatives and fetishizes localism. Lastly, Foster (2011) criticizes degrowth scholars for skirting the question of capitalism and argues that degrowth faces significant challenges confronting the current economic system. Despite these and other critiques, the degrowth movement has continued to grow and solidify. Findings from international degrowth conferences show that attendants agree that degrowth represents an anti-capitalist perspective that critiques domination and calls for a transition to a better society (Eversberg 2016).

Based on these critiques, we suggest three revisions, additions, or renovations to degrowth thinking. At a theoretical level, all three can be interpreted as outcomes of a conversation between degrowth and critical theory. First, we take seriously the issue that some degrowth literature—though far from all (e.g., Kallis 2015, Kallis 2017)—has a partial understanding of the structural need for capitalism to grow and, thus, an incomplete politics (Foster 2011). In contrast, capitalism is the starting point of our analysis. Because our explanatory framework is a structural account of capitalism's growth-dependency, our prescriptions center around structural changes in power and ownership that presuppose the possibility for degrowth. We agree with Kallis (2015:1) that degrowth must directly confront capitalism: "[d]egrowth challenges not only the outcomes, but the very spirit of capitalism. Capitalism knows no limits, it only knows how to expand, creating while destroying." Thus, we also agree with Foster (2011) that capitalism and degrowth are an "impossibility theorem" and degrowth would entail "deaccumulation."[1] Growth is not only an ideology, it is an ideology built upon the structural imperative of capitalism (Schnaiberg 1980) (see introduction).

The second revision is a response to the argument that degrowth fetishizes localism and inadequately grasps the necessity of global transformation. This critique applies to degrowth implementation, which has occurred at the local and community level. While we agree that an ecologically sustainable future would prioritize shorter and less travel, local resource use, etc., many climate change drivers and impacts (as well as those related to biodiversity loss and pollution) are extra-local and require national to global solutions and governance. This has been increasingly acknowledged in the recent degrowth literature. Here, we explicitly address the issue of scale by exploring solutions at multiple levels: local (e.g., community energy, economic democracy), national (e.g., work time reduction, nationalization of fossil fuel companies), and global (e.g., democratizing global climate governance).

A third revision of, or contribution to, degrowth is a thinking through planned economic contraction with an overlapping yet distinct theory of technology compared to those commonly deployed in degrowth (see Zoellick & Bisht 2017, Kerschner et al. 2018). Although it would be misleading to label degrowth "technophobic," degrowth proponents are generally skeptical of the potential of using modern technology to reduce environmental pressure (Weiss and Cattaneo 2017: 225). On the one hand, we share degrowth's skepticism of many "techno-fixes" (see chapters 2 and 4). However, we are also open to exploring the *potential* benefits of many already existing "green" technologies, potential benefits that are constrained by current *social* conditions. We think revisiting the work of Marcuse (cf. Ferrari & Chartier 2017), which inspired Ivan Illich (1973: 50–51), a central figure in degrowth's discussion of technology (see Deriu 2015, Kerschner et al. 2018), is a helpful entry point for integrating the truth content of both Marxian theories of technology and the theories of technology more common in degrowth thinking. Marcuse's explanatory theory of technology is detailed in chapters 2 and 4. As we will discuss in chapter 7, Marcuse also provides a sophisticated normative sociology of technology that is neither technophobic nor naively Promethean. This perspective helps us to examine how we might realize the full potential benefits of technology in a new social system.

THE (IM)POSSIBILITY OF DEGROWTH AND PATHWAYS FORWARD

We conclude by addressing a final critique of degrowth: given the current political climate, degrowth is unrealistic. As argued by van den Bergh (2011), degrowth is too radical to be relevant. When introduced to the idea of degrowth, university students often react by stating that it may address climate change, inequality, and other issues; but it will never happen. They explain that degrowth seems anti-capitalist and un-American and that the word "degrowth" has a negative association, resulting in images of life without technology and conveniences. However, as explained above, degrowth does not require intense sacrifice and ultimately involves a shift in our priorities away from never-ending profit and towards increased ecological and social well-being. Degrowth involves less unnecessary production (and associated work) and less unnecessary consumption (and associated waste). Framed as "prioritizing wellbeing before profits" or "working less and wasting less," degrowth may gain increasing favor with students and the general public. Despite how it is framed, many still dismiss degrowth as impossible. Life as we know it has been shaped around the hegemony of economic growth. However, it is important to remember that overtly prioritizing economic growth has only been a policy trend since the 1950s and "when we recognize how briefly economic growth has held such prominence in policy circles, dethroning it seems less improbable" (Victor 2010a: 371). In addition, as put by Schmelzer (2016: 258), "the very process driving the Anthropocene—capitalist economic growth—is neither self-evident, natural, nor indispensable."

This chapter is transitional, completing our analysis of ideological responses to climate change that *mask* the capital-climate contradiction (green technology, carbon markets, geoengineering, and green growth) and opening our exploration of transitional mitigation strategies that have the potential to transcend and move *beyond* the capital-climate contradiction, all of which are in some way related to degrowth. First, we discuss how mandatory reduction in work hours and the democratization of economic firms could reduce GHG emissions (chapter 6). Next, we examine community-based energy systems as well as other ways to socialize energy systems that can reduce energy use and increase ecological and social well-being (chapter 7). Lastly, we explore how public participation may be achieved in the global governance of climate change (chapter 8).

CHAPTER 6

Work Time Reduction and Economic Democracy

THE USE OF HUMAN LABOR POWER and technology for commodity production and capital accumulation ("the economy") has had tremendous impacts on the natural environment, with climate change representing the culmination of these impacts. This chapter focuses on labor, examining *work time reduction* (WTR), or, "reduction in the total levels of paid working time over the life course" (Pullinger 2014: 11), and *economic democracy*, or, shifting the control of firms from capitalists to workers, as transitional mitigation strategies to reduce GHG emissions and increase well-being. The topic of WTR is perhaps the most explicit overlap between degrowth and critical theory. When degrowth is understood as a child of various intersecting intellectual and political traditions (Demaria et al. 2013), critical theory is, at least indirectly, one of them. The term "degrowth" (*décroissance*) was first used by the French journalist and radical philosopher André Gorz in a 1972 public debate (Demaria et al. 2013: 195, Kallis et al. 2015: 1), and his ideas have influenced degrowth since this origin (Martínez-Alier 2010: 1742; Kallis et al. 2015: 1f, 8f). Gorz, a thinker that is as misrepresented as he is misunderstood (Bowring 1996), should be considered part of the broader critical theoretical tradition and he was a friend of, and influenced by, Marcuse (Granter 2009: 113). Both Marcuse (1955; see Moore 2016) and Gorz (e.g., 1982) expanded upon a central normative aim of Marx: the end, or radical reduction of, unnecessary and unfulfilling labor. Gorz makes a strong case for WTR (e.g., Gorz 1999), an idea that is becoming increasingly popular in European countries, where average working hours continue to decrease and labor unions are fighting to make even shorter working hours the standard (Harper 2017).

Along with WTR, this chapter provides a brief overview of different models for extending democratic control over the economy and explains why economic democracy would provide conditions conducive to reductions in

GHG emissions. The goal of extending democratic control to the economic sphere has a long history in socialist thought, most notably in G. D. H. Cole's (1917, 1920) model of "guild socialism." Some recent prominent proponents of economic democracy include Gar Alperovitz (2013), Richard Wolff (2012a), and the late Erik Olin Wright (2010), and it has received attention in degrowth literature (e.g., Boillat et al. 2012, Johanisova and Wolf 2012). We explore economic democracy in the context of climate change and its possible role in reviving the labor movement.

In what follows, we first review research on the overlaps and tensions between the environmental and labor movements, because successful implementation of either WTR or economic democracy presupposes a renewed labor movement. Then, we integrate research on the benefits of WTR for people and the climate as well as compare WTR with other prominent full employment strategies, job and income guarantees, in the context of climate change. Following, we discuss possible paths to economic democracy as a climate change mitigation strategy. We conclude that a renewed labor movement is necessary for WTR and economic democracy to become viable transitional mitigation strategies. Emphasizing its power to fight climate change could help to renew and strengthen the labor movement.

LABOR AND THE ENVIRONMENT

Organized labor has historically supported economic growth as a means to increase worker livelihood by claiming a portion of the generated wealth (Schnaiberg 1980, Obach 2004b, Bayon 2015). Indeed, labor is one of the three actors that make up Schnaiberg's (1980) "economic growth coalition," driving the treadmill of production. However, organized labor has also played a contradictory role by slowing the treadmill when (1) resisting labor-saving technology or demanding compensation or retraining for technological unemployment, thereby inhibiting efficiency; (2) supporting social programs like unemployment relief (diverting surpluses to non-treadmill activities); (3) promoting nonmarket values and concerns (e.g., a shorter workweek, a strategy stressed in this project); and (4) advocating for environmental goals (Obach 2004b).

The structural makeup of the treadmill has changed over time, most notably capital-state-labor alliances due to wide-ranging anti-labor policies implemented at the dawn of the neoliberal period (Schnaiberg et al. 2002,

Obach 2004b: 346–347). Although the power of organized labor is much weaker today for a number of structural reasons (see this chapter's conclusion), it has augmented its treadmill-slowing tactics due to (1) a bigger service sector that is pro-environment, (2) a smaller industrial sector that now feels more threatened by economic liberalization than environmentalism, and (3) new pro-environment union leadership (Obach 2004b). A recent study shows that unionization is negatively correlated with carbon emissions among OECD countries (Alvarez et al. 2019). Further, against the assumption that union workers are anti-environment due to worries of environmental policy-induced unemployment, a worry with limited empirical evidence (Goodstein 1999), research shows that households with unions members are just as concerned about the environment as nonunion counterparts in bad economic times, and even more concerned in a strong economy (Kojola et al. 2014).

We agree with others that it will be difficult to meet environmental goals without a class-based movement (Foster 1993, Gould et al. 2004, Obach 2004a, Jakopovich 2009, Cock 2014). A class-based movement is likely necessary for successful climate change mitigation for at least three reasons. First, as discussed in chapter 1, one underlying driver of climate change is capitalism, which is based on a class system structured around the private ownership of the means of production. Fundamentally altering the structure of the economy means altering property-based class divisions. Second, transitional mitigation strategies, like the ones proposed in this chapter, require pressure against capitalist interests, as discussed below. Third, although largely co-opted in the mid-twentieth century and then progressively and systematically disempowered since the late 1970s (see chapter 9), we are unaware of any other social group than organized labor that is in a structural position with the potential to substantially reduce the power of capital. Without question, labor should seek alliances with other social movements with similar aims and interests. The labor and environmental movements have a history of collaboration, especially on issues surrounding health, safety, pollution, and international trade, as well as conflict, especially over potential for job loss in specific sectors due to environmental regulations (for reviews, see Kojola et al. 2013: 73ff, Obach 2004a). Recent coalitions have centered around the job-creating potential of environmental and climate reforms (Gould et al. 2004), and there has been a growing discussion about the importance of union representation in "green" and "climate" job programs, e.g., in government-funded public transit projects (e.g., Cha and Skinner 2017). While we agree that the work done in renewable energy, public transportation, organic agriculture, and other sectors should be unionized or cooperatized (see below), some of the goals and framings adopted in these discussions cater to the empty promise of "green growth" (Cock 2014, Barca 2016). In contrast, some radical European labor unions openly support degrowth (Bayon 2015).

In this chapter, we illustrate how a renewed and climate-conscious labor movement could prioritize WTR and democratizing the workplace with outcomes that significantly reduce GHG emissions and increase social well-being. The remainder of this chapter explains why WTR and economic democracy should be treated as transitional mitigation strategies and that both strategies presuppose a renewed labor movement.

WORK TIME REDUCTION

WTR refers to shortening total working hours at constant or higher income levels. This can take several forms:

- "limits on the maximum number of working hours per week[. . . ,]
- the minimum number of holiday days per year,
- maternity and paternity leave,
- rights to reduce working hours (e.g., for childcare, or sickness) and
- (pre)retirement policies." (Pullinger 2014,: 14)

WTR can be implemented as a temporary policy in economic downturns, most commonly in European countries, to redistribute work time instead of increasing unemployment, or as a permanent change in collective working time (LaJeunesse 2009, ch. 5). For example, in addition to regulating collective working time, the Netherlands gives individual workers the right to adjust weekly working hours, and those who select part-time schedules have the same rights as those who select full-time schedules (Fouarge and Baaijens 2004) and, since 2006, allows employees to take long breaks from work without penalty, funded by a Life Course Savings account (Ministry of Social Affairs and Employment 2011, Pullinger 2014: 15; for additional cases, see De Spiegelaere and Piasna 2017, ch. 3). The average work time in the Netherlands is among the lowest globally, ranking right after Germany, Denmark, and Norway—all with around 1,400 work hours per year (the average U.S. citizen spends close to 1,800 hours working each year) (Smith 2018).

There are a number of social benefits to WTR (for reviews, see Coote et al. 2010, De Spiegelaere and Piasna 2017, ch. 2). WTR can address the association between longer working hours and stress and burnout (European Agency for Safety and Health at Work 2009) as well as the association between longer working hours and health issues, such as sleep shortage and hypertension (e.g., Artazcoz et al. 2009). Reduced working hours also allows for a better work-life balance (e.g., Albertsen et al. 2008). Further, work is simply less unpleasant when shortened (LaJeunesse 2009, ch. 5). In short, WTR promotes a higher quality of life. In addition to the aforementioned benefits, two WTR benefits are especially notable: (1) reductions in unemployment through "work sharing," and (2) increased autonomy. Both benefits are discussed in turn.

In our "post-Fordist" economy, many work precarious part-time jobs and would prefer not to—for example, nearly 5 million Americans are "involuntary part-time workers" (Bureau of Labor Statistics 2017)— so calls for shorter working hours may even sound threatening rather than liberating. But planned WTR with the same or higher pay is different than structural underemployment and unemployment.[1] In fact, another name for WTR is "work sharing," or reducing unemployment by reducing working hours for all (see Schor 2015). WTR is one of three proposed full employment strategies, the other two being job and income guarantees. All three strategies have been discussed as potential socially desirable means to reduce throughput (for summaries in the context of degrowth, see Alexander 2015, Schor 2015, Unti 2015). Job guarantee programs usually involve guaranteed employment for anyone willing to work via funding from national governments to decentralized employment projects (Unti 2015). The most radical proposal for an income guarantee, or establishing a universal basic income (UBI), runs as follows: "every person living permanently in a nation would receive from the state a periodic . . . payment, and this payment would be sufficient for an individual to live at a minimal though dignified standard of economic security" (Alexander 2015: 147). Job and income guarantees may play a role in the transition to a society with lower GHG emissions. For example, routes forward include combining a sufficient UBI with WTR (Gorz 1999, ch. 4) or coupling a job guarantee program with WTR (Zamora 2017). We focus on WTR because job and income guarantees must deal with the traditional problem of inflationary pressure and, most importantly in the context of climate change, currently hinge on increasing growth and consumption (LaJeunesse 2009, ch. 3; e.g., Wray 2015: 284f).[2] Work sharing through reduced working hours is an especially pertinent discussion considering: (1) job displacement via technological developments in automation and artificial intelligence (AI), and (2) even in countries that currently have low unemployment rates, work sharing will likely be a future necessity in a degrowth scenario (Fitzgerald et al. 2018).

Along with work sharing, another central social benefit of WTR is the "realm of freedom" (Marx 1981: 959) it makes available:

> [r]educing working hours will not have a liberating effect, and will not change society, if it merely serves to redistribute work and reduce unemployment. The reduction of working hours is not merely a means of managing the system, it is also an end in itself in so far as it reduces the systemic constraints and alienations which participation in the social process imposes on individuals and in so far as, on the other hand, it expands the space for self-determined activities, both individual and collective. (Gorz 1994: 61)

In other words, WTR allows for more creativity, human flourishing, and self-realization through increased leisure time. One question surrounding the "end of work" thesis concerns what activities should or would be pursued if "[freed] from the economy" (Marcuse 1964: 4, Gorz 1967: 128), with an expanded and extended "development of human powers as an end in itself" (Marx 1981: 959), due to reduced working hours? Critical theoretical visions for a post-work future all stress self-development through creative activity (see Granter 2009, Gorz 1986). This question is especially important in an environmental context.

WTR in the Context of Climate Change

WTR has gained increasing attention among environmentalists and environmental social scientists as a strategy to reduce environmental harm (e.g., Hayden 1999, Schor 2005, Robinson 2006, Rosnick and Weisbrot 2006, Hayden and Shandra 2009, LaJeuness 2009, Coote et al. 2010, Nässén and Larsson 2010, Kallis et al. 2013, Knight et al. 2013, Rosnick 2013, Pullinger 2014, Fitzgerald et al. 2015, Fitzgerald et al. 2018). Shorter working hours are associated with significant reductions in environmental pressure and resource use (Rosnick and Weisbrot 2006, Hayden and Shandra 2009, Nässén and Larsson 2010, Knight et al. 2013, Fitzgerald et al. 2015). Knight et al. (2013) found that among OECD countries, those with shorter working hours have significantly lower carbon emissions and ecological footprints. Fitzgerald et al. (2018) show that the association between working hours and carbon dioxide emissions also holds at the state-level in the United States, controlling for other factors. WTR would likely reduce total energy use as working hours are associated with energy consumption and this relationship has intensified over time (Fitzgerald et al. 2015). If the United States used productivity gains to shorten the workweek or extend vacation time, as opposed to producing more and increasing profits for the few, then the country would consume around 20 percent less energy (Rosnick and Weisbrot 2006), and, at a global level, if working hours were reduced 0.5 percent annually for the next century, it would "eliminate about one-quarter to one-half, if not more, of any warming that is not already locked in" (Rosnick 2013: 124). Recent econometric analyses show that the relationship between working hours and environmental pressure is only positive under certain conditions, and WTR policy with environmental goals must be attentive to what makes successful cases successful (e.g., see discussion of consumption and leisure below) (Shao 2017). In short, because longer working hours are generally associated with increased carbon emissions, ecological footprints, and energy use, shorter working hours represents a powerful climate change mitigation strategy.

Although nonexperimental research cannot definitively establish causality (Knight et al. 2013: 698), work time may affect environmental pressure through two channels: (1) longer working hours increase production, consumption, and income, thereby increasing environmental pressure, including GHG emissions (see chapter 5); and (2) more "time affluent" households due to fewer working hours may live more ecologically sustainable lifestyles (Schor 2010, Fitzgerald et al. 2018: 1857). Regarding the latter hypothesis, fewer working hours give people the time needed to adopt lifestyles with lower impact as "low-impact activities are often more time-consuming" (e.g., driving vs. biking/walking) (Schor 2015: 196; see also De Spiegelaere and Piasna 2017: 35). Some human activities in a society with less throughput would be more time-intensive and strenuous for humans (e.g., more biking and walking and less driving) and there would likely be more self-sufficiency practices (e.g., gardening, canning food, making soap) (Knight et al. 2013: 694). WTR not only creates conditions conducive for stable full employment via work sharing but also for reduced consumption:

> [i]f well-paid, part-time work (say 20 hours a week) became the norm there would be less scope for the capitalist to engage in exploitative tactics with any

one worker. Under the right conditions, namely an equitable distribution of material necessitates, the urgency of consumption in the private market could be diminished. (LaJeunesse 2009: 130)

However, as Knight et al. (2013: 694) note, shorter working hours do not guarantee less environmental impact because leisure may conceivably be spent doing more environmentally harmful activities (e.g., shopping, vacations via auto and air, leaving the home more) (see also Nørgård 2013: 67). Indeed, "free time" today often means consuming the many administered treats and games marketed by corporations and further encouraged by a consumer culture (Adorno 1998 :167–75). Along with the issue of leisure time, another important question moving forward, as Schor (2015) notes, is to what degree the productivity gains that make WTR possible can be powered by alternative energy sources rather than fossil fuels (e.g., see Kallis 2017).

The adjoined goals of shorter working hours and increased low-impact leisure are at odds with current priorities to increase profitability, production, and consumption at the expense of people and ecosystems. Increases in productivity through labor-saving technologies are currently used to *increase* production and consumption, which increases energy and material throughput (bad for the climate) and overworks some while systematically denying employment to others (bad for people) (e.g., Marx 1968: 477f, 1973: 704ff, 1977: 792ff; Schor 2003; Jonna and Foster 2016; Schnaiberg 2015; Stoner and Melathopoulos 2015). The adjoined goals of WTR and low-impact leisure are also antagonistic to the "work and spend" culture characteristic of American middle-class households (Schor 1991; see also Robinson 2006) and, more generally, the very ethos of capitalism, which sanctifies work, demonizes idleness, and subordinates life (an end) to utility (a means) (Lafargue 1907; Weber 1958; Scheler 1961; LaJeunesse 2009, ch. 1). If capitalism is structurally compelled to use productivity gains in environmentally and socially destructive ways and the modern ethos values work more than life, WTR, if a collective action, is a step toward inverting this ethos and a future with increased social and ecological well-being.

WTR in a Renewed Labor Movement

To be successful, WTR requires collective action (Schor 1991, ch. 6; LaJeunesse 2007, ch. 3). If WTR is decentralized and to be decided upon by individual workers or firms, it will further polarize work hours between the

unemployed/underemployed and labor market insiders and heighten existing inequalities. Those who "choose" shorter hours without collective
changes will have a difficult time benefiting financially and socially from
shorter working hours and those who "choose" to work more will be able to
increase income and benefits due to lower unemployment without engaging
in social tradeoffs (i.e., a free-rider problem) (LaJeunesse 2007, ch. 3). Because
there are structural disincentives for capitalist firms to shorten hours (see
Schor 2005: 43ff), collective WTR requires pressure from labor.

WTR was a historical goal of organized labor, and still is in Europe, but
capitalists preferred

> labor's desire for more material consumption, and they obliged by investing
> billions of dollars in marketing programs designed to induce the growing
> middle class to spend their disposable income on all manner of new com-
> modities. But the demand for leisure was not consistent with this effort and
> in this way, unions were injecting a radical antitreadmill notion into the na-
> tional psyche. Granted, this goal was never at the forefront of labor mobiliza-
> tion, and beyond securing the 40-hour workweek and some bargaining gains
> in relation to breaks and vacation time for unionized employees, labor's call
> for leisure was largely drowned out by the chorus of consumerism. (Obach
> 2004b: 344)

A renewed labor movement could embrace the goals of the environmental
movement and, once again, push for WTR, as opposed to using productivity
gains for more production and consumption (Gorz 1988: 223ff). Research on
WTR shows that the "jobs-versus-environment" is a false antagonism (see
also Goodstein 1999). When done right, WTR translates into work sharing
and lower environmental impact.

As working hours, quality of life, and climate change concerns are all
making headlines, combining labor and environmental goals now is crucial.
A rising number of European labor unions, where work times are already
standardized around 35 hours a week, have recently demanded further WTR.
For example, in 2018, the German metal workers' union IG Metall won the
right to a 28-hour workweek for up to two years (Huggler 2018). While this is
only a temporary reduction from the 35-hour week to help families during
times of transition, it represents a significant victory for the union and fore-
shadows future WTR negotiations in Germany and beyond. Labor unions in
the United Kingdom are also pursuing WTR, including the Royal Mail work-

ers (Harper 2017). As climate change concerns increase, if labor movements add climate change mitigation to their rationale for demanding WTR, they may be even more successful.

ECONOMIC DEMOCRACY

We agree with Foster (2017) that "[v]isions of a post-capitalist future that pivot on the expansion of leisure time and general prosperity, without addressing the need for meaningful work, are bound to fail." Along with increasing leisure ("liberation *from* work"), it is also pertinent to expand freedom at work ("liberation *in* work") (Gorz 1988: 229). Marx (1964) famously characterized wage labor as a structurally compelled participation in creating and reproducing a world that is hostile to our own self-development and existence, where we are alienated from our product, productive activity, "species being," and fellow humans. One means to reduce alienation at work is worker self-management, or, "economic democracy." This section briefly explains what economic democracy is and why it creates conditions conducive for reducing GHG emissions. While there is no systematic analysis of the environmental effects of economic democracy (due to a lack of a really existing democratic economy to analyze[3]), our discussion is mostly theoretical— yet important enough to warrant attention.

Economic democracy refers to "a system of governing firms in which direct control over them is redistributed . . . out of the hands of the capitalists and into the hands of their workers" (Archer 1995: 69) or, more broadly, "a system of checks and balances on economic power and support for the right of citizens to actively participate in the economy regardless of social status, race, gender, etc." (Johanisova and Wolf 2012: 564). While a helpful definition of economic democracy may include a wide range of rights and governance structures, from more extensive regulation of markets or democratic control of money creation (Johanisova and Wolf 2012), we are primarily concerned with worker self-management along with participation from those living in the area surrounding a given firm (see also Boillat et al. 2012, Wolff 2012a). Models of worker self-management include worker control of privately owned firms, worker control of publicly owned firms (whether state- or local-level), or worker control of worker-owned firms, and the degree of worker decision-making power ranges from workers receiving notification that a decision is being made to majority representation on the decision-making forum or body (Archer 1995, Schweickart 1992, Boillat et al. 2012). There are hybrid and/or transitional models as well. For example, German codetermination laws require worker representation on a firm's supervisory board of directors (Gorton and Schmid 2004). In an economic-democratic system, workers would have the right to participate in, or have democratically elected representatives participate in, decisions that have consequences for worker livelihood and the future of the firm, including work and leave schedules, work speed, hiring and firing, work task distribution, the technology and tools used, product quality and quantity, profit distribution, and investment (Stephen 1979, 23f; Schweickart 1992: 19–20). A helpful way to think about economic democracy is Wolff's (2012a) model of Workers Self-Directed Enterprises (WSDEs), where workers would serve as their own board of directors.

Economic Democracy in the Context of Climate Change

While one can make a good case for economic democracy on political, social, economic, and ethical grounds (e.g., Dahl 1985), what does it have to do with climate change? To be clear, there is nothing inherent in the structure of economic democracy that necessitates reduced throughput. For example, experiments in worker self-management in communist Yugoslavia led to rapid rates of economic growth (though to increase well-being as opposed to further "developing" an overdeveloped economy) (Schweickart 1992: 13–14). Yet, degrowth thinkers support deepening democracy (Asara et al. 2013, Demaria et al. 2013), including economic democracy (e.g., Boillat et al. 2012, Johanisova and Wolf 2012), partly because they think it will create conditions favorable to shrinking throughput in a socially desirable way. Some of the conditions related to economic democracy that would allow for reduced GHG emissions include: (1) a stronger communal bond, (2) investment decisions that are socially controlled (i.e., not for private gain), (3) freer flows of information, (4) no structural imperative to advertise to meet manufactured "needs," and (5) increases in concern with environmental degradation due to the greater involvement of people in decisions that impact their lives (Boillat et al. 2012: 602).

The most important reason economic democracy would be conducive to reducing GHG emissions was well explained by Gorz (1982: 120, 121) in an early indictment of "destructive growth" and call for "productive shrinking":

[e]conomic forecasting and political economy in general . . . are simply [concerned with] keep[ing] the machines turning over, to keep capital circulating, or to maintain a certain level of employment, [so] they manufacture the needs which correspond to any given moment to the requirements of the machinery of production and circulation. Deliberately and systematically, they supply us with new wants and new scarcities, new types of luxury and new senses of poverty, in conformity with capital's need for profitability and growth. . . . The idea that production and consumption can be decided on the basis of need is, by implication, politically subversive. It suggests that producers and consumers could meet, discuss matters and make sovereign decisions. . . . It presupposes a consensus about the nature and level of consumption to which everyone should be entitled, and hence about the limits that should not be crossed.

Rather than pursuing "production for the sake of production" (Marx 1977: 742), economic democracy allows for the subordination of the economy to social needs and ecological requirements. Similarly, Johanisova and Wolf (2012: 565) argue that economic democratic organizations like worker cooperatives

do not exist primarily to make a profit, but to deliver benefits to their cardinal stakeholder group. While . . . profit-led companies are pressured into creating demand for often spurious products or services, co-operatives (for whom profit is not a primary goal) can more easily satisfy real needs. When needs are satisfied, the call for growth is less.

Or, as Bayon (2015: 191) put it, "[i]f work were under the control of workers, human work would be much more likely to be environmentally friendly, since under capitalism's property rules and the imperative of growth, labor is forced to be environmentally harmful." Guy Debord (2004: 90) made a similar argument about the environmental potential of worker councils and Wolff (2012a: 133–34) does the same today in the context of WSDEs. In short, unlike capitalist firms, which must grow due to the profit motive, economic-democratic enterprises have the *potential* to subordinate the economy to environmental goals.

A final climate change-relevant aspect of economic democracy relates to its inequality-reducing potential. Inequality and GHG emissions are positively associated (Jorgenson et al. 2015, Jorgenson et al. 2017). Given inequality's contribution to GHG emissions and other environmental problems (Boyce 1994), there is an ecological case for reducing inequality (Jorgenson 2015, Jorgenson et al. 2017). Economic democracy is a pathway to equality enhancement. Although the Economic Democracy Index (EDI) is based on a broader conception of economic democracy than the one adopted in this chapter, preliminary evidence shows that increases in EDI are strongly associated with decreases in inequality and poverty at the national level (Cumbers 2018).

Economic Democracy in a Renewed Labor Movement

Despite its potential as a socially desirable climate change mitigation strategy, economic democracy (alone) is not a panacea. One limitation of economic democracy is that total worker self-management may be a technical impossibility in large-scale and complex production and distribution chains (Gorz 1982: 97ff, 1988: 42f). Despite this limitation, worker self-governance and self-management is worthy of pursuit at scales of organization in which it is conceivable. The form that socialization takes will likely vary based on scale and the given sector, and there are ways to integrate democracy in the workplace and macro-level changes like industry nationalization (see Wolff 2012a: 140ff).

A second limitation of economic democracy derives from the political-economic context in which firms that run along democratic lines currently operate. They are conditioned and limited by wider capitalist structures and can do little to alter them on their own (Marx 1981, ch. 27; Luxemburg 2008: 80ff; Gasper 2014; Gindin 2016). For example, the virtues and pitfalls of one of the oldest and largest worker cooperatives in the world, the Mondragon Corporation of Spain's Basque region, can be abridged with Marx's (1981: 571) assessment of worker cooperatives: they "are, within the old form, the first examples of the emergence of a new form" (e.g., Wolff 2012b), yet "naturally reproduce in all cases, in their present organization, all the defects of the existing system, and must reproduce them" (e.g., Kasmir 1996). Most importantly in the context of climate change, if worker cooperatives are the exception to traditional capitalist firms, not the norm, they will be forced to compete with capitalist firms and, thus, *grow*.

Without being part of a larger movement to change the political-economic context in which they operate, economic-democratic firms run the risk of showing that an alternative is possible yet conforming to, and reproducing, the larger system, a contradictory position akin to alternative food systems (Gunderson 2014). Like the other transitional mitigation strategies proposed in this book, worker self-management (1) will wither if pursued alone or only on a small-scale, and (2) will likely require support from the state to flourish. Further, like WTR, economic democracy is inconceivable without strong unions, in terms of membership density and/or unity and power at higher levels of organization (Cole 1917, Archer 1995). Although there have been tensions between trade unions and cooperatives throughout history, some of the earliest trade unions in the United States aimed to create a cooperative economy and set money aside to form cooperatives. Unionists and cooperators were often one and the same during the Great Depression, one of the most radical periods in American labor history (Curl 2012: 43). Using some of the profits of democratically run firms to fund trade unions and socialist and labor political parties is one proposed way to link the goal of economic democracy to larger struggles that attempt to change the social conditions in which worker-run firms operate (Gindin 2016). Economic democracy and union renewal could be conjoined goals of a renewed and powerful climate change-conscious labor movement (see also Wolff 2012a: 173ff).

LABOR MOVEMENT RENEWAL

There are clear benefits for both people and the climate if we achieve relatively low working hours in democratically controlled workplaces. Along with a number of social benefits, reduced working hours are associated with lower GHG emissions, less energy use, and a smaller ecological footprint. Economic democracy not only increases individual and group autonomy but also creates conditions conducive to lower energy and material throughput. Pairing WTR and economic democracy may overcome the false antithesis between the interests of workers and the environment.

A renewed labor movement is a necessary social and political prerequisite for WTR and economic democracy to become viable transitional mitigation strategies. It is well-known that there has been a steady decline in the power of labor in the United States and many other advanced industrial societies, especially since the late 1970s, for a number of structural reasons, including global economic liberalization, financialization of the economy, "flexible" labor markets, a rightward political shift, outdated organizing methods, demographic changes, deindustrialization, and anti-labor practices and legislation (Western 1995, Clawson and Clawson 1999, Lee 2005, Bryson et al. 2011, Moody 2017). This decline in the power of labor will undoubtedly hasten following the U.S. Supreme Court's 2018 ruling in Janus v. AFSCME, which enables workers who opt out of joining public-sector unions to not pay for collective bargaining. Given this recent development, an important discussion is how to revive or renew the labor movement through, for example, new organizing methods, organizing immigrants, bargaining strategies fitting for "flexible" post-industrial societies, and creating deeper alliances with other social movements (Clawson and Clawson 1999, Haiven et al. 2006, Lévesque and Murray 2006, Bryson et al. 2011, Moody 2017, Murray 2017). Labor renewal could be supported by efforts to: (1) continue to explicitly seek alliances with the environmental movement, (2) once again push for a shorter workweek and other WTR strategies, and (3) experiment with economic democratic models and pursue strong and explicit linkages between economic-democratic firms and trade unions. Similarly, for reasons we have stressed in this chapter, those concerned with climate change and the environment could explicitly seek alliances with labor to strengthen movements for both social and ecological well-being (Foster 1993, Gould et al. 2004, Obach 2004a, Jakopovich 2009, Cock 2014).

CHAPTER 7

Socializing Energy

OUR ENERGY SYSTEMS are at the core of the climate problem. As reviewed in chapter 2, a commonly proposed technological solution to climate change is the expansion of alternative or renewable energy development. However, as we described, there is growing evidence that renewable energy substitutes for fossil fuel-generated energy may not result in a one-to-one substitution and may even increase total energy use, a key aspect of the "energy boomerang effect" (Zehner 2012; York 2012, 2016). While technology is not an autonomous mechanism that will alone solve the environmental crisis, it remains very possible to create specific policies and programs to better realize the potential environmental gains of renewable energy development (York 2016). If renewable energy development is to contribute to significantly reducing environmental pressure, it must also be accompanied by *social* changes. The energy boomerang effect is predicated upon specific social-structural conditions and, thus, may be contained through social-structural changes. Renewable energy development along with these social-structural changes provides a possible pathway to drastically reduce GHG emissions and other forms of environmental pressure.

There are five primary sources of renewable energy: wind, solar, biomass, hydro, and geothermal. Today, about 80 percent of global energy used still comes from fossil fuels and meeting the goal of keeping global temperature increase below the 2 degree C goal would require a thirty-seven-fold increase in the annual rate of renewable energy by 2030 (Jones and Warner 2016). While currently not happening fast enough to meet this goal, renewable energy development is increasing globally and is rapidly increasing in some areas. China is currently the global leader in renewables, responsible for 40 percent of capacity growth in 2016; global solar capacity grew by 50 percent in 2016, with China accounting for half of this growth (International Energy

Agency [IEA] 2017). In the United States, states are leading the way towards a transition to renewables with California currently using 25 percent renewable energy sources with a commitment to have all utilities use 50 percent renewable energy sources by 2030 (UCS 2017b). Many European countries are also pushing for a quick transition to renewables. In Denmark, plans have been made to produce 70 percent of electricity from renewables by 2022 (IEA 2017). Growth in renewable energy has increased more rapidly in recent years due to a significant decrease in the costs of renewables, especially the costs of solar, which have decreased 73 percent since 2010; by 2020, it is expected that all renewable power technologies now in commercial use will be within range or below the cost of fossil fuels (International Renewable Energy Agency [IRENA] 2017). This could represent a significant tipping point in energy competitiveness.

Given the unrealistic increase in renewable energy use necessary to keep global temperature increase below 2 degrees C (Jones and Warner 2016), some climate change scientists and activists claim that increasing the use of nuclear energy is critical. Uranium used to create nuclear energy is not renewable; therefore, nuclear energy is generally not considered a renewable energy source. However, some leading scientists argue that decarbonization goals cannot be achieved without an increase in nuclear power generation. James Hansen and others (2015) specifically claim that "nuclear power paves the only viable path forward on climate change." However, they also acknowledge that waste and public safety issues associated with nuclear energy need to be addressed. While nuclear energy remains an option in many countries, the well-known high disaster potential associated with nuclear power generation and waste are difficult to ignore. Most of our discussion in this chapter pertains to the five renewable sources of energy listed above. It should also be noted that there are potential negative environmental impacts associated with specific renewable energy sources as well as increasing research on ways these impacts can be minimized (UCS 2018).

While others have extensively examined *what* types of alternative energy we should use, in this chapter, we focus on *how* energy technologies could be used in a transformed society to better mitigate climate change. We specifically examine how the principles of degrowth can be applied to guide the creation of new energy systems and illustrate the importance of reduced energy consumption in addition to a transition to renewables, something that most projections of future GHG emissions fail to take into account. Although not always officially linked to degrowth goals, there are a growing

number of collective-ownership energy initiatives that are increasingly suc-
ceeding in transitioning to renewable energy sources, and many are also
reducing total energy consumption. While models of collective ownership
historically developed before the more recent degrowth program, collective
ownership of energy systems as "community energy" projects are often
intentionally or unintentionally in line with degrowth goals (see Kunze and
Becker 2015, Rommel et al. 2016, Ferrari and Chartier 2017). Importantly, to
reduce total GHG emissions, these initiatives must both switch to renewables *and* reduce total energy consumption. In this chapter, we illustrate how
degrowth can guide community-based initiatives and also discuss the role of
the state to facilitate these transitions. Our aim is not to empirically demon-
strate that existing social conditions have already contained the energy boomerang effect. Instead, in line with the critical theoretical tradition, we
attempt to bring new possibilities and questions to consciousness by playing
off what is *possible* with what *is* by adopting a two-dimensional form of
thinking that assumes "that what is is fraught with tension between its
empirical reality and its potentialities" (Feenberg 2004: 87). We specifically
draw from Marcuse who envisioned a new role for science and technology in
a substantially transformed society.

MARCUSE'S NEW SCIENCE AND TECHNOLOGY

Applying critical theory illustrates how technological design, use, and
impacts are conditioned by society. For example, technology can reproduce
existing social relations or it can contribute to a more rational social order.
Technology design and use has the potential to radically change in different
social conditions (e.g., Marcuse 1964, Feenberg 1999). As discussed in chapter 4, Marcuse was neither technophobic nor naively Promethean, and his
work provides insights on how science and technology may be used to offer
alternative and nondestructive outcomes. Early critical theorists', particularly Marcuse's, views on science and technology's role in societal-
environmental interactions transcend the more recent debate of "whether
science benefits the environment or whether it is injurious to it" (Yearley
1997: 227). Science and technology embody an instrumental attitude toward
nature and, in capitalist societies, are largely destructive toward nature due
to the demands of capital and the lack of substantive and rationally formulated ends. However, Marcuse argued that science and technology, free from

their role in the organized domination of humans and nature, could aid society in building a more harmonious relationship with nature.

There is no reason to believe we can, or should want to, do away with the technological mediation of human-nature relations. For one, technological mediation of humans and the environment characterizes all of human history. Marcuse, sometimes wrongly framed as a technophobic thinker (Feenberg 1998), considered anti-technological views as "propaganda" that "serves to teach men distrust of the potential instruments that could liberate them" (Marcuse 1978: 160). Indeed, he claimed that the "'liberation of nature' cannot mean returning to a pre-technological stage, but advancing to the use of the achievements of technological civilization for freeing man and nature from the destructive abuse of science and technology in the service of exploitation" (Marcuse 1972: 60, cf. 1964: 238).

Marcuse argued that we must alter our attitudes toward the biophysical world in fundamental ways, requiring significant changes in social systems. His contention that human beings must transform the organization and purpose of their social formations in line with substantive goals without compromising the health of the natural environment is an empirically and theoretically defensible claim. Similarly, neo-Marxists and Marx (e.g., 1977: 562f, 1978: 632) argue that science and technology are embedded social projects that can be used to serve more desirable ends in a more rational society, and that technology, technique, and machines are not repressive per se but only due to the "presence" of ruling interests "in" them, determining "their number, their life span, their power, their place in life, and the need for them" (Marcuse 1969: 12). Technological development is important for developing a more harmonious relationship with the biophysical world and a number of technologies (e.g., wind power) are hindered by social relations that could be utilized more fully in society without excessive competition and growth-dependency (e.g., York and Clark 2010: 491f, Foster 2002: 101; see chapter 2). However, as Marcuse (e.g., 1989: 123, 127) controversially asserted, technology—even individual machines and instruments—are not neutral objects. Some technologies embody the irrational and destructive values of the society that created them. What Marcuse's theory of technology reveals is that the very structure and operation of science and technology, not just their application or use, has the potential to change in a new society. A new technology may require a change in our ethos and, liberated from the profit motive and pure instrumentality, could protect and foster nature rather than dominate it. Society would have the opportunity to set new substantive goals, which would also alter the creation of, the use of, and our relationship with technologies (Marcuse 1964: 232).

Marcuse recognized the liberatory potential of technology that is constrained in capitalist societies. Most fundamentally, technology has the potential to free human beings from excessive toil, which he considered the "ultimate purpose" of technology. However, like Horkheimer and Adorno, he was convinced that the mastery and exploitation of human beings and nature were interrelated and, thus, to build a better society, both would need to be liberated from a technological rationality embedded in vested interests and the profit motive. As Agger (1976: 168) put it, "[b]y damaging nature, technical rationality damages the human spirit." Marcuse argued humanity would need to develop a qualitatively different relationship with nature to unleash this potential, which he called an "aesthetic ethos" or "the new sensibility" (especially see Marcuse 1969, 1972). Drawing from early Marx (1964: 139f, 181), Marcuse argued that such an ethos could recognize nature as a "subject-object," making the extraction of natural resources in a rational society qualitatively different from capitalism: "its 'human appropriation' would be nonviolent, nondestructive: oriented on the life-enhancing, sensuous, aesthetic qualities inherent in nature" (Marcuse 1972: 67, cf. 1955: ch. 9). He proposed a distinction between a repressive mastery and liberating mastery of nature, the latter "involves the reduction of misery, violence, and cruelty" that follows the development of a new aesthetic attitude (Marcuse 1964: 236). As a social-historical human activity, Marcuse claimed a new science and technology would necessarily follow the aesthetic attitude toward nature. He imagined a new science and technology that sought to preserve and enhance life rather than dominate and destroy it.

> For freedom indeed depends largely on technical progress, on the advancement of science. But this fact easily obscures the essential precondition: in order to become vehicles of freedom, science and technology would have to change their present direction and goals; they would have to be reconstructed in accord with a new sensibility—the demands of the life instincts. (Marcuse 1969: 19)

For Marcuse, a new social order is a prerequisite for realizing the full liberatory and harmonious potential of science and technology.

A central insight of Marcuse is that technology not only impacts society but that technology design and use is influenced by social conditions (see chapter 2). In this chapter, we examine what specific social conditions and policies would be better suited to realize the environmental gains of alternative energy technology. We also specifically examine how alternative energy development may be better able to reduce environmental impacts in a degrowing economy, assuming that many of the "problems of technology can be overcome through open access and elimination of undemocratic control by corporations and elites" (Kerschner et al. 2015: 31). We conclude that while alternative energy development is a still limited and partial solution to the environmental crisis regardless of the social conditions, a healthy skepticism of techno-optimism should not extend into a rejection of the *potential* role of technology to help reduce environmental harm in different social conditions. Guided by the principles of degrowth, alternative energy technologies coupled with reduced total energy consumption have the potential to significantly reduce GHG emissions.

DEGROWTH AND ENERGY

As discussed in chapter 5, degrowth represents a movement and research program that challenges the ideological positions embedded in growth-oriented politics and economics. An organizing goal of degrowth is "dematerialization," or the absolute reduction in the total amount of material and energy utilized, especially for economic production and consumption. In terms of energy, this means an enormous reduction in fossil fuel-based energy use (decarbonization). Degrowth supports the transition to alternative energy, especially wind and solar. And increasingly, evidence indicates that degrowth would be a requirement for a renewable energy-powered future: renewable energy sources have a lower Energy Return on Investment (EROI) and a transition to renewable energy will necessitate reducing total energy use (see Hall et al. 2014). Because the EROI for solar and wind is much lower than conventional fossil fuel-based sources, for example 60:1 for coal compared to 18:1 for wind and 6:1 for solar (Hall et al. 2014), it is unlikely that a decarbonized energy supply is possible in a growth-dependent economy and, in fact, may already be incompatible with the global economy's current size (Anderson and Bows 2011, Kallis 2017). In other words, to stay within the carbon budget of 1.5 or 2 degrees Celsius requires not only a shift in the source of energy but also a total reduction in energy consumption, which is infeasible *in a growing economy* (Hickel 2019).

A degrowing economy would cast off the growth imperative and support programs to decarbonize society. Degrowth explicitly supports the absolute reduction of carbon energy (Lorek 2015). This means that a degrowth society would avoid scenarios in which fossil fuel-based energy expands despite the expansion in renewable energy (e.g., Ernsting 2015). In other words, alternative energy development would have the opportunity to expand without a simultaneous expansion in fossil fuel-based energy. A number of policy measures could be adopted to progressively reduce fossil fuel use including: eliminating financial support for fossil fuel companies, applying a carbon cap or a carbon tax, divestment from the fossil fuel industry, introducing public education programs on carbon budgets, adopting the use of "post-growth" indicators instead of GDP, and redirecting public spending from high- to low-carbon infrastructure (Alexander 2014). As discussed later in this chapter, although degrowth involves individual behavioral changes and community-based initiatives, quickly reducing GHG emissions will also require state action.

Recognizing the implications of comparatively low EROI in wind and solar (see above), a switch to renewables will need to be accompanied by a reduction in total energy consumption in order to address the energy boomerang effect. As Trainer (2012: 591) argues, "[renewables] cannot fuel a consumer society for all" (cf. Trainer 2010, Alexander 2014: 13–14). In a degrowth society, an energy system would entail reducing overall energy consumption through lifestyle changes. As described by Byrne et al. (2009: 88), a sustainable utility system "involves the creation of an institution with the explicit purpose of enabling communities to reduce and eventually eliminate use of obese energy resources and reliance on obese energy organizations." Alexander and Yacoumis (2016: 4) argue that in accordance with degrowth principles, new energy systems need to move beyond simply a switch to renewables, "transcending consumerist cultures of consumption and embracing materially sufficient but non-affluent ways of living." They suggest behavioral changes shifting to low-energy living that could involve a number of simple and low-tech changes: increasing walking and biking, using solar shower bags for hot water, insulating housing, dressing appropriately to reduce heater use, using clotheslines rather than dryers, and shifting toward nonelectronic-based entertainment. Alexander and Yacoumis (2016) estimate that these changes can reduce total household energy consumption (in Australia) by 49 percent and are easy ways households can support an overall energy descent. But significant and widespread behavioral changes often presuppose structural changes. For example, imagine residential electricity use in a degrowth scenario compared to residential electricity use in contemporary growing economies. A degrowth society would not only limit how much electricity can be produced through fossil fuel sources via appropriate ownership and governance structures but would result in less total residential electricity, including alternative energy-generated electricity, due to degrowth pathways such as cohousing (Lietaert 2010).

The energy boomerang effect could be contained given measures to progressively reduce carbon energy use, reductions in total energy use, and if there was no imperative to increase total energy throughput using money saved through alternative energy development. This is a significant consideration for macro-level energy use. Without the necessity to increase throughput predicated on the structural conditions of economic growth, alternative energy development would not put downward pressure on prices, thereby increasing total resource use. Further, it is difficult to imagine a mechanism in any social or economic sector that would spur the energy boomerang. Total energy use would likely not increase due to alternative energy development in a degrowth society, by design. Stated differently, the energy boomerang effect is not an outcome of alternative energy development per se but only of alternative energy development in a particular kind of society. Below, we examine how societies prioritizing social and environmental justice (rather than economic growth) could use decentralized and collectively owned renewable energy systems to effectively reduce GHG emissions.

COLLECTIVE OWNERSHIP OF ENERGY SYSTEMS

Collective ownership of energy systems represents a primary means by which societies could begin degrowing an alternative energy-based economy. Growth-dependency is driven in part by competition, which is predicated upon the private ownership of productive technologies (Schnaiberg 1980, Dale 2015). Because growth-dependency relies on the private ownership and control of productive technologies, addressing the issue of ownership and control is especially important to begin intentionally contracting total energy use. Collective ownership can take many forms. A range of different models of decentralized and community-based energy governance have been employed, some giving control of energy systems to citizens through public ownership and local government and others through citizen-led cooperatives. However, Kunze and Becker (2015) argue that how owner-ship structures achieve wider social and environmental goals is more impor-tant than the specific type of model employed.

Collective ownership alone is not a sufficient condition for furthering any political goal. For example, in this case, collective ownership is not a suf-ficient condition to address the energy boomerang effect. A collectively owned energy system could be engineered to grow and depend on fossil fuel energy (e.g., the Soviet model). In fact, the majority of the energy for the 900 rural electric cooperatives in the United States comes from coal, a decision representative of members' conservative beliefs (Aronoff 2016). However, collective ownership is likely a necessary condition to intentionally and sus-tainably degrow an economy and a condition conducive to implementing policies that limit the use of fossil fuel-based energy and reduce total energy use. Specific to degrowth, Kunze and Becker (2015: 427) explain, "[i]n con-trast to conventional private corporate ownership, public and collective ownership opens up possibilities for the social and ecological transforma-tion that degrowth is calling for, though it does in no way automatically guarantee the implementation of such goals." Byrne and others (2009: 90) also discuss reframing energy as a collectively owned commons but similarly mention that, "although commons institutions do not in and of themselves guarantee eradication of environmentally exploitive practices, they do offer elements for recovery of political agency in the formation of choices regard-ing energy and environmental futures and the foundation for a normative reconstitution of the good life." In a degrowth society, specific social and environmental goals would govern energy systems. These goals go beyond the production of electricity from alternative energy sources and a collective commitment to progressively reducing fossil fuel-based energy to include specific agendas for social and environmental change/justice (Kunze and Becker 2015). These goals would likely include just distribution/equity, sus-tainability, and low environmental impact. Explicit goals can foster a system where individuals act through reciprocity, rather than competition, to sup-port a range of desired social and ecological outcomes (Byrne et al. 2009).

Community energy, also called community renewable energy or community-owned renewable energy, represents an emerging means to fos-ter local control by empowering communities to promote and utilize alter-native energy sources. Seyfang et al. (2013) note that the term community energy remains contested. They suggest that it entails "projects where communities (of place or interest) exhibit a high degree of ownership and control, as well as benefiting collectively from the outcomes" (Seyfang et al. 2013: 978). Such initiatives have proliferated recently. Most of these initiatives are responsive to concerns about climate change and include goals to prioritize the use of renewable energy sources. These new systems have the potential to transition to renewable energy and also to reduce overall energy consumption: energy demand reduction is considered as *the* most important component of the community renewable energy movement (Weinrub and Giancatarino 2015).

Community energy should support what Byrne et al. (2009: 89) refer to as "community values, instead of commodity values." Doing so requires reshaping how we view energy, moving away from energy as a market-based entity to energy as a *commons*. The commons have received significant attention in this discussion partially due to Nobel laureate Elinor Ostrom's groundbreaking book *Governing the Commons* (1990), which established that Garret Hardin's (1968) argument, *The Tragedy of the Commons*, does not always hold. Drawing heavily on Ostrom's work, Bollier (2014: 15) has written about commons for a popular audience, defining a common as "paradigms that combine a distinct community with a set of social practice, values and norms that are used to manage a resource" (cf. Dietz et al. 2003). His definition highlights the social nature of commons (for further elaboration, see Choe and Yun 2017). They do not merely represent a resource but the means by which people collectively act to manage and utilize the resource for the benefit of all. The global market economy grew from enclosing and privatizing commons, which continues today with efforts to privatize water, forests, food, genetics, and more. Community energy efforts seek to reverse this trend. Byrne et al. (2009: 91) state: "[c]hoosing community governance over technocratic orders, we have the chance to do something impossible in the era of energy obesity: relocate energy-ecology-society relations in a commons space." More than simply providing energy from a different source, viewing energy from a commons perspective focuses attention on sovereignty and empowerment for communities. Further, organizations and scholars are increasingly envisioning energy as a common good. For example, the EU Horizon 2020 research project frames energy sources as common goods: "Wind, solar, hydro, biomass and geothermal energy are natural resources. They in fact belong to no one and are in principle available to all. They are common goods" (EU Horizon 2020). Going further, the Mercator Research Institute on Global Commons (2017) argues that energy is a social common good, essential for human well-being often underprovided, and at the same time, energy use affects the global commons through GHG emissions. Viewing energy as a commons, governed through democratic public decision-making and collective ownership, can help to facilitate the transition to renewables as well as reduce total energy consumption.

It is through local participatory governance that social and environmental goals can most successfully direct energy management in a degrowth society (Kunze and Becker 2015). "Energy democracy," a concept closely related to community energy, explicitly calls for the direct governance of energy by the public (for review, see Ferrari and Chartier 2017: 4f). Governance in a degrowth society would be community-run through participatory democratic means (Cattaneo et al. 2012, Deriu 2015, Johanisova and Wolf 2012, Ott 2012). This involves direct citizen participation: every community member, those interested in or potentially affected by decisions about energy use, would be included in decision-making. Byrne et al. (2009) describe a commonwealth where energy is "organized locally by and for the community" rather than by a "technocratic institution" (Byrne et al. 2009: 89). As reviewed in chapter 8, assessments of participatory environmental decision-making are generally positive. Energy democracy movements often go beyond a focus on climate change and energy use, prioritizing the restoration of community power to unrepresented and minority groups (Giancatarino 2013).

There are a growing number of community-based energy systems that illustrate many of the characteristics described above. Walker et al. (2007) identified over 500 projects in the United Kingdom in which communities have promoted renewable energy and similar projects have occurred elsewhere, including Australia (Hicks and Ison 2014) and Germany (Wen Li et al. 2013). Kunze and Becker (2015: 425) identified over one hundred European projects online that potentially met their definition of a "collective and politically motivated renewable energy project." They narrowed down their search and more intensively researched four projects. These included the Welsh community of Machynlleth, where the degrowth principles were explicitly adopted involving collective ownership, local production and governance, and changes in lifestyles to reduce consumption. Kunze and Becker (2015) also examined Somenergia, a large cooperative in Spain with photovoltaic and biogas plants, participation by all members (over 18,000), local autonomy, and engagement with social movements working on energy issues. Burke and Stephens (2017) describe a range of models being applied in the United States, including more than 2,000 community-based public power systems, community choice initiatives in California, and energy cooperatives prioritizing renewables in Oakland, California, and Cleveland, Ohio.

Citizens have also been regaining control of energy systems through local government. Municipalization involves cities controlling energy systems in the public interest. In recent years, there have been an increasing number of social movements for remunicipalization, where city residents organize and work to take energy control out of the hands of private companies and into the hands of the public. This trend has been especially apparent in Germany, with 284 remunicipalizations of energy systems between 2005 and 2016—including small municipalities and large cities like Hamburg (Becker 2017). Most all of these efforts include goals to increase the use of renewable energy sources. In the United States, the city of Boulder, Colorado, continues its battle for remunicipalization in order to meet the city's 100 percent clean energy goal (City of Boulder 2017), a development that, if successful, could have significant consequences for community energy development projects elsewhere in the United States.

A growing number of energy projects are being established in accord with degrowth principles. Treating energy systems as commons with fitting property laws and governance structures are conditions conducive to containing the energy boomerang effect. But this is only one way forward. Any successful degrowth transition—including absolute reductions in energy use and containing the energy boomerang effect—would necessarily be a socialist transition, requiring the support of labor (e.g., Trade Unions for Energy Democracy, n.d.) and leftist political parties (Latouche 2009). Collectively owned and governed energy systems are limited and shaped by wider capitalist structures (Rommel et al. 2016, Ferrari and Chartier 2017), and should be expanded as one means to overcome these structures. The reason we highlight collective ownership of energy systems in particular is to emphasize that considering degrowth as a serious social-political option implies a collective action movement aimed toward altering property and governance structures as opposed to merely reforming individual lifestyles or establishing small "alternative" communities. Again, in addition to collective ownership of energy systems and switching to renewable energy sources, these systems must also reduce total energy consumption in order to mitigate climate change. Creating energy systems that are collectively owned, democratically governed, and supported by local to national governments that eliminate fossil fuel use *and* reduce total energy use should be a central proposal of the degrowth movement.

THE ROLE OF THE STATE

Catney et al. (2014: 715) argue that projects to empower community control of energy systems represent "impoverished localist thinking" because they perpetuate the notion that the state limits local activity and should play a minimal role in such activities. The authors suggest that collective action problems often require state action, especially to ensure that inequalities are addressed. We agree that collectively owned energy systems should involve state support and there is a critical role for a degree of centralized governance. Here, we briefly discuss the role of centralized government in supporting community-based energy initiatives, creating carbon caps and carbon taxes, ending subsidies for the fossil fuel industry, and phasing out the use of fossil fuels through buying out fossil fuel companies.

Centralized governments can support and enable locally run energy systems in many ways. In the Netherlands, provincial governments created policies that formally supported local low-carbon energy initiatives; while other provinces took steps to financially incentivize such programs and established communication platforms aimed at disseminating information on best practices related to new energy initiatives (Warbroek and Hoppe 2017). Scotland has taken significant steps to promote community energy. The Community and Renewable Energy Scheme initially provided grants but has since shifted to providing preplanning loans to communities trying to establish community energy projects. The program has additional grants and financial means of support aimed at promoting community energy projects (Markantoni 2016). Across the United Kingdom more broadly, Seyfang et al. (2013) highlight policy efforts to promote community energy, including the Scottish Community and Householder Renewables Initiative, the Community Scale Renewable Energy Programme in Wales, and the Rural Community Renewable Energy Fund. The UK government also established the Low Carbon Communities Challenge and facilitated research on how to promote community energy (Seyfang et al. 2013). Overall, there is a key role for centralized government in supporting the growing diversity of community initiatives aimed at reducing dependence on fossil fuels and total energy use.

The state could play a critical role in setting prices and limits that would reduce overall energy consumption and GHG emissions. A significant carbon tax would increase the price of carbon-based resources, incentivizing the reduction of carbon consumption and increasing the demand for less expensive alternative energy sources such as renewables (Victor 2012, Anderson 2014). Energy caps or impact caps set by the state could drive reduced consumption and address the energy boomerang effect (Anderson 2014). These caps could also change over time with a progressively shrinking carbon cap (Lorek 2015). While these could be set at the national level, Burawoy (2015) convincingly argues that any climate change response needs to be global in nature. Douthwaite (2012) proposes the formation of a Global Climate Trust where fossil fuel use is controlled through a "cap and share" system. The idea involves a declining annual cap on carbon emissions from fossil fuels and allocating emissions on an equal per capita basis globally.

Another key role for the state is ending financial support for the fossil fuel industry. Government tax breaks and subsidies continue to financially support the fossil fuel industry, in many cases sharply contrasting with political rhetoric to reduce GHG emissions. In a 2017 report titled *Talk is Cheap: How G20 Countries are Financing Climate Disaster*, Doukas et al. (2017) illustrate how G20 countries provide four times the financial support to the fossil fuel industry compared to the renewable energy industry. In addition, the report states that between 2013 and 2015, the United States spent $6 billion supporting the fossil fuel industry each year compared to $1.3 billion for renewable energy. Negin (2017) reports that between 1918 and 2009, "the [fossil fuel] industry's tax breaks and other subsidies amounted to an average of $4.86 billion annually (in 2010 dollars). . . . Accounting for inflation, that would be $5.53 billion a year today." According to a 2015 report from the International Monetary Fund, fossil fuel companies receive $5.3 trillion a year in global subsidies, equivalent to $10 million a minute every day (IMF 2015). Continued government support for fossil fuel companies represents an investment in assets that, if exploited, will result in significant GHG emissions while diverting investment away from renewable energy. This is especially troubling considering that the majority of fossil fuels must remain in the ground to avert catastrophic climate change: "no more than one-third of proven reserves of fossil fuels can be consumed prior to 2050 if the world is to achieve the 2 degrees C goal" (International Energy Agency 2012). Continued financial support for the fossil fuel industry from the state will only ensure that humanity and global ecosystems will face an unavoidable climate catastrophe. Instead, this support should be eliminated and tax breaks and subsidies for renewable energy sources and community energy initiatives should be significantly increased.

Lastly, the state could play a critical role in phasing out the use of fossil fuels through buying out fossil fuel companies. Alperovitz and others (2017) detail a policy proposal they claim is similar to the response to the 2008 financial crisis: creating new money (called "quantitative easing"), but instead of bailing out big banks, use the money to buy out fossil fuel companies. They argue that fossil fuel companies are financially threatened by a "climate bubble": most of the remaining reserves of fossil fuels on the planet should not be extracted and will therefore become "stranded assets" with little to no economic value. Considering that a third of the world's wealth is currently tied up in fossil fuels, Alperovitz and others (2017) explain that state intervention now to buy out fossil fuel companies could avert a global financial crisis that would dwarf the impacts felt in 2008. They also argue that government buyouts are not uncommon and have occurred throughout U.S. history with banks, companies producing products for war, and the buyout of tobacco companies that took place between 2004 and 2014. Without this sort of intervention, it seems unlikely that fossil fuel companies will stop further exploration and extraction, resulting in climate change far beyond the 2 degree C goal. Alperovitz and others (2017) share an optimistic view that in coming years priorities may shift dramatically in the United States and beyond and open up a window of opportunity to buy out and phase out fossil fuels. Gowan (2018) also proposes nationalizing U.S. fossil fuel companies, which he states has already been proposed in the United Kingdom and is taking place in Norway. He proposed a Social Energy Fund and explains that according to takings laws, the government can purchase fossil fuel companies at market value. Gowan (2018) states that purchasing 51 percent of fossil fuel shares (a majority stake) would cost about $410 billion. He then convincingly argues that this cost is small compared to the long-term costs that climate change will incur. Gowan (2018) also thoughtfully discusses job losses in the fossil fuel industry and the importance of government support to make the transition as smooth as possible.

A NEW ETHOS FOR A NEW ENERGY SYSTEM

Alternative energy development is a commonly proposed route to address climate change. However, there is an unintended, paradoxical outcome: the "energy boomerang effect," or when alternative energy development increases total energy use. In chapter 2, we argued that this counterintuitive outcome involves a particular set of social-structural conditions that prioritize economic growth and increased energy throughput, i.e., it is not caused by wholly autonomous (asocial) technological feedback. By adopting the critical theoretical method of exploring what is possible through counterfactual comparisons of potentiality and reality, this chapter argues that economic degrowth and the collective ownership of energy systems would provide conditions *conducive to* mitigating this paradox, or to better realize the potential environmental gains of alternative energy converters. A degrowth society with a collectively owned energy system would allow for a reduction in total energy use (including non-fossil fuel-based energy use) as well as a lower ratio of fossil fuel energy to alternative energy. The state should play a critical role in this transition through supporting renewable energy, rapidly phasing out fossil fuels, and encouraging the spread of community-based energy initiatives.

Following the central influence of Illich (1973), many degrowth proponents are weary of the positive social and ecological potential of modern technologies (see Deriu 2015, Zoellick and Bisht 2017). It is indeed possible that a post-capitalist and post-growth society would prefer technical artifacts less likely to "run out of control" (i.e., smaller-scale technologies that are more easily kept under direct human control). However, as Marcuse (1964) argues, technology is always a social product, both in innovation *and* use. Marxian ideas about the social mediation and potential of technology are well-suited for thinking about the role of technology in a contracting economy. Marxian theories of technology keep open the possibility of socializing the constrained benefits afforded by larger-scale and complex technological systems. Just as job automation has the potential to be disastrous or liberating for workers, depending on social conditions and property relations (e.g., Bookchin 1971, Granter 2009), we also see this with the *potential* environmental gains of alternative energy converters. Guided by the principles of degrowth, collective ownership, and democratic governance, renewable energy systems have the potential to radically reduce total energy use and GHG emissions.

A critique of widespread techno-optimism in environmental thought should not spill over into a rejection of the potential positive employment of modern technology for contributing to the creation of an ecological society. Otherwise, one falls prey to the same ideological assumptions as the techno-optimists, who presuppose that technology is an entirely autonomous force, unconditioned by social context. While we agree with the sound reasons that we ought to be skeptical of quick technological fixes to environmental problems (e.g., Foster et al. 2010, York and Clark 2010, Dentzman et al. 2016, Gunderson et al. 2018b; see chapter 2), there are also good reasons to predict that altering social conditions would change the kinds and range of harmful or helpful environmental effects of already-existing technologies as well as foster new possibilities for technology design. Instead of a tool used for maximizing profits, technology can be used as a tool to reduce resource use. Technologies can be designed not to support the most profitable way to do something, but designed specifically to reduce consumption and GHG emissions. Marcuse (1964, 1972) argued that a harmonious relationship with technology is predicated on a cultural shift involving a change in ethos. In accord with findings from ecological economics (e.g., Herman Daly and Peter Victor), to address climate change, we need a new worldview that takes planetary boundaries into account. A new social order must operate under an understanding of limits, restraint, and downsizing. In a new society based on the principles of biophysical limits and minimal resource use, technological innovations can be used to reduce GHG emissions and harmonize the relationship between humans and nature.

CHAPTER 8

Participatory Global Climate Governance

Climate change is a global issue requiring a global response. As discussed in chapter 3, we are currently in a wave of market expansion that has involved the commodification of nature across the globe (Burawoy 2015). Fossil fuel commodification and combustion has resulted in rising GHG emissions and global climate change. According to Burawoy (2015: 24), addressing the current wave of market expansion "requires a planetary response to the global reach of finance capital and the looming environmental catastrophe that threatens the whole earth. . . . a countermovement will have to assume a global character, couched in terms of human rights since the survival of the human species is at stake." However, as explained by Dryzek and Stevenson (2011: 1), "[t]he rise to political pre-eminence of the climate change issue creates new challenges because the issue is so clearly global, and so clearly one that has eluded existing governments of all sorts, as well as existing transnational and global political processes." Global attempts to address climate change have largely taken place through the United Nations Framework Convention on Climate Change (UNFCCC). There have been twenty-five annual Conference of the Parties (COP) meetings since 1995, with up to 197 nations represented. The goal of the UNFCCC is to "prevent 'dangerous' human interference with the climate system" (UNFCCC 2018). Thousands of delegates attend COP meetings, yet delegate representation and participation in decision-making is unequal, with poor countries facing significant under-representation and under-participation (Dryzek and Stevenson 2011, Roberts and Parks 2006). There are also a growing number of international climate change initiatives taking place outside of the UNFCCC, including those led by national governments, other international organizations, and the private sector (Van Asselt and Zelli 2014).

In general, global climate governance has been criticized for being fragmented, slow, ineffective, and exclusive; dominated by the Global North (especially the United States); influenced by corporate interests; and lacking diverse perspectives and accountability (Held and Hervey 2009, Dryzek and Stevenson 2011, Van Asselt and Zelli 2014, Ciplet and Roberts 2017). Equitable global participation remains a particularly difficult challenge, yet this participation is essential to justly and effectively address an inherently global issue. In this chapter, we examine public participation in environmental governance and how participation models may be scaled up to the global level. Previous prescriptive chapters have recommended solutions for overdeveloped countries. Although some degrowth pathways such as community energy and economic democracy have applications for the Global South, degrowth as a whole is not a program designed for poor countries. This chapter, however, takes on a central procedural question related to global climate justice: How can we achieve effective and just climate change decision-making?[1]

Public participation in environmental assessment and decision-making, as opposed to technocratic state-industry negotiations and agreements, has become more common since the early 1990s (Bulkeley and Mol 2003). Public participation refers to "the practice of consulting and involving members of the public in the agenda-setting, decision-making, and policy-forming activities of the organizations or institutions responsible for such functions," which ranges from the collection of public input that may not have an influence on the outcome to the public codetermining outcomes in a deliberative process (Rowe et al. 2004: 88–89). Complex decisions about environmental problems are better formulated and more legitimate when those potentially affected by the outcome of the given decision are able to participate in the decision-making process. This position has been repeatedly endorsed by the U.S. National Research Council (US NRC) (1996, 2008), and the merits of public participation in environmental decision-making have been recognized by the Environmental Protection Agency (2003) and the International Risk Governance Council (2005). It is not only possible to bring scientists, policy makers, stakeholders, and the affected publics together to assess, evaluate, and govern environmental problems and risks, but public participation models guided by democratic principles and sensitive to context, "[improve] the quality and legitimacy of decisions and builds the capacity of all involved to engage in the policy process" (US NRC 2008: 226).

The US NRC (2008: 82f) clarified that although studies of global environmental assessments primarily focus on the relationship between scientists and policy makers (e.g., Mitchell et al. 2006, US NRC 2007), one can infer similar conclusions from their results: increasing and widening participation in decision-making will improve quality, legitimacy, and capacity outcomes. Thus, analytic-deliberative environmental decision-making research (discussed below), largely based on local, regional, and national participatory processes, has delivered an important question: How should decision-making processes be organized, and what procedures should be used when the outcome of an environmental decision has consequences for all global citizens? This question is especially pressing considering the need for new approaches to achieve multilateral agreements and other forms of international governance mechanisms that effectively address environmental challenges.

The aim of this chapter is twofold: (1) to show how research on public participation in environmental decision-making can inform discussions about how to improve global climate governance and (2) to explore how we might scale up results, themes, and principles from research on local, regional, and national public participation to address climate change. To accomplish these two goals, we explain why environmental social scientists and green political theorists have argued that reforms are needed to make global environmental governance more effective and fair. Then we explain the theoretical and conceptual foundations of research on public participation in environmental assessment and decision-making. Following, we examine the empirically documented merits of participatory approaches to addressing environmental problems. Finally, we present a series of questions that need answering to both address the problem of scale and calls for a more democratic model of global climate governance.

REFORMING GLOBAL ENVIRONMENTAL GOVERNANCE

Excluding ozone depletion, global environmental governance structures have failed to adequately tackle global environmental issues due to specific challenges. Speth (2002) outlines seven challenges: (1) global environmental problems are more difficult to tackle than national ones (more remote, invisible, and complex); (2) global environmental governance structures were designed in a top-down fashion; (3) multilateral treaties are inherently difficult to reach; (4) corporate interests actively oppose international environmental treaties; (5) the United States, since the 1970s, has failed to act as a positive leader; (6) there is ambiguity in where blame should be placed (e.g., growing population in the developing world or multinational corporate actors); and (7) it would be very expensive to effectively tackle global environmental challenges. Reforms to improve global environmental governance structures have been proposed to respond to these challenges (Carmen and Agrawal 2006: 301–2). Two common approaches are to revitalize and strengthen the UN Environment Programme (UNEP) and/or introduce a new world environmental organization with a similar function that has more power than the UNEP (Speth and Haas 2006; e.g., Biermann et al. 2012). However, many of these proposals overlook the importance of public participation.

The inclusion of global publics is critical for global climate governance. Public participation in global climate decision-making can address Speth's (2002) challenges (2), (6), and, potentially, (4) and (5) listed above. A participatory approach would fundamentally remedy challenge (2) as it would make room for a more bottom-up approach that addresses the "democratic deficit" of existing international regimes (Nanz and Steffek 2002, Lemos and Agrawal 2006: 301, Gellers 2016). Further, including local complexity and voices in global environmental discussions, including climate change, is sorely needed (Jasanoff and Martello 2004). Public participation could also address ambiguity in normative issues, challenge (6) being only one example (Chess et al. 1998, Beirrerle and Cayford 2002, Renn 2008: 335, US NRC 2008: 18, Dietz 2013). Public participation can be modeled to remove arbitrary power from deliberation and, thus, potentially address challenges (4) and (5). The qualifier "potentially" is important because it is possible corporate interests could stand in the way of real participatory global climate governance, as we will discuss later in the chapter.

A rapidly growing number of scholars have discussed deliberative and/or participatory possibilities for global governance elsewhere (e.g., Held 1995, Nanz and Steffek 2002, Martinelli 2003, Dryzek 2006, Gould 2014; for review and assessment, see Smith and Brassett 2008, Smith 2018), and democratizing global environmental governance in particular from a number of perspectives, including deliberative systems (Dryzek and Stevenson 2011, Stevenson and Dryzek 2014), juristic democracy (Baber and Bartlett 2009), and stakeholder democracy (Bäckstrand 2006). We draw from Habermas to examine the possibilities of a participatory and deliberative form of global climate governance and identify ways forward.

THE NORMATIVE-THEORETICAL BASIS OF PARTICIPATORY
ENVIRONMENTAL DECISION-MAKING

Habermas' communicative theories and discourse ethics provide a useful approach to examine public participation in environmental decision-making (Dietz 1994, Webler 1995, Beirerle 2002, Renn 2008: ch. 8).[2] Habermas argued that the possibility for human emancipation in modern societies lies in nonstrategic communication in which subjects adopt an "attitude oriented toward reaching an understanding" (communicative action) (Habermas 1984: 86, 286ff). The normative implications of these arguments are formulated in both his discourse ethics and his idea of an ideal speech situation. Habermas (1996: 107) put forth a discourse ethics where no conception of the right ought to precede his discourse principle: "[j]ust those action norms are valid to which all possibly affected persons could agree as participants in rational discourses." The ideal speech situation portrayed an inaccessible condition, though "potentially possible in ordinary interactions between speaking and acting subjects" (Pusey 1987: 73), that the public should approximate when attempting to reach mutual understanding. Regardless of economic or political power, all participants should have an equal chance to speak, interpret, justify, problematize, and explain any claim free from coercion and manipulation (see Webler, 1995: 46f). Rather than arbitrary power, conflicts and disagreements ought to be resolved in a deliberative way where "no force except that of the better argument is exercised" (Habermas 1975: 108).

Habermasian alternatives to technocratic environmental policy models (i.e., rational actor models and cost-benefit analysis) were first proposed in Dietz's (1984, 1987, 1988, 1994) discursive environmental impact assessment method and the discursive environmental decision-making models of Renn, Webler, and colleagues (e.g., Renn 1992; Webler 1993, 1995; Renn et al. 1993). There is a Habermasian focus on a participatory process that achieves *fairness* and—though undertheorized by Habermas (Webler 1995)—*competence* (e.g., Webler 1995; Renn 2008; Dietz, 2003, 2013). Two forms of fairness are stressed in analytic-deliberative environmental decision-making research: procedural fairness and fairness in outcome, though the latter, substantive fairness, is intimately linked to the former (i.e., fairness in outcome depends on the careful planning of procedural fairness) (Dietz 2003). Procedural fairness contains two essential elements: (1) that everyone who is interested in or potentially affected by the outcome of a decision—the public—can participate in a decision-making process that (2) attempts to equalize power relations so all logical and sincere arguments are taken seriously. Like fairness, competence in decision-making also includes two essential aspects: competence in facts (the use of the best methods available for validating scientific information in the decision-making process) (Webler 1995) and competence in values (acknowledging and deliberating upon uncertainty and diversity in participants' values) (Dietz 2003).

Achieving fairness and competence means that both public deliberation and science must be linked in decision-making, especially for making decisions about environmental issues, which frequently involve fact uncertainty and value diversity. The resulting approach, popularized in the US NRC's pioneering *Understanding Risk* (1996), is referred to as an "analytic-deliberative" process, where "[t]he research agenda in support of a decision is shaped by both the views of the scientific community and the information the public believes it needs to make informed decisions. In turn, public discussion engages science to build trust in scientific results and to clarify the nature of uncertainty and how best to deal with it" (Dietz 2013: 14083). This approach to environmental decision-making (a) allows values and norms to evolve, as valuation is achieved through discourse, not technique and positive science; (b) puts all participants on an equal footing, thus minimizing the influence of powerful interests; (c) "does not pretend that decisions can be made without consideration of values" (Dietz 1988: 223–24; see also Dietz 2013); (d) can subsume cost-benefit analysis; and (e) focuses on talking and pattern recognition (cognitive strength) instead of calculation (cognitive weakness) (Dietz 1994: 305).

Limitations of public participation include increased costs and resources and potential schedule delays (Fjeld et al. 2007); the possibility that an agreement will not be reached; and, even though the procedural rules are meant to equalize power relations, these processes are not immune to power (see the "social barriers question" below) (Dietz 1994; see also Baber and Bartlett 2018) (see below for expansion). Although public participation is not a panacea, the advantages for environmental decision-making are well established in the literature.

THE DOCUMENTED MERITS OF PARTICIPATORY ENVIRONMENTAL DECISION-MAKING

Deliberative public participation is supported by environmental scholars for the normative reasons discussed above, including its ability to build trust between publics and experts, the inherent value of deliberation, and the potential to reflect and act upon public values (see also Bulkeley and Mol 2003, Baber and Bartlett 2018). In addition to these normative merits, research has shown that participation in environmental assessment and decision-making increases the substantive quality of environmental decisions as well as process and other outcome measures. To date, the most extensive review and analysis of public participation and deliberation in environment assessment and decision-making is the US NRC's *Public Participation in Environmental Assessment and Decision Making* (2008). To assess the quality, legitimacy, and capacity of participatory environmental decisions, the report made recommendations based on theories of participatory democracy, decision-making, conflict resolution, and public discourse; social scientific research on topics related to public participation; public participation practitioner experience reports; comparative case studies of public participation processes; and an analysis of almost 1,000 case studies of public participation in the United States. Based on a systematic analysis of this extensive scope of theory and data, the report found that:

> [w]hen done well, public participation improves the quality and legitimacy of a decision and builds the capacity of all involved to engage in the policy process. It can lead to better results in terms of environmental quality and other social objectives. It also can enhance trust and understanding among parties. Achieving these results depends on using practices that address difficulties that specific aspects of the context can present. (US NRC 2008: 226)

Next to the US NRC's (2008) report, the most systematic and comprehensive analysis of public participation in environmental decision-making is Beirele's (2002; see also Beierle and Cayford 2002) review of 239 local, state, and federal case studies on environmental decision-making with public participation in the United States. Beierle (2002) found that, in most cases, public involvement resulted in better decision *outcomes*, including the inclusion of public values in decisions, the improvement of the substantive quality of decisions, the resolution of conflict among competing interests, and the increase of public education and information. Beierle and Cayford (2002) argued that context (the issue at hand, the institutional setting, and the quality of social relations going into the process) had little influence on decision outcomes. Instead, they contended that the "intensity" of the participatory process used (i.e., ones that are focused on reaching an agreement rather than collecting general information) was more important.

Taken together, public participation at the local, regional, and national scale has been shown to improve environmental decision-making in both process (as stressed by US NRC 2008) and substance (as stressed by Beierle 2002, Beirrerle and Cayford 2002). One important limitation of public participation research to date, however, is an almost exclusive focus on regional and local decision-making processes and related lack of attention to problem of scale (Dietz 2013). In the following section, we explore how participatory environmental governance could be scaled up to the global level.

TOWARD PARTICIPATORY GLOBAL CLIMATE GOVERNANCE: FOUR QUESTIONS OF SCALE

Findings related to local environmental governance suggest that scaling participatory principles and processes up to the global level would increase positive outcomes in climate governance. However, the daunting nature of this task is clear: making decisions about climate change affects everyone (i.e., everyone is the "directly affected public"). Here, we address the immediate problem of scale following this consideration through a series of questions. The problem of scale for participatory approaches, associated with small-scale political units, is an old one (Cook and Morgan 1971: 28f). The questions below are meant to illuminate some complex issues that must be addressed to begin approximating a plan for global participatory climate governance. We think this approach is more helpful than skepticism about the possibility of democratizing international institutions (e.g., Dahl 1999, Grant and Keohane 2005). While there are good sociological reasons to be skeptical (see the next subsection), we agree with others (e.g., Nanz and Steffek 2004, Dryzek 2008, Stevenson and Dryzek 2014) that a global democracy would operate differently than the liberal democracies of capitalist nation-states and exploring what this could look like is a beneficial exercise.

Our questions are as follows:

- *The social barriers question:* What political-economic barriers stand in the way?
- *The institutional formation question:* What institutions need (re)forming?
- *The "who" question:* Who should participate, and how should they be selected?
- *The procedural question:* How and when should the global public participate?

While we are comfortable posing answers to select questions (e.g., the "procedural question"), others are left open. In cases in which we do not have a good answer, an attempt is made to provide guidance based on normative arguments and empirical considerations. The questions are listed in the order they should be answered. In other words, if one cannot answer questions preceding a given question, it may be futile to try to answer that question. For instance, if institutional formation proves unfeasible, deciding how to evaluate the effectiveness and success of the participatory process is unnecessary.

The Social Barriers Question

What political-economic obstacles stand in the way of public participation in global climate governance? Another way of framing the social barriers question is as follows: Is the goal of participatory global climate governance in fundamental tension with the neoliberal world order? Indeed, global climate governance is increasingly neoliberal in nature (Ciplet and Roberts 2017). For critical political economists like Paterson (2000; see also Newell 2008), the structural *causes* of global environmental problems should be identified first—namely the inherent environmental destructiveness of growth-dependency discussed in the first half of this book—to find effective solutions. The implications of approaching global climate governance in this more critical way was epitomized by Conca's (2000) distinction between two irreconcilable visions of global environmental governance: trade liberalization aided by closed decision-making, as embodied by the practices and policies of the World Trade Organization (WTO), and sustainability through broad participation. Although an oversimplified and polemical division, the distinction helps illuminate the most pressing barrier to participatory global climate governance: the power of economic interests in global environmental politics (Paterson 2000; Newell 2005, 2008; Humphreys 2003; Levy and Newell 2005).

Transnational corporations (TNCs) were instrumental in watering down the 1992 Earth Summit (Hildyard 1993); there was a failure to develop a UN Corporate Accountability Convention during the 2002 Earth Summit (Newell 2005). TNCs are increasingly setting their own voluntary standards on their own terms without accountability measures in place (Clapp 2005) and have attempted to push out civil society actors from direct participation in environmental decision-making (e.g., Kuchler 2017). Miller (1995: 143–44) summarized this concern clearly:

[p]ower is shifting increasingly from nation-states to transnational actors such as TNCs, international financial markets, multilateral banks, and international media groups . . . To the extent that power continues to shift from local communities to centralized global actors, it will become that much more difficult to properly address major environmental issues.

While we agree with critical political economists that social movements are needed outside of formal global climate institutions—and global climate governance should not be reduced to international organizations and inter-state negotiations— it is important to consider the potential of democratizing formal international environmental institutions, and international institutions that cause great environmental harm (Downey 2015), in order to combat the interests of global capital or, as another means for "holding those with power in the global economy, and/or in states to account, making them legitimise their actions, democratising them, transforming their effects" (Paterson 2000: 149). In fact, broad global public participation is precisely what is needed to counteract the particularistic interests of global capital. Yet, as the critical political economists would reply, the crucial question is whether the current global political-economic order would *allow for* increased public participation in global climate governance. Similar to assuming that the nation-state is a neutral entity that exists in the interest of all citizens (e.g., Sweezy 1970), it is equally naïve and misleading to assume that global climate forums, international environmental law, etc., are neutral regimes formed and operating independently of powerful interests (Newell 2008).

If the interests of capital restrain, limit, and shape state and global environmental decision-making and policy options (Paterson 2000, Conca 2000), what does this mean for the possibility of broader public participation in global climate governance? There seems to be two answers to the social barriers question: (1) increased public participation in global climate governance is a possible route to challenge the decision-making that prioritizes particular economic over generalizable environmental interests, or (2) broader public participation in global climate governance is unrealistic without a different global political-economic order. Critical political economists must take the possibility of (1) seriously, whereas participatory and deliberative democrats must take the possibility of (2) seriously. Because these critical political economists come from the Marxist tradition, the discussion may resemble Trotsky's (1963) defense of revolutionary means and denouncement of liberal moralism and Dewey's (1988) defense of radical democracy and rejection of formulating ends based on assumed teleological historical "laws." But this need not be the case. Avenues for reconciliation were opened by those who emphasize participation as "a catalyst for an evolutionary, or even revolutionary, change of power structures in capitalist societies," what Renn (2008: 299–300) termed the "emancipatory" approach to public participation (e.g., Forester and Stitzel 1989, Fung and Wright 2001). The emancipatory approach is especially important at a global level as it emphasizes the inclusion and empowerment of less privileged voices (Renn 2008: 300) (see below).

Perhaps the first productive step forward is to examine the social and economic conditions that would enable, or disable, the possibility of broader and transnational forms of democracy (Gould 2014). For example, it is difficult to imagine a just and effective path to climate governance with extremely high levels of global inequality (Roberts and Parks 2006). The social barriers question is crucial because, on the one hand, what is supposed to be democratic decision-making is often systematically distorted by powerful interests and used as a means to simultaneously prop up and legitimate these powerful interests—indeed, modern "democracy" has often been employed to *limit* popular power (i.e., democracy); yet, on the other hand, deeper democratization is a necessary and valuable means for social transformation and an essential feature of any desirable alternative to the current order (Wood 1995).

The social barriers question should be prioritized in any attempt to scale up public participation in environmental decision-making or in more normative arguments for democratic forms of global climate governance. A statement made by the South Centre (1996: 32) stressed this concern: "an international community ridden with inequalities and injustice, institutionalizing 'global governance' without paying attention to the question of who wields power, and without adequate safeguards, is tantamount to sanctioning governance of the many weak by the powerful few." Without understanding the systemic barriers to scaling up public participation, calls for more deliberative and/or participatory forms of global climate governance will remain utopian.

The Institutional Formation Question

Do international institutions exist that could be reformed to make room for public participation or would new institutions need to be formed? Further, what would these look like? One option, proposed in Stevenson and Dryzek's *Democratizing Global Climate Governance* (2014: ch. 8), both answers and sidesteps the institutional formation question in a unique way. Putting forth a model that focuses on deliberative *systems* (see also Parkinson and Mansbridge 2012) rather than deliberative *forums* helps dispel the claim that the democratization of international institutions is technically infeasible. A deliberative system refers to a number of dispersed locations and practices—both formal and informal—from everyday talks among interested citizens to forums of negotiation. No one institution (e.g., the United Nations) can or should be the only site of democratic deliberation, an approach akin to "polycentric" approaches to global climate governance (Ostrom 2010, Dorsch and Flachsland 2017, Gunderson and Dietz 2018). To open up global climate governance to public participation, the prescriptive argument highlights the possibility of (1) Baber and Bartlett's (2009) plan for the participative formation of global environmental law, and (2) increasing public spaces for global climate governance. Both pathways are discussed in turn.

Stevenson and Dryzek emphasize the importance of "mini-publics," or "[b]odies comprised of ordinary citizens chosen through near random or stratified selection from a relevant constituency, and tasked with learning, deliberating, and issuing a judgment about a specific topic, issue, or proposal" (Warren and Gastil 2015: 562). They focus on Baber and Bartlett's (2009) proposal for citizen juries (one form of mini-publics) to deliberate, "hypothetical disputes that would arise under a variety of [environmental] regulatory approaches" that, in fact, contain the essential characteristics of actual global environmental challenges (Baber and Bartlett 2009: 119). The citizen jury judgments, formed in various countries, would be used to establish legitimate and transparent global common laws.

Regarding the creation of new public spaces for deliberation, there have been some attempts to form events and institutions that approximate participatory global environmental governance. For example, the United Nations coordinated two crowdsourcing projects, though there is much to be improved in terms of representativeness and legitimacy (Gellers 2016), and the public can participate in the Forum discussions of the World Conservation Congress (WCC), held every four years since 1996 by the International Union for Conservation of Nature (IUCN) (n.d.). Perhaps no other project has come closer to participatory global environmental governance than the three global deliberative events held by the global citizen consultation initiative World Wide Views (WWViews) (2009, 2012, 2015). These events deserve extended attention. In September of 2009, around 3,860 citizens from thirty-eight countries participated in WWViews on Global Warming (prior to the 2009 UNFCCC Conference of the Parties (COP 15) in Copenhagen) (WWViews 2009, Rask et al. 2012). Participants were provided with forty-page briefing reports prior to the event and shown videos pertaining to climate change and policy options. Sitting at tables of six to eight around the world, the participants deliberated, filled out an opinion survey about various climate change policy options, and made recommendations to policy makers. Although based on a one-day event—hardly enough time for genuine deliberation (Stevenson and Dryzek 2014)—the process itself and results are telling. There was strong support for: a binding climate change deal that kept global temperatures below 2 degrees C (90 percent of participants)—or at current or preindustrial levels (half of all participants); Annex I countries reducing emissions 25–40 percent below 1990 levels by 2020; fast-growing and low-income countries emission reductions (a proposal supported, with one exception, by participants of the Global South); financial mechanisms for funding mitigation and adaptation in Global South countries; rewards for complying countries and punishments for non-complying countries; mitigation technology available for all countries; and a stronger international climate change institution. In short, almost all participants chose more aggressive mitigation efforts than their own governments, even citizens of Global South countries.

The WWViews process was expanded before the 2012 Convention on Biological Diversity COP 11 (WWViews 2012) and again before the 2015 UNFCCC COP 21 (WWViews 2015). The latter deliberative event was massive, involving around 10,000 global citizens in seventy-six countries. The participants roughly represented the social and demographic features of their given country or region in terms of age, gender, occupation, education, and residency zone (urban vs. rural). With a similar educational and deliberation format as 2009, the results of the 2015 WWViews deliberation showed strong support for swift and deep climate action, including the following: support for a carbon tax (nearly 90 percent); belief that mitigation efforts in Global South countries should be partially or completely funded by overdeveloped countries (over 80 percent); belief that the United Nations climate negotiations have not done enough (over 70 percent); belief that their country should reduce emissions even if other countries are not reducing emissions (nearly 80 percent); and support for a legally binding target of zero emissions for developed and Global South countries by the end of the century (nearly 70 percent). Further, issues of apathy and the subjective irrelevance of environmental problems (Ollinaho 2016) were absent in a participatory and deliberative event, with almost unanimous agreement (97 percent) on the future use of deliberative processes in global climate governance. Perhaps the greatest feat of WWViews is putting to rest skepticism about the technical feasibility of structured global deliberation.

Despite the benefits of Stevenson and Dryzek's (2014) deliberative systems perspective, it is also limited. Smith and Brassett (2008) made the case that Dryzek's (2006) overall approach to global governance overemphasizes representing "discourses" while deemphasizing the possibility of formal public participation in international institutions, leaving an unclear picture as to how consequential participation would be possible. In this light, Stevenson and Dryzek's (2014) focus on mini-publics is a step in the right direction, and we share their enthusiasm for the WWViews initiative. However, formal access (what they call "empowered space," as opposed to "public space") to decision-making in already existing and/or new international organizations seems necessary for *consequential* public participation. This would mean a codetermination of climate change decisions and climate law by the global public.

The "Who" Question

Who from the global public should participate and how should they be selected? When the outcomes of environmental decisions are unambiguous, they generally do not require public participation (Beierle and Cayford 2002, Renn 2008). However, broad public participation is helpful, and some argue necessary, when environmental challenges are value diverse and conflict-ridden (Beierle and Cayford 2002, Renn 2008, US NRC 2008). Global environmental problems, climate change being a quintessential example, fit all these considerations. Thus, to restate the chief thesis of the first half of this chapter, it makes good sense to include the public. However, as detailed above, the public here *is* the global public. Because it would be technically impossible to include every voice in the discussion, it would be necessary to decide *who* should be included in the conversation and *how* these individuals and groups should be selected. It should be noted that even at the local level, small groups of the public usually "act as a proxy for the larger public" (Beierle and Cayford 2002: 65).

At the global scale, selecting a proxy public would, of course, be more complicated. Should the proxy global public be randomly selected, as is the case with citizen juries, or made to represent socioeconomic and demographic characteristics of the given population, as WWViews attempts to do? Who should the proxy global public be a proxy for? National origin, ecosystem region origin, prevalent environmental discourses, or other criteria? Any criterion chosen will lead to further questions. For example, if the chosen criterion is national origin, should indigenous peoples be viewed as citizens of nation states or "members of distinct peoples whose preferred lifeways are encumbered by [nation-states like Australia and Canada]" (Whyte 2012: 173)? Here, there must be an awareness of the tendency to treat the participation of minority and marginal peoples as a "checkbox" (Paulson et al. 2012).

The emancipatory approach to public participation provides guidance as it explicitly seeks to include and empower those who will be most harmed by climate change: the poor and marginalized (see Olsson et al. 2014). The climate justice argument that climate change is primarily caused by the Global North but will disproportionately affect the Global South has been verified empirically (Samson et al. 2011). In 2000, in conjunction with the COP 6 meetings of the UNFCCC, the first Climate Justice Summit took place, followed by the release of the Bali Principles of Climate Justice in 2002 (Beer 2014), which focus on equity and justice in response to climate change. Climate justice has become an important rallying cry in international conversations and deliberations around climate change. It is represented by different groups and sub-movements from across the globe (Klein 2014) and motivated by a desire to ensure that marginalized voices, mostly from the Global South, are heard and represented in climate change negotiations (e.g., Roberts and Parks 2006).

There is a significant technical consideration as well: Depending on how the proxy is understood, what tools could be used to select them as well as reach out to marginalized populations? There are also questions concerning the inclusion or exclusion of nonhumans (e.g., Eckersley 1999) and future generations (e.g., Beckman 2008) and, if considered part of the public, how they should be represented in decision-making.

The "who" question is complex and multi-layered. Although we do not have easy answers, we are sympathetic to models that promote extensive participation of lay people in a way that represents social location. The causes and impacts of climate change are often highly unequal and just solutions require attention to these inequalities. Broad participation based on representativeness of social location is one means to do so. The selection process employed by WWViews is especially instructive. However, there are no clear-cut answers.

The Procedural Question

In what way, and at which points, should the global public participate? The former "how" of the procedural question contains a number of components (Beierle and Cayford 2002, Fung 2006, US NRC 2008:14f), the most important being (1) the intensity of involvement (the effort made by both the public participants to be involved and the given organization to keep the public involved), (2) what type of engagement is appropriate (ranging from information input to deliberation), and (3) the extent of influence that the public has. Here, we focus on engagement types and influence. Models range considerably. Some merely allow the public to express opinions through surveys, focus groups, etc., that may not influence the outcome of the decision while others allow the public to codetermine outcomes deliberatively in consensus forums and citizen panels (Arnstein 1969, Fung 2006, Beierle and Cayford 2002, US NRC 2008, Renn 2008: Essay 10). Should the global public act as a resource for more input and information, make recommendations, or be given the power to codetermine the decision at hand?

Regarding the type of engagement, deliberation—"weighing the reasons relevant to a decision with a view to making a decision on the basis of that weighting" (Cohen 2007: 219)—will be more fitting for climate change as the latter involves a high degree of conflict and value diversity. As explained earlier, deliberation in participatory environmental decision-making allows for public values and interests to be shared in a fair process, the understanding of rationales for various positions, the learning of all relevant (and contested) claims, the creation of new solutions, fuller understanding and greater awareness of the ambiguities of the challenge, the finding of a "common moral ground," and the formation of fully informed agreements (which, at minimum, lead to a consensus about where disagreements stem from) (Beierle and Cayford 2002, US NRC 2008, Renn 2008). Additionally, deliberation allows for the development and articulation of generalizable interests as opposed to particular interests (e.g., Habermas 1975). This is important in environmental decision-making because, as Dryzek (1987: 204) has stressed, "the human life-support capacity of natural systems is *the* generalizable interest *par excellence.*" In other words, the ability of ecosystems to support human life is in everyone's best interest and may even transcend all particular interests (e.g. profit maximization).

Regarding influence, there are two good arguments for the public to codetermine decisions, or what is sometimes referred to as "consequential" influence. A helpful distinction here is between "weak publics" (those with "moral influence" through deliberative opinion-formation without legal access to administrative decision-making) and "strong publics" (those with legal access to decision-making forums) (Fraser 1992, Habermas 1996). The first argument for codetermination is normative and the second empirical. The normative argument, one made in a well-known essay by Arnstein (1969), posits that genuine public participation is marked by a redistribution of power. In other words, genuine public participation means that the public is the codetermining or determining agent in decision-making. Stated negatively, public participation without a redistribution of power is an "empty ritual" that merely preserves the status quo by allowing those in power to feign legitimacy. While the degree of influence that would best fit participatory global climate governance is an open question, Arnstein (1969) reminds us that the answer should steer clear of "manipulative" or "therapeutic" models that merely attempt to educate the public or "tokenistic" models where the public is given a voice without power. The empirical consideration is more straightforward: research shows that motivation to participate is low if the public perceives that their views will have little influence on the decision and higher influence is essential for trust building (Beierle and Cayford 2002, see also Held 1996: 268). The possibility of strong public influence and the institutional formation question are codependent.

In addition to influence and engagement type, there is also the related consideration of *when* the public should participate. The global public could be involved early on during process design and problem formation, later during information gathering, or, even later, to provide opinions about proposed decisions (US NRC 1996, 2008). As stated by the NRC (2008, 17), more participatory processes involve the public earlier in the process and at more points during the process. To provide an example of why the "when" of the procedural question matters, Paulson et al. (2012) found that only 5 percent of events related to indigenous rights at the 2008 WCC were sponsored by indigenous group organizations, with the majority being organized by the IUCN and Global North NGOs, which impacts the content and structure of deliberation. The "when" of the procedural question is equally important as the "how."

JUST AND EFFECTIVE GLOBAL CLIMATE GOVERNANCE IS
UNLIKELY BUT POSSIBLE

This chapter examined participatory environmental decision-making as a strategy to improve current models of global climate governance, which many find inadequate and unjust. Participatory models of environmental decision-making, specifically deliberative approaches, are both normatively desirable and consistently effective. However, many questions must be answered if we take seriously the possibility of scaling up public participation for global climate decision-making: (1) *the social barriers question:* what political-economic barriers stand in the way; (2) *the institutional formation question:* what institutions need (re)forming; (3) *the "who" question:* who should participate and how should they be selected; and (4) *the procedural question:* how and when should the global public participate?

While the path to the democratic governance of climate change seems daunting and participatory global climate governance is an unlikely future, we believe it is still possible and worthy of exploration. Not only have deliberative and participatory approaches to environmental governance been shown to be successful and effective at smaller scales, there are already existing yet constrained seeds to democratic forms of global climate governance. An analysis of alternatives and barriers to these alternatives allows one to engage in critical thought that evades utopianism but is open to possibilities. Many of these alternatives are already present, even if "only intermittently, partially, or potentially" (Young 2001: 10).

CHAPTER 9

Another Way Is Possible

RAPID AND RADICAL SOCIAL CHANGES are urgently required to address climate change. Critical questions remain: *Who* will participate and what social groups are in a structural position to transform the system? What *strategies* should be adopted? At what *scale* should these strategies take place? Wright's (2010, 2015) conception of social transformation highlights the importance of having several different simultaneous strategies, operating at multiple scales and from diverse actors. This includes local grassroots initiatives that create alternatives in the cracks of the current system to those working to change socioeconomic structures at the national and global levels. In the last four chapters, we have highlighted possible routes forward to address climate change taking place at a range of scales including individual lifestyle choices, community-based energy initiatives, national labor and energy policies, and participatory global governance for climate change. These efforts can also support each other: community-based projects can illustrate viable alternatives for wider application, and policies at the national and global level can make low consumptive and low carbon life the new norm. While often discussed in isolation, all of these ideas support degrowth principles and goals. To date, most degrowth activism has focused on the local level, yet, increasingly, scholars and activists are recognizing the importance of macro-level change. As explained by Alexander (2014),

> [a]ctions at the personal and household levels will never be enough, on their own, to achieve a steady-state economy. We need to create new, post-capitalist structures and systems that promote, rather than inhibit, the simpler way of life. These wider changes will never emerge, however, until we have a culture that demands them. So first and foremost, the revolution that is needed is a revolution in consciousness.

Specific to climate change, individual and community level changes are important but alone will not be enough to address this inherently global problem. Increased social consciousness is necessary, not only for lifestyle and community changes but to drive social movements that can demand the political, economic, and structural changes that are necessary to effectively address climate change. This change in social consciousness may already be occurring: recent polls in the United States and in the United Kingdom (UK) illustrate that approximately two thirds of citizens are very concerned about climate change (Milman 2019, ClientEarth 2018). However, governments have not responded to this level of concern with political action, largely due to the significant funds the fossil fuel industry continues to use to influence the political system (Brulle 2018). Due to these realities, for current governments to adopt policies like work time reduction, eliminate fossil fuel use, and reconfigure social systems in ways that support reducing production and consumption, a powerful countermovement must emerge that demands radical change. And due to the urgent realities of climate change, all of this must happen now.

While the task ahead is daunting and to many the outlook is bleak, recent events suggest there is growing momentum to pressure governments to take meaningful action on climate change. The October 2018 IPCC report triggered an unprecedented social response. In the UK, the group Extinction Rebellion has made news headlines with acts of protest, and they plan to disrupt the economy until the government meets their demands to address climate change. Initiated by Swedish teen Greta Thunberg, the youth movement "Fridays for Future" has held school strikes on Fridays demanding meaningful climate policy, with an estimated 1.6 million participants across the globe on March 15 (Haynes 2019). In the United States, the Sunrise Movement is actively promoting the Green New Deal, a possibly transformative resolution that targets both inequality and GHG emissions. As of spring 2019, these unprecedented climate change movements continue to grow and have already resulted in some responses, including the UK Parliament's declaration of a "climate emergency." While the future is impossible to predict, momentum is building to pressure governments to take bold climate action and conditions are ripening for the political and social transformations necessary.

The success of climate change movements largely relies on their ability to grow in size and scale. This growth depends on overcoming powerful forces of social reproduction, including the ideologies that inhibit action.

As discussed in the introduction, ideologies conceal the truth, including the capital-climate contradiction, and protect those who benefit from the status quo. Ideologies also stymie countermovements. Wright (2010) describes how fatalism and cynicism represent significant impediments to a growing social movement. He states that "fatalism poses a serious problem for people committed to challenging the injustices and harms of the existing social world, since fatalism and cynicism about the prospects for emancipatory change reduce the prospects for such change." In other words, believing that the way things are is inevitable and that social movements cannot be successful reduces the chances for positive social transformation. These ideologies conceal the fact that another way is indeed possible and achievable. In addition, ideologies about simply "greening" and tweaking the current system to address climate change continue to dominate discussions. Building a large-scale climate change movement that pushes policy in an effective direction requires a widespread shift in what people think *is* and what *is possible*. In other words, ideological transformation is a necessary, though not sufficient, precondition for moving beyond the capital-climate contradiction.

IDEOLOGICAL TRANSFORMATION

In the introduction of this book, we explained a negative definition of ideology and applied it in chapters 2 through 5 to illustrate how the "greening" of the current system through technology, carbon markets, and geoengineering conceals the underlying contradictions between economic growth driven by capital accumulation and climate change. We now draw from Therborn (1980: 2) who focuses on ideological transformation and uses a more general definition of ideology, which includes "everyday notions and 'experience' . . . both the 'consciousness' of social actors and the institutionalized thought-systems and discourses of a given society." In his book *The Ideology of Power and the Power of Ideology*, Therborn (1980: 19) describes a "logic of change" to ideological transformation:

> [i]n order to become committed to changing something, one must first get to know that it exists, then make up one's mind whether it is good that it exists. And before deciding to do something about a bad state of affairs, one must first be convinced that there is some chance of actually changing it.

Therborn's conception of transformation involves the replacement of one ideology with a competing ideology. However, we can also apply his work to the negative definition of ideology—ideologies that conceal systemic contradictions (Larrain 1979). Ideologies that conceal can be cast off as people realize their historically contingent and contradiction-concealing qualities. Proposed solutions to climate change involving the greening of markets and technologies that fail to address the capital-climate contradiction will ultimately fail to address climate change and represent a deceptive effort to keep profits flowing to those already benefiting from the current system.

Applying Therborn (1980) to climate change, a difficult step entails increasing awareness that green markets, technology, and growth are not viable solutions to climate change. It is an illusion that we can simply green the current system and carry on. Strong forces maintain the status quo and protect the current system from even small changes. For example, even "win-win" solutions proposed through green technology face considerable resistance: powerful political and economic interests constrain changes in infrastructure and technology because they benefit from the status quo (DeCicco and Mark 1998, Viitanen and Kingston 2014). More radical changes that address the root causes of climate change and move us beyond the capital-climate contradiction face even more resistance. Rather than increasing efforts to promote what we have illustrated to be false "win-win" solutions through carbon markets and technology, climate movements need to recognize the contradictions at play and instead focus their attention on systemic changes such as degrowth. This will require widespread recognition of the false promises of green markets, technology, and growth within the environmental movement. These false solutions are detrimental in that they conceal underlying contradictions and put off the real changes necessary to address climate change.

According to Therborn (1980), it is critical for the public to recognize that another way is possible. It is possible to fundamentally alter our social system in a way that addresses the root causes of climate change. It is possible to move beyond the capital-climate contradiction. While a growing number of scholars and activists recognize that we cannot address climate change without significantly altering the socioeconomic system (e.g., Foster 2011, Kallis et al. 2012, Li 2013, Klein 2014, Schwartzman 2014), this remains a fringe and "radical" perspective in the eyes of most citizens. Many people do not see that alternative socioeconomic systems are possible. A critical strategy of the neoliberal capitalist movement has been to extinguish any notion that other systems are possible; therefore, even if contradictions are revealed, a lack of knowledge about alternatives represents a significant barrier to change (Morgan 2013). According to Gibson-Graham (2008), making post-capitalist economic relationships more widely known is a critical step toward convincing the public that another social order is possible. Without this exposure and knowledge, people will continue to justify the current system and propose shallow solutions that will fail to adequately address climate change.

The ideological transformation necessary to support an alternative and systemic approach to address climate change faces many challenges. Accelerating capital accumulation remains the primary structurally compelled goal in society, and significant resources have been invested to maintain this goal even as scientific support for climate mitigation has intensified (Dunlap and McCright 2015). In addition to those protecting their financial interests, other citizens fear the prospect of social transformation and turn toward ideologies that allow them to avoid confronting problems and the systemic changes needed to address them. System justification theory posits that people rationalize the way things are in ways that can deter the changes necessary to address systemic issues (Feygina et al. 2010). For example, the fact that this book takes an anti-capitalist position will likely be interpreted as radical to many readers, yet, in academia as in everyday life, "supporting capitalism, an ideology that is changing the biophysical conditions that defined the Holocene and is threatening life on Earth, is considered a moderate decision!" (Prádanos 2018: 12). The challenge remains getting people to cast off ideologies that prevent change and embrace the possibility of a new and better system.

We hope that the necessary transformation can take place before we are immersed in climate change-related crises. Both Gramsci and Marx discuss how crises can, though do not necessarily, stimulate radical political change. Hegemony becomes fragile and contested, and crises can open up pathways for radical transformation. Therborn (1980: 34) also argues that material conditions are a determinant of ideological change. This suggests that when the biophysical environment changes, ideology may change with it. As climatic conditions further intensify, society will be faced with increased storms, severe droughts, unprecedented heat waves, and catastrophic floods as well as their impacts on transportation, food production, and housing (National Climate Assessment Report 2014). However, in this case, there is a significant temporal gap between the crises society faces and the causes of the crises. As emissions of GHGs today have impacts well into the future (IPCC 2013), effective responses to climate change require forethought and advanced execution. When environmental conditions have changed enough for people to realize that current strategies proposed to address climate change are insufficient, it will likely be too late to adopt the systemic changes necessary. Strategies that have hindered policy responses to address climate change may result in the eventual dismissal of any mitigation actions as they are deemed "too little too late" and there becomes a general acceptance of climate change adaptation rather than mitigation. In the case of climate change, social movements cannot afford to wait for more crises to catalyze a radical response.

THE LIKELIHOOD OF FAILURE AND THREAT OF RECUPERATION

[I]deas . . . in the face of utter hopelessness, because they confront it, know more than any others of hope.

HORKHEIMER 1974: 83

The prescriptive goal of this book was to investigate "transitional mitigation strategies," or, social alternatives already present in the existing social order but present "only intermittently, partially, or potentially" (Young 2001: 10) that, if expanded, could become more effective and just responses to climate change. We agree with Stoner and Melathopoulos (2016) that opposition to the current order and radical alternatives must also be self-critical (see also Blühdorn 2017). There are three interrelated reasons to be skeptical of the likelihood of the wide and effective adoption of transitional mitigation strategies, as well as other radical alternatives that we did not cover: (1) many if not most current political trends are at odds with transitional mitigation strategies; (2) there do not seem to be social groups with the power, organization, and/or radical consciousness necessary to implement transitional mitigation strategies, let alone at the scale and pace necessary to stay within the 2 degrees C target; and (3) transitional mitigation strategies can be easily coopted and recuperated if they are not pursued together in a collective political project. Each roadblock is discussed in turn.

First, aside from the glimmers of hope highlighted above, there are few political trends upon which one can forecast a favorable future for the global climate. Despite the seriousness of the climate crisis, mainstream responses to climate change habitually rely on ineffective techno-fixes and market-based solutions (see chapters 2 and 3), and geoengineering, a potentially catastrophic response to climate change, is "getting ever closer to the mainstream" (Preston 2016: xii; see chapter 4). Along with the commonness of ineffective climate responses, which this book attempts to explain and diagnose, there has been a rightward shift in global politics since the 1980s, a swing that has intensified in recent years, with some significant exceptions (e.g., relatively wide support for Bernie Sanders in the United States and Jeremy Corbyn in the United Kingdom). This is problematic for moving beyond the capital-climate contradiction because, as mentioned throughout the book, transitional mitigation strategies will require social-democratic or socialist state support for success. In contrast, the current administration of the most powerful country in the world is actively chipping away at decades of environmental reforms (for a running list, see Greshko et al. 2018). Further, there remains a powerful coalition between fossil fuel industries, conservative think tanks, politicians, contrarian scientists, and other actors that has developed a systematic climate change denial campaign (i.e., to deny the reality/severity of anthropogenic climate change) (for review, see Dunlap and McCright 2015). Climate change has also been a low national priority in the United States (Funk and Kennedy 2016). We acknowledge that the climate change responses discussed in the second half of this book are an unlikely outcome in such an inhospitable political climate.

A second reason to be skeptical of wide and effective future uptake of systemic responses to climate change is for the simple reason that there is not an objective basis to predict that seeds of resistance—movements in the Global South against resource privatization, indigenous resistance to extractivism, passing protests against financial capital in overdeveloped countries, red-green alliances in Europe, pockets of deliberative democratic forums, etc.—present historical alternatives to global capitalism. The immediate reason for this situation is simple, though the circumstances leading up to this situation are complex: what remains of the left is even more fractured and unorganized than during the mid-twentieth-century, and there is nothing that bears a resemblance to an international anti-capitalist movement needed to hint at the possibility of a qualitatively different historical alternative. For example, chapter 6 argues that organized labor is still in a structural position that has the potential to reduce the power of capital. Yet Marx's "gravediggers" of capital were largely co-opted by the Keynesian welfare capitalism of the mid-twentieth century through relatively higher wages and consumerism (e.g., Marcuse 1964) and then, since the late 1970s, subsequently stripped of most of the protective measures gained during capitalism's "Golden Age" (Harvey 2005: 167ff). The lack of a united social movement currently capable of overcoming capitalism is one reason why SAI or even colonizing the moon and Mars (Knapton 2017) are easier sells than the humbler aim of restructuring the economy (see also Žižek 2010). The latter may strike the reader as improbable not only due to one-dimensional thinking and ideology but also because it *is* improbable without a large and well-organized anti-system movement.

We agree with others (e.g., Foster 2009, Klein 2014, Löwy 2015, Magdoff and Williams 2017) that an active attempt should be made to identify, support, empower, link, and organize historical actors who are in structural positions capable of establishing an alternative social future. However, there is little reason to anticipate a revolution around the corner or that something great will rise out of the capital-climate contradiction. Are we not in a situation analogous to that of the first-generation Frankfurt School, who, due to the realities of monopoly capitalism, fascism, and Stalinism, were forced to alter the orthodox Marxist question (when will the revolution happen?) to the disillusioned one: Why do the workers willingly accept an alienated existence instead of revolting? Here, Stoner and Melathopoulos' (2015: 23) related "environment-society problematic" discussed in the introduction remains a key question; one we think is fruitfully addressed with the Marxist theory of ideology: Why is it "that the expansion of ecological consciousness has not yet translated into revolutionary transformation of society and culture worldwide in the face of the objective imperative to do so"? We cannot afford to assume that things will just get better because they are getting worse (Stoner and Melathopoulos 2016). One reason we target "non-reformist reforms" (Gorz 1967) that may act as part of a "transitional program" (Löwy 2015: 37) out of capitalism is due to the following impasse: mainstream climate policy is unable to address climate change yet revolution is a highly unlikely prospect for the near future, even more implausible than a wide implementation of transitional mitigation strategies. Further, any successful and desirable "ruptural" transformation will have to be built on non-reformist reforms like those discussed in this book (Wright 2010), and if the future does bring a revolutionary situation, it will only be because "social agents of revolution . . . are formed . . . in process of the transformation itself" (Marcuse 1969: 64). However, we acknowledge that the catastrophic dystopia projected in every major climate change report is more likely than either.

The threat of recuperation is a third reason that readers should be skeptical of the likelihood of the wide and effective implementation of responses to climate change. A term coined by Guy Debord, the Marxist critic of the "society of the spectacle" (Debord 1983), "recuperation" refers to the cooptation of authentic and creative activity and potentially liberatory projects (e.g., radical social movements) by "channeling . . . social revolt in a way that perpetuates capitalism" (Matthews 2005). Recuperation usually takes place through the commodification of the demands, symbols, and images of potentially liberatory projects—sometimes literally selling these images back to the manufactured spectators—thereby neutralizing the threat. In the context of social responses to climate change, the demand for degrowth may be commodified as a "green" lifestyle or small-group "politics" of personal "simplicity" without political engagement (Alexander 2011, Foster 2011); participation and interest in community energy projects may be low and restricted to middle class enthusiasts, and these projects may be structurally compelled to adopt renewables with larger environmental impacts (Rommel et al. 2016, Ferrari and Chartier 2017); and both economic democracy and paths to a more participatory global climate governance may be bureaucratized and implemented as empty and inconsequential forms of "participation" without redistributing power (Arnstein 1969). Even the demand for shorter working hours could be recuperated as a talking point for more "flexible" labor markets and used to benefit capital against labor (Wolff 2014). As discussed in chapters 5–8, each of these climate responses is constrained by the current social order and will only be successful if pursued as explicitly political collective action projects. Otherwise, these pathways forward are ripe for recuperation.

To be "reflexive," we admit that the programmatic propositions that make up the second half of this book are as much fueled by despair as they are by hope. However, as the epigraph to this section suggests, a bleak outlook today is a prerequisite for discovering anything more than the "fraudulent hope" (Bloch 1986) that reigns in mainstream climate change discourse. While dark times require that we "do what the miner's adage forbids: to work one's way through the darkness without a lamp" (Adorno 2000: 144), the weight of climate change projections compels us to report the imperfect findings. Although currently constrained by wider structures, the *potential* for a future with reduced GHG emissions and increased social well-being is present in already existing, yet currently limited, climate responses, including various degrowth pathways, WTR, economic democracy, socialized energy systems, and a more participatory global environmental governance. An analysis of alternatives as well as the barriers to their realization allows for critical analysis that evades utopianism.

ANOTHER WAY IS POSSIBLE

The responses to climate change outlined in the second half of this book are not impossible. These and related alternatives are, again, unlikely, yet worthy of serious consideration because they are possible and desirable. In other words, a desirable alternative to the existing social order is germinal within, yet still limited by, this order.

As argued by Klein (2014), the battle over climate change is directly linked to the battle over capitalism. To move beyond a society prioritizing economic growth, a strategy along multiple fronts is needed. We agree with Wright (2010, 2015) that the best hope for combating capitalism is to both create alternatives within the cracks and sidelines of the current system while also working for structural changes that move us toward a post-capitalist social order. Although we find some prospects in recent climate change movements, these movements will need to grow rapidly and increase their efforts to challenge and transform state policies and priorities.

To explore what is possible, we have focused on degrowth. Degrowth challenges the growth paradigm and offers a way forward where behavioral changes, community initiatives, and policy changes together have a chance to effectively challenge capitalism and address climate change. While not a panacea, degrowth has the potential to offer a real alternative to capitalism and to redefine what is possible. At its core, degrowth is about changing our priorities: placing social and ecological well-being above profits and increasing economic growth. To ensure well-being, we must stay within biophysical limits and therefore those who have over-appropriated resources and pushed us into ecological overshoot must reduce consumption and production in order to avoid the worst possible consequences of climate change. We stress the structural changes necessary to achieve these ends.

In agreement with Therborn (1980), Gibson-Graham (2008) and Alperovitz and Speth (2015), we argue that a critical step toward a post-capitalist transformation is widespread awareness that another world is possible. This includes an awareness of alternative economic relationships, such as those in worker cooperatives, community supported agriculture, and publicly owned utilities. Ideological transformation necessitates the imagining of alternative futures, even if indirectly through negative thinking and/or recognizing already existing yet constrained alternatives within the current order. However, a commonly shared assumption today is that society will end with capitalism. As put by philosopher Slavoj Žižek (2010), "[f]or us, it's easier to imagine the end of the world than serious social change . . . Maybe it's time to reverse our concept of what is possible and what isn't; maybe we should accept the impossibility of omnipotent immortality and consider the possibility of radical social change." As detailed in this book, it is this radical social change that is necessary to address climate change, which first requires a shift in the current conversation—away from minor reforms to the capitalist system and toward a major transformation to a new system all together. Moore (2015: 172) explains this clearly: "[s]hut down a coal plant, and you can slow global warming for a day; shut down the relations that made the coal plant, and you can stop it for good." Another way is indeed possible, but this depends on our ability to fundamentally change the current system and transcend the capital-climate contradiction.

Notes

CHAPTER 1

1. Like others, we do not see the "class relations" and "division of labor" or "trade" characterizations of capitalism as mutually exclusive (e.g., Wallerstein 1977, Bergesen 1984, Song 2015).

2. It is worth noting that value theory is complex and is not given sufficient attention here. In particular, Marx's reworking of the labor theory of value is commonly misunderstood, especially in environmental context, where he is often accused of developing an anthropocentric value theory (for a reply, see Foster and Clark 2009). However, the labor theory of value was never meant to be a labor theory of material wealth (i.e., the idea that labor is the source of all wealth) or a transhistorical value theory (Postone 1993). For example, the very concept of "value" is historicized and recast in Marx as the predominant form of wealth *particular to capitalism*, dependent on "socially general" or "abstract" labor, and argued that value had become an "increasingly less adequate measure of material wealth" primarily due to modern advances in productivity, creating more material wealth than value (Stoner and Melathopoulos 2015: 79; see Marx 1973: 704ff). Postone (1993) has done much to highlight the historical nature of Marx's value theory, as elaborated by Stoner and Melathopoulos (2015, 2016) in the context of climate change. The argument is that the system of production of value itself necessitates growth and environmental degradation. Although Postone would chastise us for employing a "traditional" Marxist framework that understands capitalism as a class-based system rooted in the private ownership of the commons, we agree with Postone that Marx's theory of value is consciously historical, the Marxist theory of domination is not only applicable to class, and a central goal of Marxism is the abolition, not affirmation, of alienated labor (see chapter 6). We thank Brett Clark, John Bellamy Foster, and Alexander M. Stoner for helpful discussions about value theory.

CHAPTER 2

1. Sometimes the Jevons Paradox and rebound effect are used as synonyms, yet two distinctions are sometimes drawn: (1) the Jevons paradox is often used to refer only to "backfires" (increases in total resource use despite efficiency gains), and (2) the *paradox* in Jevons paradox refers to something that needs to be explained whereas the term rebound *effect* already implies that increased efficiency is the *cause* of a decreased realization of efficiency gains (York and McGee 2016).

CHAPTER 4

1. However, it should be noted that this study assumes that a 4 degrees C temperature rise would be compensated via SAI, and this assumption was used in the climate model.

2. Like others (e.g., Robock 2008, Matthews 2010), we include CCS as a geo-engineering strategy, though some have argued that it is more accurately defined as a mitigation strategy (e.g., Vaughan and Lenton 2011).

CHAPTER 5

1. We thank Foster for conversation related to degrowth and capitalism.

CHAPTER 6

1. As Gorz (1999: 73) put it, "[e]ither working time can be integrated into the differentiated temporality of a multi-dimensional life . . . or the rhythms of life can be subjected to capital's need for profitability and companies' need for 'flexibility.'"

2. We are not opposed to UBI as we think it may have a potential place in transitioning. However, UBI faces numerous challenges, including the fact that it would do little to reduce work time polarization between unemployed and labor market insiders (LaJeunesse 2007: 152); the conservative approach to UBI entails replacing other social welfare systems with a low UBI, thereby forcing the unemployed to take low-paying jobs (see Gorz 1999: 81f, Ikebe 2016); and the problem of free-loading (for replies, see Gorz 1999: 98ff, Alexander 2015: 147, Calnitsky 2017).

3. An analysis of the environmental impacts of worker cooperatives compared to equivalent capitalist firms would likely bring about interesting and pertinent information. However, as argued, the potential environmental benefits of

economic democracy depend on democratically run firms being the norm as opposed to the exception.

CHAPTER 8

1. The issues surrounding global climate justice are important and complex and cannot be adequately addressed within the confines of this book (for helpful review, see Walker 2012: ch. 8). In addition to this chapter's discussion of upscaling participatory decision-making, a helpful way to interpret the prescriptive arguments in this book in the context of global climate justice is a partial program for how the Global North in particular can effectively and justly respond to climate change.

2. We would like to thank Thomas Dietz for discussions related to Habermas and the possibilities of upscaling participatory and deliberative approaches to environmental decision-making.

References

Adaman, F., and B. Ozkaynak. 2002. "The Economics–Environment Relationship: Neoclassical, Institutional, and Marxist Approaches." *Studies in Political Economy* 69: 109–35.

Adorno, T. W. 1967. *Prisms*. Cambridge: MIT Press.

Adorno, T. W. 1998. *Critical Models: Interventions and Catchwords*. New York: Columbia University Press.

Adorno, T. W. 2000. *Metaphysics*. Stanford: Stanford University Press.

Adorno, T. W., and M. Horkheimer. 2011. *Towards a New Manifesto*. New York: Verso.

Agger, B. 1976. "Marcuse and Habermas on New Science." *Polity* 9 (2): 158–81.

Albertsen, K., G. L. Rafnsdottir, A. Grimsmo, K. Tomasson, and K. Kauppinen. 2008. "Workhours and Worklife Balance." *Scandinavian Journal of Work Environment & Health*: 14–21.

Alcott, B. 2005. "Jevons' Paradox." *Ecological Economics* 54 (1): 9–21.

Alexander, S. 2011. "Property beyond Growth: Towards a Politics of Voluntary Simplicity." In *Property Rights and Sustainability*, edited by D. Grinlinton and P. Taylor, 117–48. Leiden: Brill.

Alexander, S. 2014. "Degrowth and the Carbon Budget: Powerdown Strategies for Climate Stability. In *Simplicity Institute Report 14h*: Simplicity Institute.

Alexander, S. 2015. "Basic and Maximum Incomes." In *Degrowth: A Vocabulary for a New Era*, edited by G. D'Alisa, F. Demaria, and G. Kallis, 146–48. New York: Routledge.

Alexander, S., and P. Yacoumis. 2016. "Degrowth, Energy Descent, and 'Low Tech' Living: Potential Pathways for Increased Resilience in Times of Crisis." *Journal of Cleaner Production*.

Alperovitz, G. 2013. *What Then Must We Do? Straight Talk about the Next American Revolution.* White River Junction: Chelsea Green Publishing.

Alperovitz, G., J. Guinan, and T. Hanna. 2017. "The Policy Weapon Activists Need." *The Nation.*

Alperovitz, G., and G. Speth. 2015. "The Next Systems Project." Accessed June 23, 2015. http://thenextsystem.org/

Althusser, L. 1971. "Ideology and Ideological State Apparatuses." In *Lenin and Philosophy and Other Essays.* New York: Monthly Review Press.

Alvarez, C. H., J. A. McGee, and R. York. 2019. "Is Labor Green? A Cross-National Analysis of Unionization and Carbon Dioxide Emissions. *Nature & Culture* 14 (1): 17–318.

American Council for an Energy-Efficient Economy (ACEEE). 2016. "The 2016 International Energy Efficiency Scorecard." http://aceee.org/research-report/e1602

Anderson, K., and A. Bows. 2011. "Beyond 'Dangerous' Climate Change: Emission Scenarios for a New World." *Philosophical Transactions of the Royal Society a-Mathematical Physical and Engineering Sciences* 369 (1934): 20–44.

Anderson, K., and A. Bows. 2012. "A New Paradigm for Climate Change." *Nature Climate Change* 2 (9): 639–40.

Anderson, K., and A. Bows-Larkin. 2013. "Avoiding Dangerous Climate Change Demands Degrowth Strategies from Wealthier Nations." *Kevin Anderson Blog.* https://kevinanderson.info/blog/avoiding-dangerous-climate-change-demands-de-growth-strategies-from-wealthier-nations/

Anderson, K., and G. Peters. 2016. "The Trouble with Negative Emissions." *Science* 354 (6309): 182–83.

Anderson, P. 1976. *Considerations on Western Marxism.* London: New Left Books.

Antonio, R. J., and B. Clark. 2015. "The Climate Change Divide in Social Theory." In *Climate Change and Society: Sociological Perspectives*, edited by R. E. Dunlap and R. J. Brulle. New York: Oxford University Press.

Aranoff, K. 2017. "Bringing Power to the People: The Unlikely Case for Utility Populism." *Dissent.*

Archer, R. 1995. *Economic Democracy: The Politics of Feasible Socialism.* Oxford: Clarendon Press.

Arnstein, S. R. 1969. "A Ladder of Citizen Participation." *Journal of the American Institute of Planners* 5: 216–24.

Arponen, V. P. J. 2013. "The Human Collective Causing of Environmental

Problems and Theory of Collective Action: A Critique of Cognitivism." *International Journal of Applied Philosophy* 27 (1): 47–65.

Arponen, V. P. J. 2016. "A Critique of an Epistemic Intellectual Culture: Cartesianism, Normativism and Modern Crises." *Journal for the Theory of Social Behaviour* 46 (1): 84–103.

Artazcoz, L., I. Cortez, V. Escriba-Aguir, L. Cascant, and R. Villegas. 2009. "Understanding the Relationship of Long Working Hours with Health Status and Health-Related Behaviours." *Journal of Epidemiology and Community Health* 63 (7): 521–27.

Asara, V., E. Profumi, and G. Kallis. 2013. "Degrowth, Democracy and Autonomy." *Environmental Values* 22 (2): 217–39.

Assadourian, E. 2012. "The Path to Degrowth in Overdeveloped Countries." In *State of the World 2012*, 22–37. Washington, DC: Island Press.

Association of Academies of Sciences in Asia (AASA). 2011. *Towards a Sustainable Asia: Green Transitions and Innovation*. Beijing: Science Press/Springer.

Baber, W. F., and R. V. Bartlett. 2009. *Global Democracy and Sustainable Jurisprudence: Deliberative Environmental Law*. Cambridge: MIT Press.

Baber, W. F., and R.V. Bartlett. 2018. "Deliberative Democracy and the Environment." In *The Oxford Handbook of Deliberative Democracy*, edited by A. Bachtiger, J. Dryzek, J. Mansbridge, and M. Warren, 755–67. New York: Oxford University Press.

Backstrand, K. 2006. "Democratizing Global Environmental Governance? Stakeholder Democracy after the World Summit on Sustainable Development." *European Journal of International Relations* 12 (4): 467–98.

Baik, E., D. L. Sanchez, P. A. Turner, K. J. Mach, C. B. Field, and S. M. Benson. 2018. "Geospatial Analysis of Near-Term Potential for Carbon-Negative Bioenergy in the United States." *Proceedings of the National Academy of Sciences of the United States of America* 115 (13): 3290–95.

Bajak, A. 2018. "The Dangerous Belief that Extreme Technology Will Fix Climate Change." *The Huffington Post.* https://www.huffingtonpost.com/entry/geoengineering-climate-change_us_5ae07919e4b061c0bfa3e794

Balbus, I. D. 1982. *Marxism and Domination*. Princeton: Princeton University Press.

Barca, S. 2016. "Labor in the Ae of Climate Change." *Jacobin.*

Barry, J. 2007. *Environment and Social Theory*. New York: Routledge.

Barth, H. 1976. *Truth and Ideology*. Berkeley: University of California Press.

Baykan, B. G. 2007. "From Limits to Growth to Degrowth within French Green Politics." *Environmental Politics* 16 (3): 513–17.

Bayon, D. 2015. "Unions." In *Degrowth: A Vocabulary for a New Era*, edited by G. D'Alisa, F. Demaria, and G. Kallis, 181–91. New York: Routledge.

Beck, U. 2010. "Climate for Change, or How to Create a Green Modernity?" *Theory Culture & Society* 27 (2–3): 254–66.

Becker, S. 2017. "Our City, Our Grid: The Energy Remunicipalisation Trend in Germany." In *Reclaiming Public Services*. Amsterdan and Paris: Transnational (TNI), Multinationals Observatory, Austrian Federal Chamber of Labour (AK), European Federation of Public Service Unions (EPSU), Ingenieria Sin Fronteras Cataluna (ISF), Public Services International (PSI), Public Services International Research Unit (PSIRU), We Own It, Norwegian Union for Municipal and General Employees (Fagforbundet), Municipal Services Project (MSP) and Canadian Union of Public Employees (CUPE).

Beckman, L. 2008. "Do Global Climate Change and the Interest of Future Generations Have Implications for Democracy?" *Environmental Politics* 17 (4): 610–24.

Beer, T. B. 2014. "Climate Justice, the Global South, and Policy Preferences of Kenyan Environmental NGOs." *The Global South* 8 (2): 84–100.

Bell, S. E. 2015. "Energy, Society and Environment." In *Twenty Lessons in Environmental Sociology*, edited by K. A. Gould and T. L. Lewis, 137–58. New York: Oxford University Press.

Bell, S. E., and R. York. 2010. "Community Economic Identity: The Coal Industry and Ideology Construction in West Virginia." *Rural Sociology* 75 (1): 111–43.

Bellamy, R., J. Chilvers, N. E. Vaughan, and T. M. Lenton. 2012. "A Review of Climate Geoengineering Appraisals." *Wiley Interdisciplinary Reviews: Climate Change* 3 (6): 597–615.

Beierle, T. C. 2002. "The Quality of Stakeholder-Based Decisions." *Risk Analysis* 22 (4): 739–49.

Beierle, T. C., and J. Cayford. 2002. *Democracy in Practice: Public Participation in Environmental Decisions*. Washington, DC: Resources for the Future.

Best, H. 2009. "Structural and Ideological Determinants of Household Waste Recycling: Results from an Empirical Study in Cologne, Germany." *Nature + Culture* 4 (2): 167–90.

Bickel, J. E., and L. Lane. 2009. *An Analysis of Climate Engineering as a Response to Climate Change*. Frederiksberg: Copenhagen Consensus Center.

Biello, D. 2009. "Enhanced Oil Recovery: How to Make Money from Carbon Capture and Storage Today." *Scientific American*.

Biermann, F., K. Abbott, S. Andresen, K. Backstrand, S. Bernstein, M. M. Bet-
sill, H. Bulkeley, B. Cashore, J. Clapp, C. Folke, A. Gupta, J. Gupta, P. M.
Haas, A. Jordan, N. Kanie, T. Kluvankova-Oravska, L. Lebel, D. Liverman,
J. Meadowcroft, R. B. Mitchell, P. Newell, S. Oberthur, L. Olsson, P. Patt-
berg, R. Sanchez-Rodriguez, H. Schroeder, A. Underdal, S. C. Vieira, C.
Vogel, O. R. Young, A. Brock, and R. Zondervan. 2012. "Navigating the
Anthropocene: Improving Earth System Governance." *Science* 335 (6074):
1306–7.

Bijker, W. E., T. P. Hughes, and T. Pinch, eds. 1987. *The Social Construction of
Technological Systems: New Directions in the Sociology and History of Technology*. Cambridge: MIT Press.

Biro, A. 2005. *Denaturalizing Ecological Politics: Alienation from Nature from
Rousseau to the Frankfurt School and Beyond*. Toronto: University of Toronto Press.

Blackwater, B. 2015. "Rediscovering Rosa Luxemburg." *Renewal*.

Bloch, E. 1986. *The Principle of Hope*. Cambridge: MIT Press.

Bloemmen, M., R. Bobulescu, N. T. Le, and C. Vitari. 2015. "Microeconomic
Degrowth: The Case of Community Supported Agriculture." *Ecological
Economics* 112: 110–15.

Bloomberg. 2017. "State of Clean Energy Investment." https://about.bnef.
com/clean-energy-investment/

Bluemling, B., and S. J. Yun. 2016. "Giving Green Teeth to the Tiger: A Critique of 'Green Growth' in South Korea." In *Green Growth: Ideology, Political Economy and Alternatives*, edited by G. Dale, M. V. Mathai and J. A.
Puppim de Oliveira, 114–30. London: Zed Books.

Bluhdorn, I. 2007. "Sustaining the Unsustainable: Symbolic Politics and the
Politics of Simulation." *Environmental Politics* 16 (2): 251–75.

Bluhdorn, I. 2017. "Post-Capitalism, Post-Growth, Post-Consumerism? Eco-
Political Hopes beyond Sustainability." *Global Discourses* 7 (1): 42–61.

Boillat, S., J. F. Gerber, and F. R. Funes-Monzote. 2012. "What Economic Democracy for Degrowth? Some Comments on the Contribution of Socialist Models and Cuban Agroecology." *Futures* 44 (6): 600–7.

Bollier, D. 2014. *Think Like a Commoner: A Short Introduction to the Life of the
Commons*. Gabriola Island: New Society.

Bookchin, M. 1971. *Post Scarcity Anarchism*: Ramparts Press.

Bookchin, M. 1982. *The Ecology of Freedom: The Emergence and Dissolution of
Hierarchy*. Palo Alto: Cheshire Books.

Boucher, O., D. Randall, P. Artaxo, C. Bretherton, G. Feingold, P. Forster, V. M.

Kerminen, Y. Kondo, H. Liao, U. Lohmann, P. Rasch, S. K. Satheesh, S. Sherwood, B. Stevens, and X. Y. Zhang. 2013. "Clouds and Aerosols." In *Climate Change 2013: The Physical Science Basis*, edited by T. F. Stocker, D. Qin, G. K. Plattner, M. Tignor, S. K. Allen, J. Boschung, A. Nauels, Y. Xia, V. Bex and P. M. Midgley. Cambridge and New York: Cambridge University Press.

Boules, R., and G. Cette. 2005. "A Comparison of Structural Productivity Levels in the Major Industrial Countries." *OECD Economic Studies* 41/2: 75–108.

Bowring, F. 1996. "Misreading Gorz." *New Left Review* (217):102–22.

Boyd, E. 2009. "Governing the Clean Development Mechanism: Global Rhetoric versus Local Realities in Carbon Sequestration Projects." *Environment and Planning A* 41 (10): 2380–95.

Brand, C., and B. Boardman. 2008. "Taming of the Few—the Unequal Distribution of Greenhouse Gas Emissions from Personal Travel in the UK." *Energy Policy* 36 (1): 224–38.

Brulle, R. J. 2018. "The Climate Lobby: A Sectoral Analysis of Lobbying Spending on Climate Change in the USA, 2000 to 2016." *Climatic Change* 149 (3–4): 289–303.

Bryant, G. 2016. "The Politics of Carbon Market Design: Rethinking the Techno-Politics and Post-Politics of Climate Change." *Antipode* 48 (4):877–98.

Bryson, A., B. Ebbinghaus, and J. Visser. 2011. "Introduction: Causes, Consequences and Cures of Union Decline." *European Journal of Industrial Relations* 17 (2): 97–105.

Buck, H. J. 2012. "Geoengineering: Re-Making Climate for Profit or Humanitarian Intervention?" *Development and Change* 43 (1): 253–70.

Bulkeley, H., and A. P. J. Mol. 2003. "Participation and Environmental Governance: Consensus, Ambivalence and Debate." *Environmental Values* 12 (2): 143–54.

Bunker, S. G. 1996. "Raw Material and the Global Economy: Oversights and Distortions in Industrial Ecology." *Society & Natural Resources* 9 (4): 419–29.

Burawoy, M. 2015. "Facing an Unequal World." *Current Sociology* 63 (1): 5–34.

Bureau of Labor Statistics. 2017. "The Employment Situation." https://www.bls.gov/news.release/archives/empsit_11032017.pdf

Burke, M. J., and J. C. Stephens. "Political Power and Renewable Energy Futures: A Critical Review." *Energy Research & Social Science* 35 (Jan 2018): 78–93.

Burke, P. J., M. Shahiduzzaman, and D. I. Stern. 2015. "Carbon Dioxide Emissions in the Short Run: The Rate and Sources of Economic Growth Matter." *Global Environmental Change-Human and Policy Dimensions* 33: 109–21.

Burns, W. C., and J. A. Flegal. 2015. "Climate Geoengineering and the Role of Public Deliberation: A Comment on the US National Academy of Sciences' Recommendations on Public Participation." *Climate Law* 5 (2–4): 252–94.

Byrne, J., C. Martinez, and C. Ruggero. 2009. "Relocating Energy in the Social Commons: Ideas for a Sustainable Energy Utility." *Bulletin of Science, Technology & Society* 29 (2): 81–94.

Caldeira, K., and D. W. Keith. 2010. "The Need for Climate Engineering Research." *Issues in Science and Technology* 27 (1): 57–62.

Calnitsky, D. 2017. "Debating Basic Income." *Catalyst.* https://catalyst-jour nal.com/vol1/no3/debating-basic-income

Carbon Trade Watch. 2011. "EU Trading Emissions System: Failing at the Third Attempt." http://www.carbontradewatch.org/downloads/publica tions/ETS_briefing_april2011.pdf

Carmen, M., and A. Agrawal. 2006. "Environmental Governance." *Annual Review of Environmental Resources* 3: 297–325.

Cartney, P., S. MacGregor, A. Dobson, S. M. Hall, S. Royston, Z. Robinson, M. Ormerod, and S. Ross. 2014. "Big Society, Little Justice? Community Renewable Energy and the Politics of Localism." *The International Journal of Justice and Sustainability* 19: 715–30.

Carton, W. 2014. "Environmental Protection as Market Pathology?: Carbon Trading and the Dialectics of the 'Double Movement.'" *Environment and Planning D: Society & Space* 32 (6): 1002–18.

Cattaneo, C., G. D'Alisa, G. Kallis, and C. Zografos. 2012. "Degrowth Futures and Democracy Introduction." *Futures* 44 (6): 515–23.

CDM Watch and Environmental Investigation Agency. 2010. "CDM Panel Calls for Investigation over Carbon Market Scandal." https://eia-global. org/press-releases/cdm-panel-calls-for-investigation-over-carbon-market-scandal

CDP. 2017. "The Carbon Majors Database." *CDP Carbon Majors Report 2017.*

Cha, J. M., and L. Skinner. 2017. *Reversing Inequality, Combatting Climate Change: A Climate Jobs Program for New York State.* Cornell University, ILR School: The Worker Institute.

Chen, S. 2017. "Helping Hand or Hubris?" *APS News* 26 (9).

Chess, C., T. Dietz, and M. Shannon. 1998. "Who Should Deliberate When?" *Human Ecology Review* 5 (2): 45–48.

Choe, H., and S. J. Yun. 2017. "Revisiting the Concept of Common Pool Resources: Beyond Ostrom." *Development and Society* 46 (1): 113–29.

Ciais, P., C. Sabine, G. Bala, L. Bopp, V. Brovkin, J. Canadell, A. Chabra, R. DeFries, J. Galloway, M. Heimann, C. Jones, C. Le Quere, R. B. Myneni, S. Piao, and P. Thornton. 2013. "Carbon and Other Biogeochemical Cycles." In *Climate Change 2013: The Physical Basis: Contribution of the Working Group I to the Fifth Assessment Report of the Intergovernmental Panel on Climate Change*, edited by T. F. Stocker, D. Qin, G. K. Plattner, M. Tignor, S. K. Allen, J. Boschung, A. Nauels, Y. Xia, V. Bex and P. M. Midgley. Cambridge and New York: Cambridge University Press.

Ciplet, D., and J. T. Roberts. 2017. "Climate Change and the Transition to Neoliberal Environmental Governance." *Global Environmental Change-Human and Policy Dimensions* 46: 148–56.

City of Boulder Colorado. 2017. "Boulder's Energy Future." Accessed October 12, 2017. https://bouldercolorado.gov/energy-future

Clapp, J. 2005. "The Privatization of Global Environmental Governance: ISO 14000 and the Developing World." In *The Business of Global Environmental Governance*, edited by D. L. Levy and P. J. Newell. Cambridge: MIT Press.

Clark, B., and J. B. Foster. 2001. "William Stanley Jevons and the Coal Question: An Introduction to Jevons's 'Of the Economy of Fuel.'" *Organization & Environment* 14 (1): 93–98.

Clawson, D., and M. A. Clawson. 1999. "What Has Happened to the US Labor Movement? Union Decline and Renewal." *Annual Review of Sociology* 25: 95–119.

ClientEarth. 2018. "British Public Supports Urgent Action and Litigation on Climate Change—Poll Reveals." ClientEarth, accessed May 1, 2019. https://www.clientearth.org/british-public-supports-urgent-action-and-litigation-on-climate-change-poll-reveals/

Clingerman, F., and K. J. O'Brien. 2016. *Theological and Ethical Perspectives on Climate Engineering: Calming the Storm*. Lanham: Lexington Books.

Cock, J. 2014. "The 'Green Economy': A Just Sustainable Development Path or a 'Wolf in Sheep's Clothing'?" *Global Labour Journal* 51 (1): 23–44.

Cohen, P. 2007. "Deliberative Democracy." In *Deliberation, Participation, and Democracy: Can the People Govern?*, edited by S. W. Rosenberg. New York: Palgrave Macmillan.

Cohen, P. 2018. "U.S. Economy Grew at 2.6% Rate in Fourth Quarter." *New York Times*, January 26. https://www.nytimes.com/2018/01/26/business/economy/gdp-economy.html

Cole, G. D. H. 1917. *Self-Government in Industry*. London: G. Bell and Sons.

Cole, G. D. H. 1920. *Guild Socialism Re-Stated*. London: George Allen & Unwin.

Conca, K. 2000. "The WTO and the Undermining of Global Environmental Governance." *Review of International Political Economy* 7 (3): 484–94.

Connerton, P. 1976. *Critical Sociology: Selected Readings*. New York: Penguin.

Connolly, K. 2017. "Geoengineering Is Not a Quick Fix for Climate Change, Experts Warn Trump." *The Guardian*, October 14. https://www.theguardian.com/environment/2017/oct/14/geoengineering-is-not-a-quick-fix-for-climate-change-experts-warn-trump

Cook, T. E., and P. M. Morgan. 1971. *Participatory Democracy*. San Francisco: Canfield Press.

Coote, A., J. Franklin, and A. Simms. 2010. *21 Hours: Why a Shorter Working Week Can Help Us All to Flourish in the 21st Century*. London: New Economics Foundation.

Corner, A., K. Parkhill, N. Pidgeon, and N. E. Vaughan. 2013. "Messing with Nature? Exploring Public Perceptions of Geoengineering in the UK." *Global Environmental Change-Human and Policy Dimensions* 23 (5): 938–47.

Corner, A., and N. Pidgeon. 2010. "Geoengineering the Climate: The Social and Ethical Implications." *Environment* 52 (1): 24–37.

Corporate Europe Observatory. 2015. "EU Emissions Trading: 5 Reasons to Scrap the ETS." Accessed May 8, 2017. https://corporateeurope.org/environment/2015/10/eu-emissions-trading-5-reasons-scrap-ets

Cottrell, W. F. 1972. *Technology, Man and Progress*. Columbus: Charles Merrill Publishing.

Crutzen, P. J. 2006. "Albedo Enhancement by Stratospheric Sulfur Injections: A Contribution to Resolve a Policy Dilemma?" *Climatic Change* 77 (3–4): 211–19.

Cuellar-Franca, R. M., and A. Azapagic. 2015. "Carbon Capture, Storage and Utilisation Technologies: A Critical Analysis and Comparison of Their Life Cycle Environmental Impacts." *Journal of CO2 Utilization* 9: 82–102.

Curl, J. 2012. *For All the People: Uncovering the Hidden History of Cooperation, Cooperative Movements, and Communalism in America*. Oakland: PM Press.

Cutler, M. J. 2016. "Class, Ideology, and Severe Weather: How the Interaction of Social and Physical Factors Shape Climate Change Threat Perceptions among Coastal US Residents." *Environmental Sociology* 2 (3): 275–85.

Dahl, R. A. 1985. *A Preface to Economic Democracy*. Berkeley: University of California Press.

Dahl, R. A. 1999. "Can International Organizations Be Democratic? A Skeptic's View." In *Democracy's Edges*, edited by I. Shapiro and C. Hacker-Cordon. New York: Cambridge University Press.

Dale, G. 2010. *Karl Polanyi: The Limits of the Market*. Cambridge: Polity Press.

Dale, G. 2015. "Origins and Delusions of Green Growth." *International Socialist Review*, accessed November 20, 2016. http://isreview.org/issue/97/ori gins-and-delusions-green-growth

Dale, G. 2016. *Reconstructing Karl Polanyi: Excavation and Critique*. London: Pluto Press.

Dale, G., M. V. Mathai, and J. P. de Oliveira, eds. 2016. *Green Growth: Ideology, Political Economy and the Alternatives*. London: Zed Books.

Daly, H. 2013. "A Further Critique of Growth Economics." *Ecological Economics* 88: 20–24.

Davis, M. 2007. "Home-Front Ecology." *Sierra Club Magazine*.

Debord, G. 1983. *Society of the Spectacle*. Detroit: Black and Red.

Debord, G. 2004. *A Sick Planet*. London: Seagull Books.

de Coninck, H., and S. M. Benson. 2014. "Carbon Dioxide Capture and Storage: Issues and Prospects." In *Annual Review of Environment and Resources, Vol. 39*, edited by A. Gadgil and D. M. Liverman, 243–70.

DeCicco, J., and J. Mark. 1998. "Meeting the Energy and Climate Challenge for Transportation in the United States." *Energy Policy* 26 (5): 395–412.

De Spiegelaere, A., and S. Piasna. 2017. "The Why and How of Working Time Reduction." European Trade Union Institute, accessed March 6, 2017. https://www.etui.org/content/download/32642/303199/file/Guide_Working+time-web-version.pdf

Demaria, F., F. Schneider, F. Sekulova, and J. Martinez-Alier. 2013. "What Is Degrowth? From an Activist Slogan to a Social Movement." *Environmental Values* 22 (2): 191–215.

Dentzman, K., R. Gunderson, and R. Jussaume. 2016. "Techno-Optimism as a Barrier to Overcoming Herbicide Resistance: Comparing Farmer Perceptions of the Future Potential of Herbicides." *Journal of Rural Studies* 48: 22–32.

Department of Energy (DOE). 2018. *Energy Department Announces Intent to Fund Enhanced Oil Recovery Research*. Washington, DC: United Stated Department of Energy.

Deriu, M. 2015. "Conviviality." In *Degrowth: A Vocabulary for a New Era*, edited by G. D'Alisa, F. Demaria, and G. Kallis. New York: Routledge.

Dewey, J. 1988. "Means and Ends." In *The Later Works, 1938–1939*, edited by J. A. Boydston. Carbondale: Southern Illinois University Press.

Dietz, T. 1984. "Social Impact Assessment as a Tool for Rangelands Management." In *Developing Strategies for Rangelands Management*, edited by National Research Council. Boulder: Westview.

Dietz, T. 1987. "Theory and Method in Social Impact Assessment." *Sociological Inquiry* 57: 54–69.

Dietz, T. 1988. "Social Impact Assessment as Applied Human Ecology: Integrating Theory and Method." In *Human Ecology: Research and Applications*, edited by R. J. Borden and J. Jacobs. College Park: Society for Human Ecology.

Dietz, T. 1994. "What Should We Do?: Human Ecology and Collective Decision Making." *Human Ecology Review* 1 (2): 301–9.

Dietz, T. 2003. "What Is a Good Decision?: Criteria for Environmental Decision Making." *Human Ecology Review* 10 (1): 33–39.

Dietz, T. 2013. "Bringing Values and Deliberation to Science Communication." *Proceedings of the National Academy of Sciences of the United States of America* 110: 14081–87.

Dietz, T. 2015. "Prolegomenon to a Structural Human Ecology of Human Well-Being." *Sociology of Development* 1 (1): 123–48.

Dietz, T., E. Ostrom, and P. C. Stern. 2003. "The Struggle to Govern the Commons." *Science* 302 (5652): 1907–12.

Dietz, T., E. A. Rosa., and R. York. 2009. "Environmentally Efficient Well-being: Rethinking Sustainability as the Relationship between Human Well-being and Environmental Impacts." *Human Ecology Review* 16 (1): 114–23.

Dietz, T., E. A. Rosa, and R. York. 2012. "Environmentally Efficient Well-being: Is There a Kuznets Curve?" *Applied Geography* 32 (1): 21–28.

Dobson, A. 1993. "Critical Theory and Green Politics." In *Politics of Nature: Explanations in Green Political Theory*, edited by A. Dobson and P. Lucardie. New York: Routledge.

Dorsch, M. J., and C. Flachsland. 2017. "A Polycentric Approach to Global Climate Governance." *Global Environmental Politics* 17 (2): 45–64.

Doukas, A., K. DeAngelis, and N. Ghio. 2017. "Talk Is Cheap: How G20 Governments Are Financing Climate Disaster." Oil Change International, Friends of the Earth U.S., the Sierra Club, WWF European Policy Office. http://priceofoil.org/2017/07/05/g20-financing-climate-disaster/

Douthwaite, R. 2012. "Degrowth and the Supply of Money in an Energy-Scarce World." *Ecological Economics* 84: 187–93.

Downey, L. 2015. *Inequality, Democracy, and the Environment.* New York: NYU Press.

Dryzek, J. S. 1987. *Rational Ecology: Environment and Political Economy.* Oxford: Blackwell Basil.

Dryzek, J. S. 2006. *Deliberative Global Politics.* Malden: Polity.

Dryzek, J. S., and H. Stevenson. 2011. "Global Democracy and Earth System Governance." *Ecological Economics* 70 (11): 1865–74.

Dunlap, R. E., and A. M. McCright. 2015. "Challenging Climate Change: The Denialist Countermovement." In *Climate Change and Society: Sociological Perspectives,* edited by R. E. Dunlap and R. J. Brulle. New York: Oxford University Press.

Easterlin, R. A., L. A. Mcvey, M. Switek, O. Sawangfa, and J. S. Zweig. 2010. "The Happiness-Income Paradox Revisited." *Proceedings of the National Academy of Sciences of the United States of America* 107 (52): 22463–68.

Eckersley, R. 1992. *Environmentalism and Political Theory: Toward an Ecocentric Approach.* New York: SUNY Press.

Eckersley, R. 1999. "The Discourse Ethic and the Problem of Representing Nature." *Environmental Politics* 8 (2): 24–49.

Ellison, K. 2018. "What on Earth? Why Climate Change Skeptics Are Backing Geoengineering." *National Observer,* accessed May 1, 2018. https://www. nationalobserver.com/2018/03/30/news/what-earth-why-climate-change-skeptics-are-backing-geoengineering

Elster, J. 1985. *Making Sense of Marx.* Cambridge: Cambridge University Press.

Ernsting, A. 2015. "Renewables Cannot Sustain the Globalized Growth Economy." Degrowth Web Portal, accessed January 12, 2018. https://www.degrowth.info/en/2015/02/renewables-cannot-sustain-the-globalized-growth-economy/

EU Commission. 2010. *Europe 2020: A European Strategy for Smart, Sustainable and Inclusive Growth.* COM.

EU Horizon. 2020. Accessed October 12, 2017. https://ec.europa.eu/pro grammes/horizon2020/

European Agency for Safety and Health at Work. 2009. "OSH in Figures: Stress at Work—Facts and Figures." Office for Official Publications of the European Communities. https://osha.europa.eu/en/tools-and-publica tions/publications/reports/TE-81-08-478-EN-C_OSH_in_figures_stress_at_ work

Eversberg, D. 2016. "Critical Self Reflection as a Path to Anti-capitalism: The Degrowth Movement." Accessed April 20, 2017. https://www.degrowth. de/en/2016/02/critical-self-reflection-as-a-path-to-anti-capitalism-the-de growth-movement/

Fairbrother, M. 2016. "Externalities: Why Environmental Sociology Should Bring Them In." *Environmental Sociology* 2 (4): 375–84.

Feenberg, A. 1999. *Questioning Technology.* New York: Routledge.

Feenberg, A. 2004. *Heidegger and Marcuse: The Catastrophe and Redemption of History.* New York: Routledge.

Ferrari, C. A., and C. Chartier. 2017. "Degrowth, Energy Democracy, Technology and Social-Ecological Relations: Discussing a Localised Energy System in Vaxjo, Sweden." *Journal of Cleaner Production.* https://www.sci encedirect.com/science/article/pii/S0959652617310405

Ferraro, A. J., E. J. Highwood, and A. J. Charlton-Perez. 2014. "Weakened Tropical Circulation and Reduced Precipitation in Response to Geoengineering." *Environmental Research Letters* 9 (1).

Feygina, I., J. T. Jost, and R. E. Goldsmith. 2010. "System Justification, the Denial of Global Warming, and the Possibility of 'System-Sanctioned Change.'" *Personality and Social Psychology Bulletin* 36 (3): 326–38.

Fitzgerald, J. B., A. K. Jorgenson, and B. Clark. 2015. "Energy Consumption and Working Hours: A Longitudinal Study of Developed and Developing Nations, 1990–2008." *Environmental Sociology* 3 (1): 213–23.

Fitzgerald, J. B., J. B. Schor, and A. K. Jorgenson. 2018. "Working Hours and Carbon Dioxide Emissions in the United States, 2007–2013." *Social Forces* 96 (4): 1851–74.

Fjeld, R. A., N. A. Eisenberg, and K. L. Compton. 2007. *Quantitative Environmental Risk Analysis.* Hoboken: John Wiley & Sons.

Forester, J., and D. Stitzel. 1989. "Beyond Neutrality—the Possibilities of Activist Mediation in Public Sector Conflicts." *Negotiation Journal: On the Process of Dispute Settlement* 5 (3): 251–64.

Foster, J. B. 1993. "The Limits of Environmentalism without Class: Lessons from the Ancient Forest Struggle of the Pacific Northwest." *Capitalism Nature Socialism* 4 (1): 11–41.

Foster, J. B. 2002. *Ecology against Capitalism.* New York: Monthly Review Press.

Foster, J. B. 2009. *The Ecological Revolution: Making Peace with the Planet.* New York: Monthly Review Press.

Foster, J. B. 2010. "Why Ecological Revolution." *Monthly Review* 61 (8).

Foster, J. B. 2011. "Capitalism and Degrowth: An Impossibility Theorem." *Monthly Review* 62 (8): 26–33.

Foster, J. B. 2017. "The Meaning of Work in a Sustainable Society." *Monthly Review* 69 (4).

Foster J. B. 2018. Making War on the Planet: Geoengineering and Capitalism's Creative Destruction of the Earth. *Science for the People.* https://mag azine.scienceforthepeople.org/making-war-on-the-planet/

Foster, J. B., and B. Clark. 2009. "The Paradox of Wealth: Capitalism and Ecological Destruction." *Monthly Review* 61 (6): 1–18.

Foster, J. B., B. Clark, and R. York. 2009. "The Midas Effect: A Critique of Climate Change Economics." *Development and Change* 40 (6): 1085–197.

Foster, J. B., B. Clark, and R. York. 2010. "Capitalism and the Curse of Energy Efficiency: The Return of the Jevons Paradox." *Monthly Review: An Independent Socialist Magazine* 62 (6): 1–12.

Fourage, D. J. A. G., and C. Baaijens. 2004. "Changes in Working Hours and Job Mobility: The Effect of Dutch Legislation." OSA Working Paper 2004-23.

Fournier, V. 2008. "Escaping from the Economy: The Politics of Degrowth." *International Journal of Sociology and Social Policy* 28 (11/12): 528–45.

Fragniere, A., and S. M. Gardiner. 2016. "Why Engineering Is Not 'Plan B.'" In *Climate Justice and Geoengineering: Ethics and Policy in the Atmospheric Anthropocene*, edited by C. J. Preston, 15–32. London: Rowman & Littlefield.

Fraser, N. 1992. "Rethinking the Public Sphere." In *Habermas and the Public Sphere*, edited by C. Calhoun. Cambridge: MIT Press.

Fraser, N. 2014. "Can Society Be Commodities All the Way Down? Post-Polanyian Reflections on Capitalist Crisis." *Economy and Society* 43 (4): 541–58.

Freeman, R., M. Yearworth, and C. Preist. 2016. "Revisiting Jevons' Paradox with System Dynamics: Systemic Causes and Potential Cures." *Journal of Industrial Ecology* 20 (2): 341–53.

Fridahl, M., and M. Lehtveer. 2018. "Bioenergy with Carbon Capture and Storage (BECCS): Global Potential, Investment Preferences, and Deployment Barriers." *Energy Research & Social Science* 42: 155–65.

Friedman, L. 2017. "Trump Team to Promote Fossil Fuels and Nuclear Power at Bonn Climate Talks." *New York Times*, November 2, 2017. https://www.nytimes.com/2017/11/02/climate/trump-coal-cop23-bonn.html

Fung, A. 2006. "Varieties of Participation in Complex Governance." *Public Administration Review* 66: 66–75.

Fung, A., and E. O. Wright. 2001. "Deepening Democracy: Innovations in Empowered Local Governance." *Politics and Society* 29 (1): 5–41.

Funk, C., and B. Kennedy. 2016. "Public Views on Climate Change and Climate Scientists." Pew Research Center. http://www.pewinternet. org/2016/10/04/public-views-on-climate-change-and-climate-scientists/

Fuss, S., J. G. Canadell, G. P. Peters, M. Tavoni, R. M. Andrew, P. Ciais, R. B. Jackson, C. D. Jones, F. Kraxner, N. Nakicenovic, C. Le Quere, M. R. Raupach, A. Sharifi, P. Smith, and Y. Yamagata. 2014. "Commentary: Betting on Negative Emissions." *Nature Climate Change* 4 (10): 850–53.

Galey, P. 2019. "415.26 Parts per Million: CO2 Levels Hit Historic High." Phys. org, accessed May 30, 2019. https://phys.org/news/2019-05-million-co2-historic-high.html

Gardiner, S. M. 2011. "Some Early Ethics of Geoengineering the Climate: A Commentary on the Values of the Royal Society Report." *Environmental Values* 20 (2): 163–88.

Gasper, P. 2014. "Are Workers' Cooperatives the Alternative to Capitalism?" *International Socialist Review* 93, accessed March 10, 2018. https://isreview. org/issue/93/are-workers-cooperatives-alternative-capitalism

Gellers, J. C. 2016. "Crowdsourcing Global Governance: Sustainable Development Goals, Civil Society, and the Pursuit of Democratic Legitimacy." *International Environmental Agreements: Politics Law and Economics* 16 (3): 415–32.

Georgescu-Roegen, N. 2011. "The Steady State and Ecological Salvation: A Thermodynamic Analysis." *BioScience* 27 (4): 266–70.

Giancatarino, A. 2013. "Community-Scale Energy: Models, Strategies, and Racial Equity—a Scan of Community Innovation around Efficiency and Renewable Energy." Center for Social Inclusion. www.centerforsocialin clusion.org

Gibson-Graham, J. K. 2008. "Diverse Economies: Performative Practices for 'Other Worlds.'" *Progress in Human Geography* 32 (5): 613–32.

Gindin, S. 2016. "Chasing Utopia." *Jacobin*, accessed March 10, 2018. https:// www.jacobinmag.com/2016/03/workers-control-coops-wright-wolff-alpero vitz/

Goldman Sachs. 2017. "The Wind and Solar Boom." http://www.goldmansachs. com/our-thinking/pages/alberto-gandolfi-wind-and-solar-boom.html

Goodstein, E. 1999. *The Trade-Off Myth: Fact and Fiction about Jobs and the Environment*. Washington, DC: Island Press.

Gore, T. 2015. "Extreme Carbon Inequality." Oxfam International. https://oxf.am/2FMYtY2

Gorton, G., and F. A. Schmid. 2004. "Capital, Labor, and the Firm: A Study of German Codetermination." *Journal of the European Economic Association* 2 (5): 863–905.

Gorz, A. 1967. *Strategy for Labor*. Boston: Beacon Press.

Gorz, A. 1982. *Farewell to the Working Class*. London: Pluto.

Gorz, A. 1986. "The Socialism of Tomorrow." *Telos* 67: 199–206.

Gorz, A. 1988. *Critique of Economic Reason*. New York: Verso.

Gorz, A. 1999. *Reclaiming Work: Beyond the Wage-Based Society*. Malden: Polity Press.

Gould, C. G. 2014. *Interactive Democracy: The Social Roots of Global Justice*. New York: Cambridge University Press.

Gould, K. A., D. N. Pellow, and A. Schnaiberg. 2008. *The Treadmill of Production*. Boulder: Paradigm.

Gowan, P. 2018. "A Plan to Nationalize Fossil-Fuel Companies." *Jacobin*. https://www.jacobinmag.com/2018/03/nationalize-fossil-fuel-companies-climate-change

Grant, R. W., and R. O. Keohane. 2005. "Accountability and Abuses of Power in World Politics." *American Political Science Review* 99 (1): 29–43.

Granter, E. 2009. *Critical Social Theory and the End of Work*. Burlington: Ashgate.

Greenfield, A. 2017. *Radical Technologies: The Design of Everyday Life*. New York: Verso.

Greening, L. A., D. L. Greene, and C. Difiglio. 2000. "Energy Efficiency and Consumption—the Rebound Effect—a Survey." *Energy Policy* 28 (6–7): 389–401.

Greenpeace International. 2008. "False Hope: Why Carbon Capture and Storage Won't Save the Climate." Greenpeace International, accessed April 1, 2019. https://www.greenpeace.org/archive-international/Global/international/planet-2/report/2008/5/false-hope.pdf

Greshko, M., L. Parker, and B. C. Howard. 2018. "A Running List of How Trump Is Changing the Environment." *National Geographic*, accessed April 25, 2018. https://news.nationalgeographic.com/2017/03/how-trump-is-changing-science-environment/

Gunderson, R. 2014. "Problems with the Defetishization Thesis: Ethical

Consumerism, Alternative Food Systems, and Commodity Fetishism." *Agriculture and Human Values* 31 (1): 109–17.

Gunderson, R. 2015. "Environmental Sociology and the Frankfurt School 2: Ideology, Techno-Science, Reconciliation." *Environmental Sociology* 2 (1): 64–76.

Gunderson, R. 2017. "Ideology Critique for the Environmental Social Sciences: What Reproduces the Treadmill of Production?" *Nature + Culture* 12 (3): 263–89.

Gunderson, R., and T. Dietz. 2018. "Deliberation and Catastrophic Risks." In *The Oxford Handbook of Deliberative Democracy*, edited by A. Bachtiger, J. Mansbridge, M. Warren and J. Dryzek, 768–88. New York: Oxford University Press.

Gunderson, R., B. Petersen, and D. Stuart. 2018a. "A Critical Examination of Geoengineering: Economic and Technological Rationality in Social Context." *Sustainability* 10 (1).

Gunderson, R., D. Stuart, and B. Petersen. 2018b. "Ideological Obstacles to Effective Climate Policy: The Greening of Markets, Technology, and Growth." *Capital and Class* 42 (1): 133–60.

Gunderson, R., D. Stuart, and B. Petersen. 2019. "Materialized Ideology and Environmental Problems: The Cases of Solar Geoengineering and Agricultural Biotechnology." *European Journal of Social Theory*.

Gunderson, R., and S. J. Yun. 2017. "South Korean Green Growth and the Jevons Paradox: An Assessment with Democratic and Degrowth Policy Recommendations." *Journal of Cleaner Production* 144: 239–47.

Habermas, J. 1975. *Legitimation Crisis*. Boston: Beacon Press.

Habermas, J. 1984. *The Theory of Communicative Action, Vol. 1*. Boston: Beacon Press.

Habermas, J. 1996. *Between Facts and Norms*. Cambridge: MIT Press.

Haiven, L., C. Levesque, and N. Roby. 2006. "Paths to Union Renewal: Challenges and Issues—Introduction." *Relations Industrielles/Industrial Relations* 61 (4): 578–88.

Hale, B. 2012. "The World that Would Have Been: Moral Hazard Arguments against Geoengineering." In *Engineering the Climate: The Ethics of Solar Radiation Management*, edited by C. J. Preston, 113–31. Plymouth: Lexington Books.

Hall, C. A. S., J. G. Lambert, and S. B. Balogh. 2014. "EROI of Different Fuels and the Implications for Society." *Energy Policy* 64:141–52.

Hallegatte, S., G. Heal, M. Fay, and D. Treguer. 2011. "From Growth to Green Growth: A Framework." The World Bank, Sustainable Development Network, Office of the Chief Economist. Policy Research Working Paper 5872.

Hamilton, C. 2013a. *Earthmasters: The Dawn of the Age of Climate Engineering.* Padstow: Yale University Press.

Hamilton, C. 2013b. "Geoengineering: Our Last Hope, or a False Promise." *New York Times*, May 27, 2013. Accessed May 24, 2017. http://www.nytimes.com/2013/05/27/opinion/geoengineering-our-last-hope-or-a-false-promise.html

Hamilton, C. 2014. "Geoengineering and the Politics of Science." *Bulletin of the Atomic Scientists* 70 (3): 17–26.

Hansen, J., K. Emanuel, K. Caldeira, and T. Wigley. 2015. "Nuclear Power Paves the Only Viable Path Forward on Climate Change." *The Guardian*, December 3.

Hansen, J., M. Sato, P. Kharecha, D. Beerling, R. Berner, V. Masson-Delmotte, M. Pagani, M. Raymo, D. L. Royer, and J. C. Zachos. 2008. "Target Atmospheric CO2: Where Should We Aim?" *The Open Atmospheric Science Journal* 2: 217–31.

Hardin, G. 1968. "The Tragedy of the Commons." *Science* 162: 1243–48.

Harding, A., and J. B. Moreno-Cruz. 2016. "Solar Geoengineering Economics: From Incredible to Inevitable and Half-Way Back." *Earths Future* 4 (12): 569–77.

Harper, A. 2017. "Germany's Biggest Union Is Fighting for a 28 Hour Working Week—Here's How the UK Could Follow Suit." *The Independent*, October 12. https://www.independent.co.uk/voices/four-day-working-week-german-union-28-hours-uk-fight-for-the-same-a7996261.html

Harvey, D. 1982. *The Limits to Capital.* Oxford: Basil Blackwell.

Harvey, D. 1996. *Justice, Nature and the Geography of Difference.* Malden: Blackwell.

Harvey, D. 2005. *A Brief History of Neoliberalism.* Oxford: Oxford University Press.

Hawken, P., A. Lovins, and L. H. Lovins. 1999. *Natural Capitalism.* Boston: Little, Brown and Co.

Hayden, A. 1999. *Sharing the Work, Sparing the Planet.* London: Zed Books.

Haynes, S. 2019. "'It's Literally Our Future.' Here's What Youth Climate Strikers around the World Are Planning Next." *Time Magazine*, March 20.

Heede, R. 2014. "Tracing Anthropogenic Carbon Dioxide and Methane

Emissions to Fossil Fuel and Cement Producers, 1854–2010." *Climatic Change* 122 (1–2): 229–41.

Held, D. 1995. *Democracy and the Global Order: From the Modern State to Cosmopolitan Governance.* New York: Cambridge University Press.

Held, D. 1996. *Models of Democracy.* Stanford: Stanford University Press.

Held, D., and A. Harvey. 2011. "Democracy, Climate Change and Global Governance: Democratic Agency and the Policy Menu Ahead." *The Governance of Climate Change*: 89–110.

Hickel, J. 2016. "Clean Energy Won't Save Us—Only a New Economic System Can." *The Guardian*, July 15.

Hickel, J. 2017. "The Paris Climate Deal Won't Save Us—Our Future Depends on Degrowth." *The Guardian*, July 15. Accessed May 1, 2018. https://www.theguardian.com/global-development-professionals-network/2017/jul/03/paris-climate-deal-wont-work-our-future-depends-degrowth

Hickel, J. 2019. "Degrowth: A Theory of Radical Abundance." *Real-World Economic Review* 87: 54–68.

Hickel, J., and G. Kallis. 2019. "Is Green Growth Possible?" *New Political Economy.*

Hicks, J., and N. Ison. 2011. "Community-Owned Renewable Energy (CRE): Opportunities for Rural Australia." *Rural Society* 20: 244–55.

Hildyard, N. 1993. "Foxes in Charge of the Chickens." In *Global Ecology*, edited by W. Sachs. London: Zed Books.

Hoffman, U. 2011. "Some Reflections on Climate Change, Green Growth Illusions and Development Space." Discussion paper at the United Nations Conference on Trade and Development, no. 205. United Nations.

Hoffman, U. 2016. "Can Green Growth Really Work?" In *Green Growth: Ideology, Political Economy and the Alternatives*, edited by G. Dale, M. Mathai and J. Oliviera. London: Zed Books.

Holm, S. O., and G. Englund. 2009. "Increased Ecoefficiency and Gross Rebound Effect: Evidence from USA and Six European Countries 1960–2002." *Ecological Economics* 68 (3): 879–87.

Holmes, C. 2012. "Problems and Opportunities in Polanyian Analysis Today." *Economy and Society* 41 (3):468–84.

Hook, M., J. Li, K. Johansson, and S. Snowden. 2012. "Growth Rates of Global Energy Systems and Future Outlooks." *Natural Resources Research* 21 (1):23–41.

Horkheimer, M. 1947. *Eclipse of Reason.* New York: Continuum.

Horkheimer, M. 1972. "Materialism and Metaphysics." In *Critical Theory: Selected Essays*, 10–46. New York: Continuum.

Horkheimer, M. 1993. "Beginnings of the Bourgeois Philosophy of History." In *Between Philosophy and Social Science: Selected Early Writings*, 313–88. Cambridge: MIT Press.

Horkheimer, M., and T. W. Adorno. 1969. *Dialectic of Enlightenment*. New York: Continuum.

Hornborg, A. 1992. "Machine Fetishism, Value and the Image of Unlimited Good—towards a Thermodynamics of Imperialism." *Man* 27 (1): 1–18.

Hornborg, A. 2001. *The Power of the Machine: Global Inequalities of Economy, Technology, and Environment*. Walnut Creek: AltaMira Press.

Hornborg, A. 2003. "Cornucopia or Zero-Sum Game? The Epistemology of Sustainability." *Journal of World-Systems Research* 9: 205–16.

Hornborg, A. 2009. "Zero-Sum World Challenges in Conceptualizing Environmental Load Displacement and Ecologically Unequal Exchange in the World-System." *International Journal of Comparative Sociology* 50 (3–4): 237–62.

Hueting, R. 2010. "Why Environmental Sustainability Can Most Probably Not Be Attained with Growing Production." *Journal of Cleaner Production* 18 (6): 525–30.

Hulme, M. 2014. *Can Science Fix Climate Change: A Case against Climate Engineering*. Hoboken: John Wiley & Sons.

Humphreys, D. 2003. "Life Protective or Carcinogenic Challenge? Global Forests Governance under Advanced Capitalism." *Global Environmental Politics* 3 (2): 40–55.

ICAP. 2018. "International Carbon Action Partnership." https://icapcarbonac tion.com/en/news-archive/524-first-joint-auction-of-california-quebec-and-ontario-sold-out

Ikebe, S. 2016. "The Wrong Kind of UBI." *Jacobin*, accessed March 7, 2018. https://www.jacobinmag.com/2016/01/universal-basic-income-switzerland-finland-milton-friedman-kathi-weeks/

Illich, I. 1973. *Tools for Conviviality*. New York: Harper and Row.

Intergovernmental Panel on Climate Change (IPCC). 2012. "Meeting Report of the Intergovernmental Panel on Climate Change Expert Meeting on Geoengineering." In *IPCC Working Group III Technical Support Unit, Postdam Institute for Climate Impact Research*, edited by O. Edenhofer, R. Pichs-Madruga, Y. Sokona, C. Field, V. Barrros, T. F. Stocker, Q. Dahe, J. Minx, K. Mach, G. K. Plattner, S. Schlomer, G. Hansen and M. Mastrandrea, 99. Postdam, Germany.

Intergovernmental Panel on Climate Change (IPCC). 2014. "Climate Change 2014: Synthesis Report. Edited by R. K. Pachauri and L. A. Meyer. Geneva, Switzerland: IPCC.

International Energy Agency (IEA). 2012. World Energy Outlook 2012. Paris, France: International Energy Agency.

International Energy Agency (IEA). 2015. *Storing CO2 through Enhanced Oil Recovery: Combining EOR with CO2 Storage (EOR+) for Profit.* Paris, France: International Energy Agency.

International Energy Agency (IEA). 2017. *Renewables 2017: Analysis and Forecast to 2022.* Paris, France: International Energy Agency.

International Monetary Fund (IMF). 2015. *IMF Survey: Counting the Cost of Energy Subsidies.* International Monetary Fund.

International Renewable Energy Agency (IRENA). 2018. "Renewable Power Generation Costs 2017." Abu Dhabi: International Renewable Energy Agency.

International Risk Governance Council. 2005. "Risk Governance—towards an Integrative Approach. White Paper no. 1, O. Renn with an Annex by P. Graham, IRGC, Geneva.

Irfan, U. 2018. "Sucking CO_2 Out of the Atmosphere, Explained." Vox, accessed May 2, 2019. https://www.vox.com/energy-and-environ ment/2018/10/24/18001538/climate-change-co2-removal-negative-emis sions-cdr-carbon-dioxide

Irvine, P., K. Emanuel, J. He, L. W. Horowitz, G. Vecchi, and D. Keith. 2019. "Halving Warming with Idealized Solar Geoengineering Moderates Key Climate Hazards." *Nature Climate Change* 9 (4): 295–99.

Jackson, T. 2009. *Prosperity without Growth.* London: Earthscan.

Jacobs, M. 2013. "Green Growth." In *Handbook of Global Climate and Environmental Policy,* edited by R. Falkner. Malden: Wiley-Blackwell.

Jakopovick, D. 2009. "Uniting to Win: Labour Environmental Alliances." *Capitalism Nature Socialism* 20 (2): 74–96.

Jameson, F. 2003. "Future City." *New Left Review* (21): 65–80.

Janicke, M. 2012. "'Green growth': From a Growing Eco-Industry to Economic Sustainability." *Energy Policy* 48: 13–21.

Jaramillo, P., W. M. Griffin, and S. T. McCoy. 2009. "Life Cycle Inventory of CO_2 in an Enhanced Oil Recovery System." *Environmental Science & Technology* 43 (21): 8027–32.

Jarvis, H. 2017. "Sharing, Togetherness and Intentional Degrowth." *Progress in Human Geography.*

Jasanoff, S., and M. L. Martello, eds. 2004. *Earthly Politics: Local and Global in Environmental Governance*. Cambridge: MIT Press.

Jay, M. 1973. *The Dialectical Imagination: History of the Frankfurt School and the Institute of Social Research 1923–1950*. Boston: Little, Brown and Company.

Jevons, W. S. 1906. *The Coal Question: An Inquiry Concerning the Progress of the Nation, and the Probable Exhaustion of our Coal-Mines*. New York: Macmillan.

Johanisova, N., and S. Wolf. 2012. "Economic Democracy: A Path for the Future?" *Futures* 44 (6): 562–70.

Jones, G. A., and K. J. Warner. 2016. "The 21st Century Population-Energy-Climate Nexus." *Energy Policy* 93:206–12.

Jonna, R. J., and J. B. Foster. 2016. "Marx's Theory of Working-Class Precariousness." *Monthly Review*.

Jorgenson, A. K. 2015. "Inequality and the Carbon Intensity of Human Well-being." *Journal of Environmental Studies and Sciences* 5 (3): 277–82.

Jorgenson, A. K., and B. Clark. 2012. "Are the Economy and the Environment Decoupling? A Comparative International Study, 1960–2005." *American Journal of Sociology* 118 (1): 1–44.

Jorgenson, A. K., J. Schor, and X. R. Huang. 2017. "Income Inequality and Carbon Emissions in the United States: A State-Level Analysis, 1997–2012." *Ecological Economics* 134: 40–48.

Jorgenson, A. K., J. B. Schor, X. R. Huang, and J. Fitzgerald. 2015. "Income Inequality and Residential Carbon Emissions in the United States: A Preliminary Analysis." *Human Ecology Review* 22 (1): 93–105.

Kallis, G. 2011. "In Defence of Degrowth." *Ecological Economics* 70 (5): 873–80.

Kallis, G. 2017. "Radical Dematerialization and Degrowth." *Philosophical Transactions of the Royal Society a-Mathematical Physical and Engineering Sciences* 375 (2095).

Kallis, G. 2018. *Degrowth*. Newcastle: Agenda Publishing.

Kallis, G., F. Demaria, and G. D'Alisa. 2015. "Introduction: Degrowth." In *Degrowth: A Vocabulary for a New Era*, edited by G. D'Alisa, F. Demaria and G. Kallis, 1–17. New York: Routledge.

Kallis, G., M. Kalush, H. O. Flynn, J. Rossiter, and N. Ashford. 2013. "Friday Off': Reducing Working Hours in Europe." *Sustainability* 5 (4): 1545–67.

Kallis, G., C. Kerschner, and J. Martínez-Alier. 2012. "The Economics of Degrowth." *Ecological Economics* 84: 172–80.

Kallis, G., and H. March. 2015. "Imaginaries of Hope: The Utopianism of Degrowth." *Annals of the Association of American Geographers* 105 (2): 360–68.

Kasmir, S. 1996. *The Myth of Mondragon: Cooperatives, Politics, and the Working Class Life in a Basque Town.* Albany: SUNY Press.

Kaup, B. 2015. "Markets, Nature, and Society: Embedding Economic and Environmental Sociology." *Sociological Theory* 33 (3): 280–96.

Keary, M. 2016. "The New Prometheans: Technological Optimism in Climate Change Mitigation Modelling." *Environmental Values* 25 (1): 7–28.

Keith, D. W. 2010. "Photophoretic Levitation of Engineered Aerosols for Geoengineering." *Proceedings of the National Academy of Sciences of the United States of America* 107 (38): 16428–431.

Keith, D. W. 2013. *Climate Engineering.* Boston: MIT Press.

Keith, D. W., G. Holmes, D. S. Angelo, and K. Heidel. 2018. "A Process for Capturing CO_2 from the Atmosphere." *Joule* 2 (8): 1573–94. doi: 10.1016/j.joule.2018.05.006.

Keith, D. W., and D. G. MacMartin. 2015. "A Temporary, Moderate and Responsive Scenario for Solar Geoengineering." *Nature Climate Change* 5 (3): 201–6.

Kenis, A., and E. Mathijs. 2014. "Climate Change and Post-Politics: Repoliticizing the Present by Imagining the Future?" *Geoforum* 52: 148–56.

Kerschner, C., P. Wachter, L. Nierling, and M. H. Ehlers. 2015. "Special Volume: Technology and Degrowth." *Journal of Cleaner Production* 108: 31–33.

Kerschner, C., P. Wächter, L. Nierling, and M. H. Ehlers. 2018. "Degrowth and Technology: Towards Feasible, Viable, Appropriate and Convivial Imaginaries." *Journal of Cleaner Production.* 197 (Part 2): 1619–36.

Kiehl, J. T. 2006. "Geoengineering Climate Change: Treating the Symptom over the Cause?" *Climatic Change* 77 (3–4): 227–28.

Kintisch, Eli. 2010. *Hack the Planet: Science's Best Hope—or Worst Nightmare—for Averting Climate Catastrophe.* Hoboken: John Wiley & Sons.

Klein, N. 2011. "Capitalism vs. the Climate." *The Nation.*

Klein, N. 2014. *This Changes Everything: Capitalism vs. the Climate.* New York: Simon and Schuster.

Knapton, S. 2017. "Human Race Is Doomed if We Do Not Colonise the Moon and Mars, Says Stephen Hawking." *The Telegraph*, June 20, 2017. https://www.telegraph.co.uk/science/2017/06/20/human-race-doomed-do-not-colonise-moon-mars-says-stephen-hawking/

Knight, K. W., E. A. Rosa, and J. B. Schor. 2013. "Could Working Less Reduce Pressures on the Environment? A Cross-National Panel Analysis of OECD Countries, 1970–2007." *Global Environmental Change-Human and Policy Dimensions* 23 (4): 691–700.

Knight, K. W., and J. B. Schor. 2014. "Economic Growth and Climate Change:

A Cross-National Analysis of Territorial and Consumption-Based Carbon Emissions in High-Income Countries." *Sustainability* 6 (6): 3722–31.

Knox-Hayes, J. 2010. "Constructing Carbon Market Spacetime: Climate Change and the Onset of Neo-Modernity." *Annals of the Association of American Geographers* 100 (4): 953–62.

Kojola, E., C. Y. Xiao, and A. M. McCright. 2014. "Environmental Concern of Labor Union Members in the United States." *Sociological Quarterly* 55 (1): 72–91.

Kosoy, N., and E. Corbera. 2010. "Payments for Ecosystem Services as Commodity Fetishism." *Ecological Economics* 69 (6): 1228–36.

Kuchler, M. 2017. "Stakeholding as Sorting of Actors into Categories: Implications for Civil Society Participation in the CDM." *International Environmental Agreements: Politics Law and Economics* 17 (2): 191–208.

Kunze, C., and S. Becker. 2015. "Collective Ownership in Renewable Energy and Opportunities for Sustainable Degrowth." *Sustainability Science* 10 (3): 425–37.

Lafargue, P. 1907. *The Right to be Lazy and Other Studies*. Chicago: Charles H. Kerr & Company.

LaJeunesse, R. 2009. *Work Time Regulation as Sustainable Full Employment Strategy: The Social Effort Bargain*. New York: Routledge.

Langman, L. 2015. "An Overview: Hegemony, Ideology and the Reproduction of Domination." *Critical Sociology* 41 (3): 425–32.

Larrain, J. 1979. *The Concept of Ideology*. London: Hutchinson & Co.

Larrain, J. 1982. "On the Character of Ideology: Marx and the Present Debate in Britain." *Theory, Culture & Society* 1 (1): 5–22.

Larrain, J. 1983. *Marxism and Ideology*. London: Macmillan.

Latouche, S. 2009. *Farewell to Growth*. Cambridge: Polity.

Latouche, S. 2010. "Special Issue: Growth, Recession, or Degrowth for Sustainability and Equity?" *Journal of Cleaner Production* 18 (6): 519–22.

Lee, C. S. 2005. "International Migration, Deindustrialization and Union Decline in 16 Affluent OECD Countries, 1962–1997." *Social Forces* 84 (1): 71–88.

Leiss, W. 1974. *The Domination of Nature*. New York: Braziller.

Leiter, A. M., A. Parolini, and H. Winner. 2011. "Environmental Regulation and Investment: Evidence from European Industry Data." *Ecological Economics* 70 (4): 759–70.

Lemos, M. C., and A. Agrawal. 2006. "Environmental Governance." *Annual Review of Environment and Resources* 31: 297–325.

Leung, D. Y. C., G. Caramanna, and M. M. Maroto-Valer. 2014. "An Overview of Current Status of Carbon Dioxide Capture and Storage Technologies." *Renewable & Sustainable Energy Reviews* 39: 426–43.

Levesque, C., and G. Murray. 2006. "How Do Unions Renew? Paths to Union Renewal." *Labor Studies Journal* 31 (3): 1–13.

Levitt, S. D., and S. J. Dubner. 2011. *Superfreakonomics: Global Cooling, Patriotic Prostitutes, and Why Suicide Bombers Should Buy Life Insurance.* New York: HarperCollins.

Levy, D. L., and P. J. Newell. 2005. *The Business of Global Environmental Governance.* Cambridge: MIT Press.

Liao, S. M., A. Sandeberg, and R. Roache. 2013. "Human Engineering and Climate Change." In *Designer Biology*, edited by J. Sasl and R. Sandler. Lanham: Lexington Books.

Lichtheim, G. 1965. "The Concept of Ideology." *History and Theory* 4 (2): 164–83.

Lietaert, M. 2010. "Cohousing's Relevance to Degrowth Theories." *Journal of Cleaner Production* 18 (6): 576–80.

Lohmann, L. 2005. "Marketing and Making Carbon Dumps: Commodification, Calculation and Counterfactuals in Climate Change Mitigation." *Science as Culture* 14 (3): 203–35.

Lohmann, L. 2010. "Uncertainty Markets and Carbon Markets: Variations on a Polanyian Theme." *New Political Economy* 15 (2): 225–54.

Long, J. C. S., and D. Scott. 2013. "Vested Interests and Geoengineering Research." *Issues in Science and Technology* 29 (3): 45–52.

Lorek, S. 2015. "Dematerialization." In *Degrowth: A New Vocabulary for a New Era*, edited by G. D'Alisa, F. Demaria, and G. Kallis, 83–85. New York: Routledge.

Lowy, M. 2009. "Eco-Socialism and Democratic Planning." *Socialist Register* 43 (43).

Lowy, M. 2015. *Ecosocialism: A Radical Alternative to Capitalist Catastrophe.* Chicago: Haymarket Books.

Lukacs, G. 1971. *The Theory of the Novel.* Cambridge: MIT Press.

Lukacs, M. 2012. "World's Biggest Geoengineering Experiment 'Violates' UN Rules." *The Guardian*, October 15. Accessed May 1, 2018. https://www.theguardian.com/environment/2012/oct/15/pacific-iron-fertilisation-geoengineering

Lukacs, M. 2017. "Trump Presidency 'Opens Door' to Planet-Hacking Geoengineer Experiments." *The Guardian*, March 27. https://www.theguardian.com/environment/true-north/2017/mar/27/trump-presidency-opens-door-to-planet-hacking-geoengineer-experiments

Lukes, S. 1974. *Power: A Radical View.* New York: Macmillan.

Luxemburg, R. 2008. "Reform or Revolution." In *The Essential Rosa Luxemburg*, edited by H. Schott, 41–104. Chicago: Haymarket Books.

MacKenzie, D. 1984. "Marx and the Machine." *Technology and Culture* 25: 473–502.

MacKenzie, D., and J. Wajcman, eds. 1985. *The Social Shaping of Technology*. Bristol: Open University Press.

Madlener, R., and B. Alcott. 2009. "Energy Rebound and Economic Growth: A Review of the Main Issues and Research Needs." *Energy* 34 (3): 370–76.

Magdoff, F., and C. Williams. 2017. *Creating an Ecological Society: Towards a Revolutionary Transformation*. New York: Monthly Review Press.

Magill, B. 2018. "Carbon Removal Firms See Opportunity in U.N. Climate Report." Accessed May 2, 2019. https://news.bloombergenvironment.com/environment-and-energy/carbon-removal-firms-see-opportunity-in-un-climate-report

Malm, A. 2016. *Fossil Capital: The Rise of Steam Power and the Roots of Global Warming*. London: Verso Books.

Malm, A. 2018. "Marx on Steam: From the Optimism of Progress to the Pessimism of Power." *Rethinking Marxism* 30 (2): 166–85.

Mannheim, K. 1936. *Ideology and Utopia*. New York: Harcourt, Brace & World.

Marcu, A. 2016. "Carbon Market Provisions in the Paris Agreement (Article 6)." Center for European Policy Studies, Special Report, no. 128.

Marcuse, H. 1955. *Eros and Civilization*. New York: Vintage.

Marcuse, H. 1964. *One-Dimensional Man*. Boston: Beacon Press.

Marcuse, H. 1968. "Industrialization and Capitalism in Max Weber." In *Negations: Essays in Critical Theory*, 201–26. Boston: Beacon Press.

Marcuse, H. 1969. *An Essay on Liberation*. Boston: Beacon Press.

Marcuse, H. 1972. *Counterrevolution and Revolt*. Boston: Beacon Press.

Marcuse, H. 1978. "Some Social Implications of Modern Technology." In *The Essential Frankfurt School Reader*, edited by A. Arato and E. Gebhardt, 138–62. New York: Urizen Books.

Marcuse, H. 1989. "From Ontology to Technology: Fundamental Tendencies of Industrial Society." In *Critical Theory and Society: A Reader*, edited by E. Bronner and D. Kellner, 119–27. New York: Routledge.

Marcuse, H. 1992. "Ecology and the Critique of Modern Society." *Capitalism Nature Socialism* 3 (3): 29–38.

Marcuse, H. 1994. "Ecology and Revolution." In *Ecology: Key Concepts in Critical Theory*, edited by C. Merchant, 51–54. Atlantic Heights: Humanities Press.

Marcuse, H. 2001. "The Problem of Social Change in the Technological Society." In *Towards a Critical Theory of Society: Collected Papers of Herbert Marcuse, Vol. 2*, edited by D. Kellner and C. Pierce. New York: Routledge.

Marcuse, H. 2011. "On Science and Phemonology." In *Philosophy, Psychoanalysis and Emancipation*, edited by D. Kellner and C. Pierce, 145–54. New York: Routledge.

Markantoni, M. 2016. "Low Carbon Governance: Mobilizing Community Energy through Top-Down Support?" *Environmental Policy and Governance* 26 (3): 155–69.

Martinelli, A. 2003. "Markets, Governments, Communities and Global Governance." *International Sociology* 18 (2): 291–23.

Martínez-Alier, J. 2009. "Socially Sustainable Economic De-growth." *Development and Change* 40 (6): 1099–119.

Martínez-Alier, J., H. Healy, L. Temper, M. Walter, B. Rodriguez-Labajos, J. F. Gerber, and M. Conde. 2010. "Between Science and Activism: Learning and Teaching EcologicalEconomics with Environmental Justice Organisations." *Local Environment* 16 (1): 17–36.

Martínez-Alier, J., U. Pascual, F. D. Vivien, and E. Zaccai. 2010. "Sustainable De-growth: Mapping the Context, Criticisms and Future Prospects of an Emergent Paradigm." *Ecological Economics* 69 (9): 1741–47.

Marx, K. 1964. *The Economic and Philosophic Manuscripts of 1844*. New York: International.

Marx, K. 1968. *Theories of Surplus Value, Vol. 2*. Moscow: Progress Publishers.

Marx, K. 1973. *Grundrisse*. New York: Vintage.

Marx, K. 1977. *Capital, Vol. 1*. New York: Vintage.

Marx, K. 1981. *Capital, Vol. 3*. New York: Vintage.

Marx, K., and F. Engels. 1977. *The German Ideology*. New York: International Publishers.

Matthews, H. D. 2010. "Can Carbon Cycle Geoengineering Be a Useful Complement to Ambitious Climate Mitigation?" *Carbon Management* 1 (1): 135–44.

Matthews, J. A. 2012. "Green Growth Strategies: Korean Initiatives." *Futures* 44: 761–69.

Matthews, J. D. 2005. "An Introduction to the Situationists." theanarchistlibrary.org

McCright, A. M., and R. E. Dunlap. 2010. "Anti-reflexivity: The American Conservative Movement's Success in Undermining Climate Science and Policy." *Theory Culture & Society* 27 (2–3): 100–33.

McCright, A. M., and R. E. Dunlap. 2011. "The Politicization of Climate Change and Polarization in the American Public's Views of Global Warming, 2001–2010." *Sociological Quarterly* 52 (2): 155–94.

McCright, A. M., S. T. Marquart-Pyatt, R. L. Shwom, S. R. Brechin, and S. Allen. 2016. "Ideology, Capitalism, and Climate: Explaining Public Views about Climate Change in the United States." *Energy Research & Social Science* 21: 180–89.

McCusker, K. E., K. C. Armour, C. M. Bitz, and D. S. Battisti. 2014. "Rapid and Extensive Warming Following Cessation of Solar Radiation Management." *Environmental Research Letters* 9 (2).

Melathopoulos, A. P., and A. M. Stoner. 2015. "Critique and Transformation: On the Hypothetical Nature of Ecosystem Service Value and Its Neo-Marxist, Liberal and Pragmatist Criticisms." *Ecological Economics* 117: 173–81.

Mercator Research Institute on Global Commons and Climate Change. 2017. "The Mercator Research Institute." Accessed October 12, 2017. https://www.mcc-berlin.net/en/research.html

Miller, M. A. L. 1995. *The Third World in Environmental Politics*. Boulder: Lynne Rienner Publishers.

Mills, P. J. 1991. "Feminism and Ecology: On the Domination of Nature." *Hypatia* 6 (1): 162–78.

Milman, O. 2019. "Americans' Climate Change Concerns Surge to Record Levels, Poll Shows." *The Guardian*, January 22.

Ministry of Social Affairs and Employment. 2011. "Q+A Life Scheme." Accessed March 5, 2018. https://www.government.nl/binaries/government/documents/leaflets/2011/10/20/q-a-life-course-savings-scheme/q-a-life-course-savings-scheme-doc.pdf

Mitchell, R. B., W. C. Clark, D. W. Cash, and N. M. Dickson, eds. 2006. *Global Environmental Assessments: Information and Influence*. Cambridge: MIT Press.

Mol, A. P. J. 1995. *The Refinement of Production*. Utrecht: Van Arkel.

Monbiot, G. 2019. "Averting Climate Breakdown by Restoring Ecosystems: A Call to Action." Natural Climate Solutions. https://www.naturalclimate.solutions/the-science

Moody, K. 2017. *On New Terrain: How Capitalism Is Reshaping the Battleground of Class War*. Chicago: Haymarket Books.

Moore, J. 2015. *Capitalism in the Web of Life*. London: Verso.

Moore, R. 2016. "Eros and Civilization for a Jobless Future: Hebert Marcuse and the Abolition of Work." *Heathwood Journal of Critical Theory* 1 (2).

Murray, G. 2017. "Union Renewal: What Can We Learn from Three Decades of Research?" *Transfer-European Review of Labour and Research* 23 (1): 9–29.

Muuls, M., J. Colmer, R. Martin, and U. Wagner. 2016. "Evaluating the EU Emissions Trading System: Take It or Leave It? An Assessment of the Data after Ten Years." Grantham Institute Briefing Paper 21. Imperial College London.

Nanz, P., and J. Steffek. 2004. "Global Governance, Participation and the Public Sphere." *Government and Opposition* 39 (2): 314–35.

Nassen, J., and J. Larsson. 2015. "Would Shorter Working Time Reduce Greenhouse Gas Emissions? An Analysis of Time Use and Consumption in Swedish Households." *Environment and Planning C-Government and Policy* 33 (4): 726–45.

National Academies of Sciences, Engineering, and Medicine. 2018. *Negative Emissions Technologies and Reliable Sequestration: A Research Agenda*. Washington, DC: National Academies Press.

National Aeronautics and Space Administration (NASA). 2017. "What Are the Effects of Climate Change." https://climate.nasa.gov/effects/

National Climate Assessment. 2014. https://nca2014.globalchange.gov/

National Iron & Steel Heritage Museum. 2012. "Bessemer Process." National Iron & Steel Heritage Museum, accessed May 30, 2019. https://www.steel-museum.org/railroad_exhibit_2015/process_bessemer.cfm

National Oceanic and Atmospheric Administration (NOAA). 2013. "Global Climate Report—Annual 2013." National Oceanic and Atmospheric Administration. https://www.ncdc.noaa.gov/sotc/global/201313

National Oceanic and Atmospheric Administration (NOAA). 2017. "Global Climate Report—Annual 2017." National Oceanic and Atmospheric Administration. https://www.ncdc.noaa.gov/sotc/global/201713

National Oceanic and Atmospheric Administration (NOAA). 2019. "2018 Was 4th Hottest Year on Record for the Globe." NOAA, accessed March 30. https://www.noaa.gov/news/2018-was-4th-hottest-year-on-record-for-globe

Negin, E. 2017. "Memo to EPA Chief Pruitt: Let's End Subsidies for Fossil Fuels, Not Renewables." *Huffington Post*. https://www.huffingtonpost.com/entry/memo-to-epa-chief-pruitt-lets-end-subsidies-for-fossil_us_59ee9567e4b0b8a51417bcc6

Nelson, E. S. 2011. "Revisiting the Dialectic of Environment: Nature as Ideology and Ethics in Adorno and the Frankfurt School." *Telos* (155): 105–26.

Nerlich, B., and R. Jaspal. 2012. "Metaphors We Die By? Geoengineering, Metaphors, and the Argument from Catastrophe." *Metaphor and Symbol* 27 (2): 131–47.

Newell, P. 2008. "The Political Economy of Global Environmental Governance." *Review of International Studies* 34 (3): 507–29.

Newell, P. J. 2005. "Business and International Environmental Governance: The State of the Art." In *The Business of Global Environmental Governance*, edited by D. L. Levy and P. J. Newell. Cambridge: MIT Press.

Newell, R. G., W. A. Pizer, and D. Raimi. 2013. "Carbon Markets 15 Years after Kyoto: Lessons Learned, New Challenges." *Journal of Economic Perspectives* 27 (1): 123–46.

Nicolas, B., B. Cheze, and J. Chevallier. 2014. "The CO_2 Emissions of the European Power Sector: Economic Drivers and the Climate-Energy Policies' Contribution." CDC Climate Research. Working Paper N 2014-17.

Nordhaus, W. 2007. *A Question of Balance*. New Haven: Yale University Press.

Norgaard, K. M. 2011. *Living in Denial: Climate Change, Emotions and Everyday Life*. Cambridge: MIT Press.

Norgaard, K. M. 2018. "The Sociological Imagination in a Time of Climate Change." *Global and Planetary Change* 163: 171–76.

Norgard, J. S. 2013. "Happy Degrowth through More Amateur Economy." *Journal of Cleaner Production* 38: 61–70.

Nyberg, D., and C. Wright. 2013. "Corporate Corruption of the Environment: Sustainability as a Process of Compromise." *The British Journal of Sociology* 64 (3): 405–24.

Obach, B. K. 2004a. *Labor and the Environmental Movement: The Quest for Common Ground*. Cambridge: MIT Press.

Obach, B. K. 2004b. "New Labor: Slowing the Treadmill of Production?" *Organization & Environment* 17(3): 337-354.

O'Connor, J. 1998. *Natural Causes: Essays in Ecological Marxism*. New York: Guilford Press.

Ollinaho, O. I. 2016. "Environmental Destruction as (Objectively) Uneventful and (Subjectively) Irrelevant." *Environmental Sociology* 2 (1): 53–63.

O'Neill, D. W. 2012. "Measuring Progress in the Degrowth Transition to a Steady State Economy." *Ecological Economics* 84: 221–31.

Orcutt, M. 2017. "Why This Geoengineering Pioneer's Worst Nightmare Is a Trump Tweet." *MIT Technology Review*. https://www.technologyreview. com/s/609379/why-this-geoengineering-pioneers-worst-nightmare-is-a-trump-tweet/

Organization for Economic Co-operation and Development. 2011. *Towards Green Growth*. Paris: OECD.

Osborne, T. 2015. "Tradeoffs in Carbon Commodification: A Political Ecology of Common Property Forest Governance." *Geoforum* 67: 64–77.

Ostrom, E. 1990. *Governing the Commons: The Evolution of Institutions for Collective Action*. Cambridge: Cambridge University Press.

Ostrom, E. 2010. "Polycentric Systems for Coping with Collective Action and Global Environmental Change." *Global Environmental Change-Human and Policy Dimensions* 20 (4): 550–57.

Ott, K. 2012. "Variants of De-growth and Deliberative Democracy: A Habermasian Proposal." *Futures* 44 (6): 571–81.

Ott, K. 2018. "On the Political Economy of Solar Radiation Management." *Frontiers in Environmental Science*.

Owen, D. 2011. *The Conundrum: How Scientific Innovation, Increased Efficiency, and Good Intentions Can Make Our Energy and Climate Problems Worse*. New York: Riverhead Books.

Owen, D. 2011. "The Efficiency Dilemma: If Our Machines Use Less Energy, Will We Just Use Them More?" *The New Yorker*.

Paris Climate Agreement. 2016. https://treaties.un.org/Pages/ViewDetails. aspx?src=TREATY&mtdsg_no=XXVII-7-d&chapter=27&lang=_en&clang=_ en

Parkinson, J. and J. Mansbridge. 2012. *Deliberative Systems: Deliberative Democracy at the Large Scale*. New York: Cambridge University Press.

Paterson, M. 2000. *Understanding Global Environmental Politics: Domination, Accumulation, Resistance*. London: Macmillan Press.

Paulson, N., A. Laudati, A. Doolittle, M. Welsh-Devine, and P. Pena. 2012. "Indigenous Peoples' Participation in Global Conservation: Looking beyond Headdresses and Face Paint." *Environmental Values* 21 (3): 255–76.

Payne, C. R., R. Shwom, and S. Heaton. 2015. "Public Participation and Norm Formation for Risky Technology: Adaptive Governance of Solar-Radiation Management." *Climate Law* 5 (2–4): 210–51.

Polanyi, K. 2001. *The Great Transformation: The Political and Economic Origins of Our Time*. Boston: Beacon Press.

Polimini, J. M., K. Myumi, M. Giampietro, and B. Alcott. 2008. *The Jevons Paradox and the Myth of Resource Efficiency Improvements*. London: Earthscan.

Postone, M. 1993. *Time, Labor, and Social Domination*. New York: Cambridge University Press.

Powell, H. 2008. "Will Ocean Iron Fertilization Work?" *Oceanus Magazine* 46 (1): 10–13.

Prádanos, L. I. 2018. *Postgrowth Imaginaries: New Ecologies and Counterhegemonic Culture in Post-2008 Spain*. Liverpool: Liverpool University Press.

Preston, C. J., ed. 2012. *Engineering the Climate: The Ethics of Solar Radiation Management*. Plymouth: Lexington Books.

Preston, C. J. 2016. *Climate Justice and Geoengineering: Ethics and Policy in the Atmospheric Anthropocene*. London: Rowman & Littlefield.

Pullinger, M. 2014. "Working Time Reduction Policy in a Sustainable Economy: Criteria and Options for its Design." *Ecological Economics* 103: 11–19.

Pusey, M. 1987. *Jurgen Habermas*. Chichester: Ellis Horwood Limited.

Rask, M., R. Worthington, and M. Lammi. 2012. *Citizen Participation in Global Environmental Governance*. London: Earthscan.

Reiner, D. M. 2016. "Learning through a Portfolio of Carbon Capture and Storage Demonstration Projects." *Nature Energy* 1.

Renn, O. 1992. "Risk Communication: Towards a Rational Dialogue with the Public." *Journal of Hazardous Materials* 29 (3): 465–519.

Renn, O. 2008. *Risk Governance: Coping with Uncertainty in a Complex World*. London: Earthscan.

Renn, O., T. Webler, H. Rakel, P. Dienel, and B. Johnson. 1993. "Public-Participation in Decision-Making—a 3 Step Procedure." *Policy Sciences* 26 (3): 189–214.

Research & Degrowth. 2010. "Degrowth Declaration of the Paris 2008 Conference." *Journal of Cleaner Production* 18 (6): 523–24.

Research & Degrowth. 2018. https://degrowth.org/

Reuters. 2017. "EU Strikes Deal on Carbon Market Reform." https://www.reuters.com/article/us-eu-carbon/eu-strikes-deal-on-carbon-market-reform-idUSKBN1D90PK

Reynolds, J. L., J. L. Contreras, and J. D. Sarnoff. 2018. "Intellectual Property Policies for Solar Geoengineering." *Wiley Interdisciplinary Reviews: Climate Change* 9 (2).

Reynolds, J. L., J. L. Contreras, and J. D. Sarnoff. 2017. "Solar Climate Engineering and Intellectual Property: Towards a Research Commons." *Minnesota Journal of Law, Science and Technology* 18.

Reynolds, J. L., A. Parker, and P. Irvine. 2016. "Five Solar Engineering Tropes that Have Outstayed Their Welcome." *Earth's Future* 4 (12): 562–68.

Roberts, J. T., and B. Parks. 2006. *A Climate of Injustice: Global Inequality, North-South Politics, and Climate Policy*. Cambridge: MIT Press.

Robertson, M. M. 2004. "The Neoliberalization of Ecosystem Services: Wetland Mitigation Banking and Problems in Environmental Governance." *Geoforum* 35 (3): 361–73.

Robinson, T. 2006. *Work, Leisure and the Environment*. Northhampton: Edward Elgar.

Robock, A. 2008a. "Geoengineering: It's Not a Panacea." *Geotimes* 53 (7): 58–58.

Robock, A. 2008b. "20 Reasons Why Geoengineering May Be a Bad Idea." *Bulletin of the Atomic Scientists* 64 (2): 14–18.

Robock, A., M. Bunzl, B. Kravitz, and G. L. Stenchikov. 2010. "A Test for Geoengineering?" *Science* 327 (5965): 530–31.

Robock, A., A. Marquardt, B. Kravitz, and G. Stenchikov. 2009. "Benefits, Risks, and Costs of Stratospheric Geoengineering." *Geophysical Research Letters* 36.

Romano, O. 2012. "How to Rebuild Democracy, Re-thinking Degrowth." *Futures* 44 (6): 582–89.

Romm, J. 2010. "Bill Gates Disses Energy Efficiency, Renewables, and Near Term Climate Action while Embracing the Magical Thinking of Bjorn Lomborg (and George Bush)." *Think Progress*, accessed May 24, 2014. http://thinkprogress.org/climate/2010/01/26/205380/bill-gates-energy-effi ciency-insulation-renewables-and-global-climate-action-bjorn-lomborg/

Romm, J. 2011. "Pro-Geoengineering Bill Gates Disses Efficiency, 'Cute' Solar Development, Deployment—Still Doesn't Know How He Got Rich." *Think Progress*, accessed May 24, 2014. http://thinkprogress.org/cli mate/2011/05/05/208032/bill-gates-efficiency-cute-solar/

Rommel, J., J. Radtke, G. Von Jorck, F. Mey, and O. Yildtiz. 2016. "Community Renewable Energy at a Crossroads: A Think Piece on Degrowth, Technology, and the Democratization of the German Energy System." *Journal of Cleaner Production*.

Rosa, E. A., T. K. Rudel, R. York, A. K. Jorgenson, and T. Dietz. 2015. "The Human (Anthropogenic) Driving Forces of Global Climate Change." In *Climate Change and Society: Sociological Perspectives*, edited by R. E. Dunlap and R. J. Brulle. Cambridge: Cambridge University Press.

Rosen, J. 2019. "The Real Climate Change Controversy: Whether to Engineer the Planet in Order to Fix It." *Los Angeles Times*, April 24.

Rosenberg, N. 1994. *Exploring the Black Box: Technology, Economics, and History*. Cambridge: Cambridge University Press.

Rosnick, D. 2013. "Reduced Work Hours as a Means of Slowing Climate Change." *Real-World Economic Review* 63: 124–33.

Rosnick, D., and M. Weisbrot. 2006. *Are Shorter Working Hours Good for the Environment? A Comparison of U.S. and European Energy Consumption*. Washington, DC: Center for Economic and Policy Research.

Rowe, G., R. Marsh, and L. J. Frewer. 2004. "Evaluation of a Deliberative Conference." *Science Technology & Human Values* 29 (1): 88–121.

Royal Society. 2009. *Geoengineering the Climate: Science, Governance and Uncertainty*. London: The Royal Society.

Salleh, A. K. 1988. "Epistemology and the Metaphors of Production: An Eco-Feminist Reading of Critical Theory." *Studies in the Humanities* 15 (2): 130–39.

Samson, J., D. Berteaux, B. J. McGill, and M. M. Humphries. 2011. "Geographic Disparities and Moral Hazards in the Predicted Impacts of Climate Change on Human Populations." *Global Ecology and Biogeography* 20 (4): 532–44.

Santarius, T. 2012. *Green Growth Unraveled: How Rebound Effects Baffle Sustainability Targets When the Economy Keeps Growing*. Berlin: Wuppertal Institute.

Scheler, M. 1961. *Ressentiment*. New York: Schocken Books.

Schmelzer, M. 2016. *The Hegemony of Growth: The Making and Remaking of the Economic Growth Paradigm and the OECD, 1948–2010*. Cambridge: Cambridge University Press.

Schnaiberg, A. 1980. *The Environment: From Surplus to Scarcity*. New York: Oxford University Press.

Schnaiberg, A. 2015. "Labor Productivity and the Environment." In *Twenty Lessons in Environmental Sociology*, edited by K. A. Gould and T. L. Lewis. New York: Oxford University Press.

Schnaiberg, A., D. Pellow, and A. Weinberg. 2002. "The Treadmill of Production and the Environmental State." In *The Environmental State Under Pressure*. 15–32. Emerald Group Publishing Limited.

Schneider, F., G. Kallis, and J. Martinez-Alier. 2010. "Crisis or Opportunity? Economic Degrowth for Social Equity and Ecological Sustainability. Introduction to this Special Issue." *Journal of Cleaner Production* 18 (6): 511–18.

Scholte, S., E. Vasileiadou, and A. C. Petersen. 2013. "Opening Up the Social Debate on Climate Engineering: How Newspaper Frames Are Changing." *Journal of Integrative Environmental Sciences* 10 (1): 1–16.

Schor, J. 1991. *The Overworked American: The Unexpected Decline in Leisure*. New York: Basic Books.

Schor, J. 2003. "The (Even More) Overworked American." In *Take Back Your Time: Fighting Overwork and Poverty in America*, edited by J. de Graaf, 6–11. San Francisco: Berrett-Koehler Publishers.

Schor, J. 2005. "Sustainable Consumption and Worktime Reduction." *Journal of Industrial Ecology* 9 (1–2): 37–50.

Schor, J. 2010. *Plenitude: The New Economics of True Wealth*. New York: Penguin Press.

Schor, J. 2015. "Work Sharing." In *Degrowth: A Vocabulary for a New Era*, edited by G. D'Alisa, F. Demaria and G. Kallis, 195–97. New York: Routledge.

Schwartzman, D. 2012. "A Critique of Degrowth and Its Politics." *Capitalism Nature Socialism* 23 (1): 119–25.

Schwartzman, D. 2014. "Is Zero Economic Growth Necessary to Prevent Climate Catastrophe?" *Science & Society* 78 (2): 235–40.

Schweickart, D. 1992. "Economic Democracy—a Worthy Socialism that Would Really Work." *Science & Society* 56 (1): 9–38.

Sekulova, F. 2015. "Happiness." In *Degrowth: A Vocabulary for a New Era*, edited by G. D'Alisa, F. Demaria, and G. Kallis, 113–16. New York: Routledge..

Seliger, M. 1976. *Ideology and Politics*. London: Free Press.

Seyfang, G., J. J. Park, and A. Smith. 2013. "A Thousand Flowers Blooming? An Examination of Community Energy in the UK." *Energy Policy* 61: 977–89.

Showstack, R. 2016. "High Energy Growth, Fossil Fuel Dependence Forecast through 2040." *EOS*. https://eos.org/articles/high-energy-growth-fossil-fuel-dependence-forecast-through-2040

Siegel, R. P. 2018. "The Fizzy Math of Carbon Capture: Once Seen as Cost-Prohibitive, Pulling Carbon Dioxide out of Air Could Become Feasible Thanks to a Growing Secondary Market." *Grist*, accessed May 2, 2019. https://grist.org/article/direct-air-carbon-capture-global-thermostat/

Sikka, T. 2012a. "A Critical Discourse Analysis of Geoengineering Advocacy." *Critical Discourse Studies* 9 (2): 163–75.

Sikka, T. 2012b. "A Critical Theory of Technology Applied to the Public Discussion of Geoengineering." *Critical Discourse Studies* 9 (2): 163–75.

Shao, Q. 2017. "Recession, Working Time and Environmental Pressure: Econometric Contributions." PhD thesis, Universitat Autonoma de Barcelona, Barcelona, Spain.

Smith, N. 2007. "Nature as Accumulation Strategy." *Socialist Register* 16: 19–41.

Smith, W. 2018. "Transnational and Global Deliberation." In *The Oxford Handbook of Deliberative Democracy*, edited by A. Bachtiger, J. Dryzek, J. Mansbridge and C. R. Warren, 856–68. New York: Oxford University Press.

Smith, W., and J. Bassett. 2008. "Deliberation and Global Governance: Liberal, Cosmopolitan, and Critical Perspectives." *Ethics & International Affairs* 22 (1): 69–92.

Smith, W., and G. Wagner. 2018. "Stratospheric Aerosol Injection Tactics and Costs in the First 15 years of Deployment." *Environmental Research Letters* 13 (12).

Sorrell, S. 2007. *The Rebound Effect: An Assessment of the Evidence for Economy-Wide Energy Savings from Improved Energy Efficiency*. London: UK Energy Research Centre.

South Centre. 1996. *For a Strong and Democratic United Nations: A South Perspective on UN Reform*. Geneva: South Centre.

Speth, J. G. 2002. "The Global Environmental Agenda: Origins and Prospects." In *Global Environmental Governance: Options & Opportunities*, edited by D. C. Etsy and M. H. Ivanova. Yale School of Forestry and Environmental Studies: New Haven.

Speth, J. G., P. M. Haas. *Global Environmental Governance*. London: Island Press.

Steffen, W., J. Rockstrom, K. Richardson, T. M. Lenton, C. Folke, D. Liverman, C. P. Summerhayes, A. D. Barnosky, S. E. Cornell, M. Crucifix, J. F. Donges, I. Fetzer, S. J. Lade, M. Scheffer, R. Winkelmann, and H. J. Schellnhuber. 2018. "Trajectories of the Earth System in the Anthropocene." *Proceedings of the National Academy of Sciences of the United States of America* 115 (33): 8252–59.

Stephens, J. C., and N. Markusson. 2018. "Technological Optimism in Climate Mitigation: The Case of Carbon Capture and Storage." In *The Oxford Handbook of Energy and Society*, edited by Debra J. Davidson and Matthias Gross, 503–17. Oxford University Press.

Stephens, J. D. 1979. *The Transition from Capitalism to Socialism*. London: Macmillan.

Stern, N. 2006. *Stern Review on the Economics of Climate Change*. Cambridge: Cambridge University Press.

Stevenson, H., and J. Dryzek. 2014. *Democratizing Global Climate Governance*. New York: Cambridge University Press.

Stiglitz, J. 2009. "Rethink GDP Fetish." *The Cap Times*.

Stilgoe, J. 2016. "Geoengineering as Collective Experimentation." *Science and Engineering Ethics* 22 (3): 851–69.

Stone, A. 2018. "Negative Emissions Won't Rescue Us from Climate Change." *Forbes*, accessed May 2, 2019. https://www.forbes.com/sites/andys tone/2018/10/29/negative-emissions-wont-rescue-us-from-climate-change/#88cf13636268

Stoner, A., and A. Melathopoulos. 2016. "If Climate 'Changes Everything,' Why Does So Much Remain the Same?" *Logos* 15(1). http://logosjournal. com/2016/stoner/

Stoner, A. M., and A. Melathopoulos. 2015. *Freedom in the Anthropocene: Twentieth-Century Helplessness in the Face of Climate Change*. New York: Palgrave Macmillan.

Stuart, D. 2018. "Climate Change and Ideological Transformation in US Agriculture." *Sociologia Ruralis* 58 (1): 63–82.

Stuart, D., R. C. H. Denny, M. Houser, A. P. Reimer, and S. Marquart-Pyatt. 2018. "Farmer Selection of Sources of Information for Nitrogen Management in the US Midwest: Implications for Environmental Programs." *Land Use Policy* 70: 289–97.

Stuart, D., R. L. Schewe, and M. McDermott. 2014. "Reducing Nitrogen Fertilizer Application as a Climate Change Mitigation Strategy: Understanding Farmer Decision-Making and Potential Barriers to Change in the US." *Land Use Policy* 36: 210–18.

Sunderlin, W. D. 2003. *Ideology, Social Theory, and the Environment*. Lanham: Rosman & Littlefield.

Surprise, K. 2018. "Preempting the Second Contradiction: Solar Geoengineering as Spatiotemporal Fix." *Annals of the American Association of Geographers* 108 (5): 1228–44.

Sweezy, P. M. 1970. *The Theory of Capitalist Development*. New York: Modern Reader Paperbacks.

Teller, E. 1998. "Sunscreen for Planet Earth." *Hoover Digest* 1.

Temple, J. 2017. "GOP Embraces Geoengineering . . . which Terrifies Geoengineering Researchers." *Technology Review*. https://www.technologyreview. com/the-download/609431/gop-embraces-geoengineering-which-terrifies-geoengineering-researchers/

Therborn, G. 1980. *The Ideology of Power and the Power of Ideology*. London: Verso.

Thompson, J. B. 1984. *Studies in the Theory of Ideology*. Cambridge: Polity Press.

Trainer, T. 2010. "Can Renewables etc. Solve the Greenhouse Problem? The Negative Case." *Energy Policy* 38 (8): 4107–14.

Trainer, T. 2012. "De-growth: Do you Realise What It Means?" *Futures* 44 (6): 590–99.

Trotsky, L. 1963. "Their Morals and Ours." In *The Basic Writings of Trotsky*, edited by I. Howe. New York: Schocken Books.

Turner, P. A., K. J. Mach, D. B. Lobell, S. M. Benson, E. Baik, D. L. Sanchez, and C. B. Field. 2018. "The Global Overlap of Bioenergy and Carbon Sequestration Potential." *Climatic Change* 148 (1–2): 1–10.

Union of Concerned Scientists (UCS). 2017a. "Global Warming Impacts." Union of Concerned Scientists. https://www.ucsusa.org/our-work/global-warming/science-and-impacts/global-warming-impacts#.Wx7NvIMvyRs

Union of Concerned Scientists (UCS). 2017b. "Clean Energy Momentum." Union of Concerned Scientists. www.ucsusa.org/EnergyProgress

Union of Concerned Scientists (UCS). 2018. "Environmental Impacts of Renewable Energy." Union of Concerned Scientists. https://www.ucsusa.org/clean-energy/renewable-energy/environmental-impacts#.WyFa51MvyRs

United Nations Environment Programme (UNEP). 2011. "Towards a Green Economy: Pathways to Sustainable Development and Poverty Eradication." UNEP, accessed June 23, 2016. http://www.unep.org/greeneconomy/Portals/88/documents/ger/ger_final_dec_2011/Green%20EconomyReport_Final_Dec2011.pdf

United Nations Framework Convention on Climate Change (UNFCCC). 2015. "The Paris Agreement." https://unfccc.int/process-and-meetings/the-paris-agreement/the-paris-agreement

United Nations Framework Convention on Climate Change (UNFCCC). 2018. "What Is the United Nations Framework Convention on Climate Change?" https://unfccc.int/process/the-convention/what-is-the-united-nations-framework-convention-on-climate-change

Unti, B. J. 2015. "Job Guarantee." In *Degrowth: A Vocabulary for a New Era*, edited by G. D'Alisa, F. Demaria and G. Kallis, 172–74. New York: Routledge.

U.S. National Research Council. 1996. *Understanding Risk: Informing Decisions in a Democratic Society*. Edited by P. C. Stern and H. V. Fineberg. Washington, DC: National Academy Press.

U.S. National Research Council. 2007. "Analysis of Global Change Assessments: Lessons Learned." In *Committee on the Analysis of Global Change Assessments. Board on Atmospheric Sciences and Climate. Division on Earth and Life Sciences*. Washington, DC: National Academies Press.

U.S. National Research Council. 2008. *Public Participation in Environmental Assessment and Decision Making*. Edited by T. Dietz and P. C. Stern. Washington, DC: National Academy Press.

van Asselt, H., and F. Zelli. 2014. "Connect the Dots: Managing the Fragmentation of Global Climate Governance." *Environmental Economics and Policy Studies* 16 (2): 137–55.

van den Bergh, J. 2001. "Ecological Economics: Themes, Approaches, and Differences with Environmental Economics." *Regional Environmental Change* 2 (1): 13–23.

van den Bergh, J. 2011. "Environment versus Growth—A Criticism of 'Degrowth' and a Plea for 'A-growth.'" *Ecological Economics* 70 (5): 881–90.

van Griethuysen, P. 2010. "Why Are We Growth-Addicted? The Hard Way towards Degrowth in the Involutionary Western Development Path." *Journal of Cleaner Production* 18 (6): 590–95.

Vaughan, N. E., and T. M. Lenton. 2011. "A Review of Climate Geoengineering Proposals." *Climatic Change* 109 (3–4): 745–90.

Veblen, T. 1939. *Imperial Germany and the Industrial Revolution*. Ann Arbor: University of Michigan Press.

Victor, P. A. 2010a. "Questioning Economic Growth." *Nature* 468 (7322): 370–71.

Victor, P. A. 2010b. "Ecological Economics and Economic Growth." In *Ecological Economics Reviews*, edited by K. Limburg and R. Costanza, 237–45.

Victor, P. A. 2012. "Growth, Degrowth and Climate Change: A Scenario Analysis." *Ecological Economics* 84: 206–12.

Vidal, J. 2009. "Global Warming Could Create 150 Million 'Climate Refugees' by 2050." *The Guardian*. https://www.theguardian.com/environment/2009/nov/03/global-warming-climate-refugees

Videira, N., F. Schneider, F. Sekulova, and G. Kallis. 2014. "Improving Understanding on Degrowth Pathways: An Exploratory Study Using Collaborative Causal Models." *Futures* 55: 58–77.

Viitanen, J., and R. Kingston. 2014. "Smart Cities and Green Growth: Outsourcing Democratic and Environmental Resilience to the Global Technology Sector." *Environment and Planning A* 46 (4): 803–19.

Vlachou, A. 2014. "The European Union's Emissions Trading System." *Cambridge Journal of Economics* 38 (1): 127–52.

Vlachou, A., and G. Pantelias. 2017a. "The EU's Emissions Trading System, Part 1: Taking Stock." *Capitalism Nature Socialism* 28 (2): 84–102.

Vlachou, A., and G. Pantelias. 2017b. "The EU's Emissions Trading System, Part 2: A Political Economy Critique." *Capitalism Nature Socialism* 28 (3): 108–27.

Vogel, S. 1996. *Against Nature: The Concept of Nature in Critical Theory*. New York: SUNY Press.

Walker, G. 2012. *Environmental Justice: Concepts, Evidence and Politics*. New York: Routledge.

Walker, G., S. Hunter, P. Devine-Wright, B. Evans, and H. Fay. 2007. "Harnessing Community Energies: Explaining and Evaluating Community-Based Localism in Renewable Energy Policy in the UK." *Global Environmental Politics* 7 (2): 64–82.

Wallerstein, I. 1979. *The Capitalist World Economy*. New York: Cambridge University Press.

Wallerstein, I. 2004. *World-Systems Analysis: An Introduction*. Durham: Duke University Press.

Warbroek, B., and T. Hoppe. 2017. "Modes of Governing and Policy of Local and Regional Governments Supporting Local Low-Carbon Energy Initiatives: Exploring the Cases of the Dutch Regions of Overijssel and Fryslan." *Sustainability* 9 (1).

Warren, M. E., and J. Gastil. 2015. "Can Deliberative Minipublics Address the Cognitive Challenges of Democratic Citizenship?" *Journal of Politics* 77 (2): 562–74.

Weber, M. 1958. *The Protestant Ethic and the Spirit of Capitalism*. New York: Charles Scribner's Sons.

Webler, T. 1993. "Habermas Put into Practice: A Democratic Discourse for Environmental Problem Solving." In *Human Ecology: Crossing Boundaries*, edited by S. D. Wright, T. Dietz, R. Borden, G. Young and G. Guagnano. Fort Collins: Society for Human Ecology.

Webler, T. 1995. "'Right' Discourse in Citizen Participation: An Evaluative Yardstick." In *Fair and Competent Citizen Participation: Evaluating New Models for Environmental Discourse*, edited by O. Renn, T. Webler and P. Wiedmann. Dordrecht: Kluwer.

Weinrub, A., and A. Giancatarino. 2015. "Toward a Climate Justice Energy Platform: Democratizing Our Energy Future." localenergy.org

Weis, T. 2010. "The Accelerating Biophysical Contradictions of Industrial Capitalist Agriculture." *Journal of Agrarian Change* 10 (3): 315–41.

Weisenstein, D. K., D. W. Keith, and J. A. Dykema. 2015. "Solar Geoengineering Using Solid Aerosol in the Stratosphere." *Atmospheric Chemistry and Physics* 15: 11835–59.

Weiss, M., and C. Cattaneo. 2017. "Degrowth—Taking Stock and Reviewing an Emerging Academic Paradigm." *Ecological Economics* 137: 220–30.

Wennersten, R., Q. Sun, and H. L. Li. 2015. "The Future Potential for Carbon Capture and Storage in Climate Change Mitigation—an Overview from

Perspectives of Technology, Economy and Risk." *Journal of Cleaner Production* 103: 724–36.

Western, B. 1995. "A Comparative Study of Working-Class Disorganization: Union Decline in Eighteen Advanced Capitalist Countries." *American Sociological Review* 60: 179–201.

Whyte, K. P. 2012. "Indigenous Peoples, Solar Radiation Management, and Consent." In *Engineering the Climate*, edited by C. J. Preston. Lanham: Lexington Books.

Whyte, K. P., R. Gunderson, and B. Clark. 2017. "Is Technology Insidious?" In *Philosophy, Technology, and the Environment*, edited by D. M. Kaplan. Cambridge: MIT Press.

Wiedmann, T. O., H. Schandl, M. Lenzen, D. Moran, S. Suh, J. West, and K. Kanemoto. 2015. "The Material Footprint of Nations." *Proceedings of the National Academy of Sciences of the United States of America* 112 (20): 6271–76.

Wiggershaus. 1994. *The Frankfurt School*. Cambridge: MIT Press.

Wilding, A. 2008. "Ideas for a Critical Theory of Nature." *Capitalism Nature Socialism* 19 (4): 48–67.

Wolff, R. 2012a. *Democracy at Work: A Cure for Capitalism*. Chicago: Haymarket Books.

Wolff, R. 2012b. "Yes, There Is an Alternative to Capitalism: Mondragon Shows the Way." *The Guardian*. Accessed March 11, 2018. https://www.theguardian.com/commentisfree/2012/jun/24/alternative-capitalism-mondragon

Wolff, R. 2014. "Four-Day Workweeks: Change for the Better?" *Truthout*. https://truthout.org/articles/four-day-workweeks-change-for-the-better/

Wood, E. M.1995. *Democracy against Capitalism: Renewing Historical Materialism*. New York: Cambridge University Press.

World Bank. 2012. *Inclusive Green Growth: The Pathway to Sustainable Development*. Washington, DC: World Bank.

World Wide Views. 2009. "World Wide Views on Global Warming: From the World's Citizens to the Climate Policy-Makers." The Danish Board of Technology, accessed February 9, 2018. http://globalwarming.wwviews.org/files/AUDIO/WWViews%20Policy%20Report%20FINAL%20-%20Web%20version.pdf

World Wide Views. 2012. "World Wide Views on Global Biodiversity: From the World's Citizens to the Climate Policy-Makers." The Danish Board of

Technology, accessed February 9, 2018. http://biodiversity.wwviews.org/wp-content/uploads/2012/11/WWViews_on_Biodiversity_ResultsReport_WEB_11-2012.pdf

World Wide Views. 2015. "World Wide Views on Climate and Energy: From the World's Citizens to the Climate and Energy Policymakers and Stake Holders." The Danish Board of Technology, accessed February 9, 2018. http://climateandenergy.wwviews.org/wp-content/uploads/2015/09/WWviews-Result-Report_english_low.pdf

Wray, L. R. 2015. *Modern Money Theory: A Primer on Macroeconomics for Sovereign Monetary Systems*. New York: Palgrave Macmillan.

Wright, C., Nyberg, D., 2014. Creative self-destruction: corporate responses to climate change as political myths. *Environmental Politics* 23, 205–23.

Wright, C., and D. Nyberg. 2015. *Climate Change, Capitalism, and Corporations: Processes of Creative Self-Destruction*. Cambridge: Cambridge University Press.

Wright, E. O. 2015. *Envisioning Real Utopias*. London: Verso.

Wright, E. O. 2015. "How to Be an Anticapitalist Today." *Transcend Media Services* 14.

Yearley, S. 1997. "Science and the Environment." In *The International Handbook of Environmental Sociology*, edited by M. R. Redclift and G. Woodgate, 227–36. Northhampton: Edward Elgar.

York, R. 2006. "Ecological Paradoxes: William Stanley Jevons and the Paperless Office." *Human Ecology Review* 13 (2): 143–47.

York, R. 2009. "Evert Van de Vliert: Climate, Affluence, and Culture." *Human Ecology* 37 (6): 795–96.

York, R. 2010. "Three Lessons from Trends in CO_2 Emissions and Energy Use in the United States." *Society & Natural Resources* 23 (12): 1244–52.

York, R. 2012. "Do Alternative Energy Sources Displace Fossil Fuels?" *Nature Climate Change* 2 (6): 441–43.

York, R. 2016. "Decarbonizing the Energy Supply May Increase Energy Demand." *Sociology of Development* 2 (3): 265–72.

York, R., and S. E. Bell. 2019. "Energy Transitions or Additions? Why a Transition from Fossil Fuels Requires More than the Growth of Renewable Energy." *Energy Research & Social Science* 51:40–43.

York, R., and B. Clark. 2010. "Critical Materialism: Science, Technology, and Environmental Sustainability." *Sociological Inquiry* 80 (3): 475–99.

York, R., and B. Clark. 2010. "Nothing New under the Sun." *Review* 33 (2–3): 203–24.

York, R., C. Ergas, E. A. Rosa, and T. Dietz. 2011. "It's a Material World: Trends in Material Extraction in China, India, Indonesia, and Japan." *Nature + Culture* 6 (2): 103–22.

York, R., and P. Mancus. 2009. "Critical Human Ecology: Historical Materialism and Natural Laws." *Sociological Theory* 27 (2): 122–49.

York, R., and J. A. McGee. 2016. "Understanding the Jevons paradox." *Environmental Sociology* 2 (1): 77–87.

York, R., and J. A. McGee. 2017. "Does Renewable Energy Development Decouple Economic Growth from CO2 Emissions?" *Socius: Sociological Research for a Dynamic World* 3:1–6.

York, R., E. A. Rosa, and T. Dietz. 2003. "Footprints on the Earth: The Environmental Consequences of Modernity." *American Sociological Review* 68 (2): 279–300.

York, R., E. A. Rosa, and T. Dietz. 2010. "Ecological Modernization Theory: Theoretical and Empirical Challenges." *International Handbook of Environmental Sociology, 2nd Edition*, 77–90.

Young, G. 1976. "The Fundamental Contradiction of Capitalist Production." *Philosophy & Public Affairs* 5 (2): 169–234.

Young, I. M. 2001. *Inclusion and Democracy*. New York: Oxford University Press.

Young, O. R. 2013. "Sugaring Off: Enduring Insights from Long-Term Research on Environmental Governance." *International Environmental Agreements: Politics Law and Economics* 13 (1): 87–105.

Young, R. M. 2014. "Is Nature a Labour Process?" *Review (Fernand Braudel Center)* 37 (3–4): 293–320.

Yun, S. J. 2010. "Not So Green: A Critique of South Korea's Growth Strategy." *Global Asia* 5 (2): 70–74.

Zamora, D. 2017. "The Case against Basic Income." *Jacobin*, accessed March 7, 2018. https://www.jacobinmag.com/2017/12/universal-basic-income-in equality-work

Zehner, O. 2012. *Green Illusions: The Dirty Secrets of Clean Energy and the Future of Environmentalism*. Lincoln: University of Nebraska Press.

Zhang, Z. H., J. C. Moore, D. Huisingh, and Y. X. Zhao. 2015. "Review of Geoengineering Approaches to Mitigating Climate Change." *Journal of Cleaner Production* 103: 898–907.

Žižek, S. 2010. "The End of Nature." *New York Times*, December 2. Accessed March 20, 2018. http://www.nytimes.com/2010/12/02/opinion/global/ 02iht-GA12zizek.html

Zoellick, J. C., and A. Bisht. 2017. "It's Not (All) about Efficiency: Powering and Organizing Technology from a Degrowth Perspective." *Journal of Cleaner Production.*

Index

Printed and bound by CPI Group (UK) Ltd, Croydon, CR0 4YY

13/04/2025

14656530-0001